THE GENTLE ART OF FLAVORING

Basil

The Gentle Art of Flavoring

A Guide to Good Cooking

By

ROBERT LANDRY

Translated by BRUCE H. AXLER

ABELARD-SCHUMAN
London   New York   Toronto

Translation: Copyright © 1970 by Abelard-Schuman
Limited
Library of Congress Catalog Card Number: 76-122498
ISBN 0 200716999

Originally published in French by Robert Laffont as:
Les Soleils de la Cuisine
Copyright © 1967 by Robert Laffont

LONDON	**NEW YORK**	**TORONTO**
Abelard-Schuman	Abelard-Schuman	Abelard-Schuman
Limited	Limited	Canada Limited
8 King St. WC2	257 Park Ave. So.	228 Yorkland Blvd.

An Intext Publisher

Printed in the United States of America

Translator's Note

Shortly before his death in the early nineteenth century, the jurist Brillat-Savarin, who was a preeminent writer on gastronomy, wrote a significant sentence:

"And you, too, gastronomes of 1825, sated in the bosom of plenty, already dreaming of new dishes, not for you the mysteries science shall reveal in 1900, mineral esculences perchance, or liqueurs distilled from a hundred atmospheres; not yours to see what travelers yet unborn shall bring from that half of the globe that still remains to be discovered or explored. How I pity you!"

Foursquare and fully in the tradition of Brillat-Savarin, Robert Landry has summed up here what Savarin could only predict. Too often, of late, have cookbook authors tended to make French cooking into a narrow collection of museum pieces, combinations of a few major ingredients plus a few overworked aromatics, each dish masquerading under a half-dozen different names.

Landry offers the flavoring keys to a vital modern French cuisine—that is to say, an international cuisine—presenting today's herbs, spices and aromatics, a world of which Savarin could only dream. In consulting this concise encyclopedic presentation (which is also a fascinating book to be read from cover to cover), you will find the herbs and exotic spices you read about but probably know little about; here are the liqueurs and spirits of good cooking and how to use them; here are the principles of The Gentle Art of Flavoring, detailed by a master.

Finally, in one volume, we have about 90 per cent of what is known today about spices and seasonings. Brillat-Savarin can relax, at last.

B.H.A.

Illustrations chosen from:

A NEW FAMILY HERBAL: Or Popular Account of the Natures and Properties of the Various Plants Used in Medicine, Diet, and the Arts *by Robert John Thornton, M. D., 1810.*

LEAVES FROM GERARD'S HERBALL *by Marcus Woodward, 1931,* with illustrations after the original woodcuts in THE HERBALL *by John Gerard, 1597.*

Author's Preface

This book is positive evidence of an art of living. Thirty years ago it would hardly have interested most of the public. Today, our stores are full of aromatics, spices and other specialty goods of all kinds. Their customers, returning from sunny shores with sun-tanned faces, belong to a new civilization of leisure and comfort. They are quite demanding.

As Professor Moulin of Bruges has said, the European is now tending to eat as much to amuse himself as for nourishment.

Along with the introduction of exotic cuisines, regional cuisines are returning in favor, strengthening our menus. A number of old food authors are being republished and many products with vaguely familiar or forgotten names are now offered to the housewife as well as to the professional cooks. Both confess to being overwhelmed by the many experiments suggested to them.

The author has tried to provide a useful book whose only ambition is to help them to delve more deeply into the meaning of a word, to understand the product they want to know about. We have taken into account the various spellings and many different bents of foreign cuisines by introducing numerous complementary or recapitulative articles.

This broadening by introducing novel tastes is not a negation of the remarkable French cuisine but, on the contrary, contributes to its perfection. At a time when foreigners tend to be conquering —and very rapidly—the gastronomic independence of France, the French must avoid routine and narrowness. This is the price for remaining the first cooks of the world.

R.L.

Abahan

Or *Habahan, Al-Bakhan,* etc., names given pure cardamom or cardamom mixed with other spices, in Egypt and other Arab countries. On the shores of the Nile, abahan and the seeds of the mastic tree flavor the thick stews made of *gamousse* (meat from a sort of buffalo) and tomatoes, with an abundance of garlic.

Abalones

This word, apparently of Spanish origin, refers to the savory mollusks that abound on the coasts of the Pacific. These "sea ears," close to the French *ormeaux* and *oreilles de mer,* are enjoyed by Americans and Japanese. In Europe, some gourmet shops stock dried or canned abalones, which can be used to add interest to soups, bisques, a sea-food pilaf, or even chicken-with-garlic made like the North Vietnamese dish.

Aceto Dolce

A very popular Italian condiment made of small fruits, young onions, and pieces of vegetables pickled in vinegar before being preserved in the must (unfermented wine) of muscat grapes mixed with coriander, mustard, and honey. In my opinion, *aceto dolce* is only suitable for white meats. It goes especially well with roast veal with spinach (*rôti de veau à la florentine*) already seasoned with rosemary or with a saddle of veal. In Italy, it is nowadays being replaced more and more by *sotto aceti,* Italian pickles.

Agar-Agar

A gelatinous food made from seaweed of the Far East (*Gelidum corneum, Fucus spinosus, Gracilaria lichenoises,* etc.). In France, it is also known as Japanese moss (*mousse du Japon*). Agar-agar is generally sold as white crinkled thongs, which swell in lukewarm water and are dissolved by long boiling. While agar-agar is largely tasteless, it has a number of culinary uses. When it is added to a Japanese or Chinese soup just off the fire, it provides a gelatinous consistency that is very attractive to Oriental gourmets. If cooled after being dissolved by cooking, it can be used in preparations that usually call for gelatin, such as an aspic.

Agar-agar is often used in birds' nest soup by unscrupulous restaurateurs instead of the very expensive swallow's nests. The sea swallow builds its nest by using those same algaes from the China Sea. A touch of monosodium glutamate, a few Chinese mushrooms with their strong iodine taste, a sprig of burnet, a handful of agar-agar in some chicken broth, and you have the famous birds' nest soup "reconstituted." (*See* GELATIN, KOMBOU, *and* PLANKTON.)

Aging Game

A process intended to cause the flesh of wild animals to begin to decompose. Veterinarians and doctors call this process *mortification.* Aging is said to make the meat more flavorful and more tender, but this is questionable. The opinions of the great modern chefs seem divided. However, all agree with Dumas, who said, "Pheasant eaten within three days after its death has nothing to distinguish it." On the other hand, they argue wisely about how

10

long a hare should be aged and how long a saddle of hare should be marinated before being made into a *civet*.

Aging is the process of the breakdown of muscle fibers by enzymes present in the animal's body.

Since we are convinced that gastronomy and health go hand in hand, let us offer only three guides to the reader:

1. Preferably use game that does not need aging. These include patridge, or birds killed in autumn when they are fat and stuffed with flavorful berries. Young hares and wild rabbits can be cooked after only 24 to 36 hours of aging. In tropical countries, game ages quickly, and it should be protected from insects with a covering of banana or papaya leaves for 3 or 4 hours at most.

2. Let hare and young boar hang—and not putrify—2 days in the cellar (Trans. note: about 55⁰ F.) or 3 days in the refrigerator. (Even butchers let a filet of beef hang.) Then marinate game for 4 or 5 hours, without wine or vinegar, simply in a mixture of oil, aromatics, and lemon juice.

3. Follow the same procedure with a large piece of game (a quarter of deer or wild boar). Then trim it and cut it in parts before marinating it for 2 days in strong wine with aromatics, onions, oil, etc. The oil floats on the surface and prevents the bacteria in the atmosphere from mixing with agents of fermentation that are already numerous. Besides, the disinfectant elements contained in the aromatics will retard decomposition while the flesh becomes more tender.

As for woodcock—which need not be cleaned—and pheasant, it is a matter of personal choice or experience. It requires a "kind of instinct," said Brillat-Savarin, to discern when, first, odors and then change in the color of the bird's belly reveal the proper time of aging at which to cook the game.

Agrimony

(*Agrimonia eupatoria;* French, *Aigremoine;* German, *Ackermenning*) A common small perennial plant with grapelike bunches of yellow flowers. In France, it is also called *eupatoire, soubeirette,* and *thé des bois.* Among those who value the medicinal properties of herbs, agrimony is an astringent and appetite stimulant. It is also an element in arquebuse liqueur. An exotic variety, the *aya-pana,* or *eupatoire de l'île Bourbon,* was widely appreciated in the last century. Dumas said that it "communicates an exceedingly agreeable aroma to soufflés and desserts."

In spite of its slightly bitter taste, small quantities of agrimony can be used in marinades and court-bouillons. (*See* ARQUEBUSE.)

Aïoli, Aïlloli

A word in the dialect of the South of France that is a combination of *ailet* (garlic) and *oli* (oil). This preparation, which Mistral thought "intoxicated the mind, saturated the body with warmth and bathed the soul with enthusiasm" is really no more than a garlic mayonnaise. Mother Besson, the valiant restaurateur from Cannes, in the message that accompanies her menus, says, "Lots of garlic, pounded in a mortar, salt, pepper, drop after drop of olive oil, with a strong arm behind the pestle, and the aïoli is made." In Provence, this mayonnaise with its typical southern aroma traditionally accompanies the Friday meatless dish: salt cod, hard-cooked egg, carrots, potatoes in their skins, cauliflower, beans, Jerusalem artichokes and, according to the season and the market, snails, mussels, squid, and artichokes.

Jean-Noël Escudier* tells us that in Provence celebrations a *grand aïoli* used to be served. The same ingredients were accompanied by a variety of boiled meats: beef, mutton, etc. The same author notes another old tradition, the *"coù dôu mitan,"* the equivalent of the "Norman Hole" (Trans. note: *trou normand,* a break in the middle of the meal for a glass of spirits, usually Calvados), during which a little glass of marc was drunk in the middle of the banquet.

SOME ADVICE: *When making aïoli don't use too many egg yolks in preparing the sauce. They kill the aroma of the aïoli, without increasing its digestibility in the least. One yolk is enough for a large bowl. A boiled potato can be added, as in Toulon, where this is often done.*
In the South of France, aïoli is also called beurre de Provence *and* pommade d'or.

* See APPENDIX.

Ajinomoto

(*See* MONOSODIUM GLUTAMATE.)

Ajonjoli

(*See* SESAME:)

Ajowan, Ajwain

(*Carum copticum ajowan*) An umbelliferous plant of India and the Middle East (Persian, *Zinian;* Arabian, *Talib-el Koubs*). Its grayish-brown fruit resembles that of parsley, and gives off an odor of thyme when it is crushed. Thymol, a chemical used in perfumes, is often an extract of ajowan seeds. Under the name *ammi des Indes,* ajowan formerly was widely used in medicine. Orientals use it extensively, notably in making those varied spice "cocktails" known under the generic name of *curry.* I don't believe ajowan is presently widely available in Western shops.

Alcohol

A great number of types of alcohol—cognac, Armagnac, vermouth—are traditionally used in cooking. Their help is invaluable; they are used to swish cooking dishes, to flame (*flambée*) meats, and all add their particular aroma. In cooking, the alcohol itself evaporates and its ether-salts remain.

Alcohol should not be used too liberally, as it may tend to toughen red meats, game, and particularly kidneys.

In flaming a food, the alcohol content of the spirit used is important. Sometimes the flaming fails because the spirit is heated too quickly or too little is used. One way to solve the problem is to add pure medicinal alcohol to the liquid being flamed. This is what insensitive restaurateurs abroad do when they serve a *steak au poivre* or *bananes flambées,* etc. (Trans. note: Medicinal alcohol is not readily available in the U.S.A. Use a high-proof brandy, Cognac or other liqueur.)

Algae

Marine vegetables will certainly enjoy as important a role in the future in human nutrition as they now figure in foreign specialities: *mousse du Japon* or agar-agar, the Irish carrageen moss, Japanese *kombu* and *dashi*, Russian fruit pastes, snacks, and candies made of seaweed from Hawaii, and many diet foods. Because algae are rich in iodine and mineral salts, there is really more of interest for the doctor than the cook. It is difficult to discern any real flavor in algae, sea lettuce, or *chlorella.* Nevertheless, the Japanese and Hawaiians use them in several gastronomic capacities.

Alliaire (Sauce-Alone)

(*Alliaria officinalis;* French, *Allaire;* German, *Lauchhederig*) A crucifer with little white bunches of flowers, very common beside hedgerows and in humid forests. Its soft, stringy, lacy leaves give off a strong smell of garlic when rubbed. Alliare has been used as a substitute for garlic for a long time. Its leaves add interest to usual salad mixtures. Finely chopped, they can give a delicate aroma to a soup or a sauce. The name Sauce-Alone gives some indication of its usefulness, and it is rather a shame that this plant is not more widely used.

Allspice

(*Pimenta officinalis;* French, *Piment de la Jamaïque;* German, *Pimentpfeffer*) In France, allspice is also called *poivre-giroflée*, but allspice is neither a pepper nor a red pepper. This spice is purely American, coming from the pimento of the Caribbean isles (not the pepper pimiento, but a fine tree), that grows almost by itself in Jamaica, Honduras, southern Mexico, and the Leeward Islands. Belonging to the noble family of *Myrtaceae*, like the modest Mediterranean myrtle and the clove tree, its leaves and fruits contain an aromatic ether from which vanillin and eugenol are commercially extracted.

The "seeds" of the allspice sold in groceries are dried, immature berries. If one of these little spheres is cut, a woody shell the size of a pea and two very black seeds held in little niches are revealed. These seeds are oily, sweet, and much less aromatic than the woody parts. Together they give off a strong odor, somewhere between cloves, nutmeg, and cinnamon. The name allspice indicates the wonderment of the cooks who first used it.

COOKING USES: *Allspice is rather strong and should be used carefully. Anglo-Saxon and Nordic people consume between five and six times more allspice than Latins, according to the Food and Agriculture Organization. They use it in preparations of beef and pork, in delicatessen, in cured meats, even in vanilla ice cream, and in flavoring slices of lemon to liven up tea! Bakers use it a great deal, notably for plum cake. In Germany, allspice is used in mayonnaise for serving with cold fish, and with spinach, carrots, and game. In France, this berry is found mostly in flavored vinegars and for flavoring pickles; also it is used in the spice mixture known as* quatre-épices. *Three allspice berries might be added to the family* pot-au-feu, *even four or five if it is a large family! Allspice goes well with shallots in a Bercy sauce or in the peppery vinegar to go with oysters; a seed or two, finely milled, is quite enough.*

Almond (Sweet)

(*Amygdalus communis;* French, *Amande douce;* German, *Mandel;* Italian, *Mandorla*) Aside from having a valuable role in pastry-making, the almond often figures in cooking itself. In general, the almond is used in stuffings and forcemeats, as well as other preparations that accompany fish, crustaceans, snails, etc. However, there are several exceptions to this rule. In French cuisine, trout with almonds (*truite aux amandes*) is well known, but highly criticized by demanding gourmets. No less famous is Jewish-style carp (*carpe à la juive*), stuffed with onions, raisins, and almonds. Without doubt, this dish must remind Jews that Joseph received almonds from his companions after having conducted their flight. In the Balkans, one can enjoy filets of *silure* (a sort of fresh water lamprey) fried with paprika and shredded almonds.

Spanish Basques prepare salt cod with Bell peppers, tomatoes, and a mixture of grated hazelnuts and almonds. This savory dish is called *bacalao à la vizcaina.* In the South of France, they make a sauce of almonds and filets of anchovies called *saussoun* as well as a delicious fresh almond soup, made by pounding blanched almonds in a mortar and cooking them with a little milk

Almond

and stewed onions. In Turkey and Syria, grilled and crushed almonds are dusted on skewered lamb for *chachi-kebassi,* otherwise known as shish-kebab.

To brown almonds, first blanch and string them before putting them in a heavy frying pan with a good-sized lump of butter and reducing the preparation; finally, swish the pan with white wine or sherry. Almond butter can be made by combining pounded almonds with fresh butter, and passing it through a very fine sieve. This butter can be added to a hollandaise sauce or a spicy mayonnaise. Almond powder (*poudre d'amandes*) can be used for stuffings, and for terrines made with pork, veal, or rabbit, imparting an agreeable flavor to them.

The whole almond has a role in Arabian stews, Moroccan chicken with almonds, and the Algerian *mechmachya.* It is generally combined with powdered coriander in these dishes.

N.B. The bitter almond, fruit of the variety *amara,* is proscribed for cooking. It contains prussic acid; only the essence of bitter almonds is used in pastry and elsewhere. (Trans. note: Essence of bitter almonds can be bought in most drug stores.)

Alpine Mugwort

(*Artemisia spicata;* French, *Genepi*) A particularly aromatic mountain variety of wormwood, with bright folliage. It is used in phytotherapy as an antifebrile and stomach tonic. It used to be sought after by distillers for the manufacture of *fée verte,* but nowadays it is used only in certain vermouths and in chartreuse. (*See* WORMWOOD *and* MUGWORT.)

Alsatian Plum

(*See* QUETSCHE.)

Ambergris

(French, *Ambre-gris;* German, *Ambra)* The soft, waxy secretion of sperm whales' liver (while they enjoy cuttlefish and squid, they are victims of their gluttony!). Balls of ambergris, sometimes weighing 6 or 8 pounds, are found inside large crustaceans or floating on the waters and ice floats of Antarctica. Because of its use as a fixative in perfume, the price of ambergris is very high. The Chinese were the first to know ambergris, which they called "perfume of dragon's saliva." They sent it to Arabia where the sultans ate it in their sherbets. The Crusaders in their turn became familar with this precious commodity. Until the eighteenth century, in France, ambergris was used in cooking, especially in candy-making. Its virtues as a tonic and "revitalizer" brought about its use in the famous "chocolate for the ill," *chocolat des affligés,* which Brillat-Savarin noted. Dumas himself invented an elixir containing ambergris, rooster broth, and sugar candy to invigorate husbands "who had overdone it."

Today, ambergris is only known in the kitchens of rich Chinese in Hong Kong and perhaps, in Grasse, the French perfume capital, where nothing keeps cooks from perking up a chicken consommé with a pinch of ambergris!

Amber Seed

Amber seed or musk seed (*ambrette,* in French) is a strongly scented seed with an odor something like ambergris. It is also called *abelmosch* after the bush on which it grows. In Egypt and the Middle East, amber seed is often used to perfume Turkish coffee. (*See* VEGETABLE MUSK.)

Ambrosia

(French, *Ambroisie;* German, *Ambrosia*) The food of the Olympian gods. This substance, nine times sweeter than honey, is the solid counterpart of *nectar,* the most exquisite drink.

The name ambrosia is sometimes given to mugwort (which see) as well as to a decoction of fine wine, sugar, and spices that was enjoyed in the Middle Ages.

For botanists, this word also means Mexican tea (*Chenopodium ambrosioides;* French, *thé du Mexique*). This herbaceous plant, which grows in the South of France, is used to make a little-known liquor, *moquine* (named after its creator M. Moquin-Tandon). (*See* HYPO-CRAS.)

Amonum

An Asian variety of plants with rhizomes, of the *Zingiberaceae* family whose seeds are used in pharmacy and in cooking. The thick roots furnish an edible, starchlike arrowroot. The most well known amonum is cardamom.

Anchovy

(French, *Anchois;* German, *Anschove;* Italian, *Acciuga*) A small fish of the *Clupeidae* family that differs from the sardine in that its body is thin and its mouth split right to the gills. The Mediterranean variety is said to have 45 vertebrae, the ocean type 47 or 48. Anchovies are fished for in the Mediterranean and in the Scandinavian Straits. Preserved in brine, the anchovy brings a delicate bouquet to our tables. It is so fine, so distinguished that it contributes to innumerable sauces and condiments. (*See* BAGNA CAUDO, GARUM, NUÖC-MAM, PISSALAT, SAUSSOUN, TAPENADO, *and* WORCESTERSHIRE SAUCE.)

The filet of anchovies seems to be predestined to be incorporated directly in veal: roast veal Italian-style, veal cutlets, particularly Milanese-style, traditionally served with a round of lemon, a filet of anchovy, and a pitted green olive; and *osso-bucco,* Milanese-style. It figures in many other preparations: *hors d'oeuvre, escargots à la provençale, steak tartare,* etc.

ANCHOVY BUTTER which is sold already prepared, can be used to season broiled foods, and *fondue bourguignonne.* It can also be used like mustard, to season a white meat (saddle of rabbit or veal steaks for barbecue) before cooking. This usage (Trans. note: The anchovy butter or paste is smeared on the meat) is typically Latin and recalls the uses of the *garum* of the Romans. Anchovy butter is an aromatic decoction that most cooks find very useful. It delicately flavors a soup or a sauce, as well as highlighting the taste of a marine animal or fowl.

ANCHOIADE PROVENÇALE is a fine cocktail snack from the South of France made of toasted bread covered with a purée of anchovies and garlic, and on occasion, a crumbled hard egg and chopped parsley.

Angelica

(*Angelica archangelica;* French, *Angélique;* German, *Engelwurz*) Another umbelliferous plant that is close to celery and to lovage. Its fleshy stem supports finely divided leaves. It is occasionally found wild, but it has been cultivated for several centuries. It is the *herbe aux anges* (angel's grass) in the gardens of ancient monasteries. If it has not been proved that it can neutralize snake bites, as Olivier de Serres* believed, its virtues for the stomach are certain.

Gourmets are interested in angelica because of its many uses in candy-making, pastry, and the manufacture of several liqueurs for the digestion (*vespétro, chartreuse, eau de mélisse,* etc.). It is seldom used in cooking itself. On rare occasions, it is used to reduce the sharpness of ginger or to reinforce, if there is a need, some of the sweet and sour sauces the English enjoy. People of the Balkans, who have a demanding palate, prefer angelica to lovage (which see).

WILD ANGELICA (French, *Angélique sauvage*) and Cow's Parsnip [(*Berce*) *Angelica sylvestris*, also *Heracleum sphondilium*] are adventitious plants, but much less strong. In Scandinavia and in Siberia, the young shoots are eaten stewed, and the dried, pulverized roots are used to flavor biscuits.

Angostura

A medicinal tincture that has tonic and antifebrile properties. It comes from the base of certain Venezuelan trees (*Galipea febrifuga*), which should not be confused with false angostura, made from the bark of the Indian tree *Nux vomica*. All bartenders and

* See APPENDIX.

20

lovers of cocktails are familiar with the name Angostura, an elixir that is prepared in the United States but known all over the world. The firm that produces it recalls that it was perfected in 1824 by Doctor Johann Siegert, personal physician to Simon Bolivar, liberator of South America. (The Venezuelan city called Ciudad Bolivar was renamed Angostura in the last century.) The bitters called *Angostura* notably contains the bark of the *galipea,* extract of gentian, cloves, and several secret aromatics.

Anglo-Saxon cooks use these bitters to liven up a tomato soup or a sauce. Because it is slightly diluted with alcohol, angostura keeps well.

Anise

(*Pimpinella anisum;* French, *Anis*) This umbelliferous plant which originally came from Asia Minor, is found all over the Mediterranean as well as farther north. Its leaves resemble those of parsley and can be used like it, especially to liven up the taste of carrots, turnips, and rutabagas.

The seed of the green anise is rounded, brownish, and downy. When pressed, it separates into two seed vessels. Anise is widely used by pastry chefs, candy-makers, and liqueur manufacturers. It is used in biscuits, spice breads, and even for an anise bread.

Anise is strongly challenged for cookery by star anise, an exotic seed with a similar odor, perhaps a little stronger. Either is used in making *anisette* liqueur. In cooking itself, it plays a very minor role, figuring only in Chinese mixed spices. Nevertheless, a product with an anise base, the famous *pastis* of Marseilles, adds a delicate touch to certain recipes in the South of France.

VOSGES ANISE (*Anis des Vosges*) The seed of a cuminlike plant. (*See* CARAWAY.)

PEPPERED ANISE (*Zantoxylum piperitum;* French, *Anis poivré*) The crushed seed of an Asiatic tree whose leaves are used as a substitute for hops by the Chinese. It is one of the elements of the Chinese five spices; it is also called *poivré-clavalier,* Chinese pepper.

21

Anona

A group of very tasty fruits with a vanilla-flavored pulp, from American trees, which are often grown in the Orient: the custard apple (paw-paw), cherimoya, purple apple, Bullock's heart. These are delicious desserts that should not be confused with amonum, whose seeds are used as spices (cardamom) and whose roots are made into edible starches.

Aphrodisiac

For the ancient Greeks, Aphrodite (the Venus of the Romans) was the goddess of beauty and love. Her name, with a little bit of literary license, became the word aphrodisiac, the name of a substance suitable for stimulating romantic ardor.

Both tradition and some modern writers agree that a number of foods and spices are light aphrodisiacs: truffles, crustaceans, rams' gonads, pepper and red pepper, nutmeg, ginger, ginseng, cumin, musk seed, chocolate, alcohol, etc.

As for the Orientals, they argue about a host of specific stimulants such as shark fins, ambergris, musk, Spanish fly, yohimbé bark, even whisper of the very questionable powdered rhinocerous horn. These unsavory items, which often contain dangerous alkaloids, demonstrate that the violence of love's victuals has nothing in common with true gastronomy.

Apple

(*Malus communis;* French, *Pomme-fruit;* German, *Apfel*) A pip fruit from a tree known since the beginning of time; it is mentioned in Genesis. A ripe apple contains 8 per cent sugar, 85 per cent water, malic acid, and some vitamins. Apples are cultivated over a vast part of Europe and North America.

USES: *The apple has so many uses in desserts and sweets that there is no need to mention them all here. The tastiest, in our opinion, is the Viennese apple strudel. In cooking itself, the fruit accompanies pork, less commonly fowl, cabbage, and raw vegetable hors d'oeuvres. It is enough to mention the apple sauce that is served with blood sausage or game; pork chops with quartered apples enjoyed in Normandy and Canada; fresh sauerkraut with apples, an Alsatian specialty; Guinea hen stuffed with apples and Corinth raisins, etc. The English enjoy mackerel with quartered apples and gooseberries. The* andouillette *(Trans. note: a type of tripe sausage) can be broiled right along with buttered or greased apple slices. Let us not forget those compound salads that contain peeled and spiced apples; German salad* (salade allemande) *of apple, beet, and onion slices; Port Royal salad—apple, potato, and green beans in a mayonnaise spiced with mustard. The agreeable pungent smell goes well with a touch of powdered sugar and cinnamon as well as with dry white wine, and vinegar. Celery, in all forms, is always ready to liven up apple sauce, stuffings, salads, if not all the dishes in which this fruit that made us lose divine grace is found.*

Aquavit

A Scandinavian spirit made from wheat and potatoes, about eighty proof, lightly flavored with juniper or caraway. The best aquavit certainly comes from Aalborg, Denmark. Several other Swedish and Norwegian spirits resemble aquavit: *snaps, brännvin*, or *bourdaquavit* (aged in the hold of the ships that circle the world). These strong drinks marvelously liven up the Scandinavian cold table, an imposing collection of local hors d'oeuvre: salted herrings, salami, and Danish delicatessen, smoked reindeer from Norway, cheese with cumin, accompanied by radishes, smoked eel, etc. The best Nordic cooks use aquavit to flame feathered game before it goes on the spit. A dish of sauerkraut and smoked pork (*choucroute*) is improved by a sprinkling of aquavit a few minutes before it is finished.

Areca

The generic name of *Arec catechu* and several other palm trees of Asia and Oceania. Their stems are made into sago starch. Their fruits, the size of a hen's egg, are sometimes eaten preserved. Finally, the nuts of this fruit contains an almond with a bitter taste from which the famous *cachou* is made. The areca nut, or the "hazelnut of India" (*noisette d'Inde*), is pulverized and mixed with powdered betel nut to make the preparation many people in India chew. It also figures in Oriental condiments: curry, chutney, etc. (*See* BETEL.)

Armagnac

A distinguished French spirit produced from acid white wines in three wine-growing regions of lower Armagnac, Tenareze, and upper Armagnac. It is aged in oak, darker, more earthy, but also often with an aroma more subtle than cognac, Armagnac figures in a number of old regional recipes. Among them *steak au poivre*, unexcelled if it is grilled before being flamed on a fire of *picquepoul* (Trans. note: a vine of Armagnac), *civet de lièvre à l'armagnac, Estouffat de boeuf* as it is made for Christmas in Nérac, thrushes and woodcock flamed with Armagnac before being put on the spit, *langouste dorée à l'armagnac,* and the manufacture of savory blood sausages, etc. Because of its unique taste, Armagnac contributes a distinct note to many preparations. It requires a very moderate use of aromatic herbs (thyme, bay, marjoram, etc.). Some famous chefs like to cut the Armagnac with whiskey before using it for cooking.

Aromatic Woods and Barks

Aromatics and spices are for the most part seeds, fruits, leaves, and roots or flowers. The bark and the wood of trees and bushes do not add much to gastronomy, with one important exception: cinnamon, and the several minor exceptions listed below:

ALOES WOOD This is not the American aloe, which is a cactus that is used to make Mexican *pulque* and *tequila.* It includes several exotic hardwoods, such as the *agalloch, garo, calambac.* These highly scented woods are used to make the chests in which the Hindu grocers keep their aromatics. It is said that the sawdust of aloe wood is found in certain cheap curries.

HICKORY WOOD The American white walnut; it has a role in barbecuing and smoking. (*See* HICKORY.)

LOGWOOD (French, *Bois de campêche*) Red-brown or black, smelling like iris or violet, this wood is a coloring agent. It dyes bad wines, sometimes dried raisins and, more usefully, Russian Easter eggs. It flavors and colors certain stews in Latin America where red victuals are appreciated.

SANDALWOOD (French, *Bois de santal*) A generally red wood extracted from the *Ptérocarpus santalinus.* It is burned by the Chinese in Buddhist temples. Its smell is spicy and lasting. In the last century, it set off many pharmaceutical preparations. The Indians use it as a substitute for cardamom with certain fish. In Morocco, sandalwood is used to flavor the fresh water in the earthenware pitchers used as water coolers (*gargoulettes*).

TULIP WOOD (*Dalbergia latifolia;* French, *Bois de rose*) A reddish wood, from India, streaked with gold. It is used like aloes wood.

YELLOW WOOD (French, *Bois jaune*) The sap wood and bark of the tulip tree (*Liriodendron tulipifera*). It is eaten like a vegetable or used in flavoring liquors in the Caribbean, as well as *sapinette,* a Canadian beer made from pine buds. Yellow wood smells like *cedrat* and is used like it.

BLACK CHERRY WOOD The scented wood of a kind of cherry tree grown in the Vosges and in the Antilles (*Prunus maheleb* or *padue*). The leaves are used in Alsatian cooking and the fruits in *Marasquin* liqueur. (*See* CHERRY.)

TEAKWOOD (French, *Bois de teck*) Taken from the Indian oak (*Tectona grandis*), it is hard and rotproof. The Chinese and Malays make containers of it, and it gives a slightly bitter taste to the water they hold. It is often used in the construction of restaurant cars.

LICORICE WOOD (French, *Bois de réglisse*) The root of a Mediterranean plant. (*See* LICORICE.)

MAHOGANY WOOD With the *rotra* of Madagascar and a variety of other unusual ingredients, mahogany is used to give a color and taste to rum, which is naturally white.

BITTER-ASH (French, *Ecorce de quassia*) A bitter tonic furnished by the *Quassia amara,* a tropical American bush. Small quantities are used in certain *apéritifs.*

PINE BARK Taken from the *Pinus sylvestris* or *P. arcticus,* it used to be ground by the *Kvenes* (Laplander and Finnish half-breeds) to make *Misery Bread,* when a part of the buckwheat harvest had

25

frozen in the field. A taste for pine bark followed its use, and now certain country dishes are always flavored with it. The people of the South of France, who are better off, use pine nuts in cooking and pastry. (*See* PINE NUTS.)

QUININE (French, *Ecorce de quinquina*) A very active antifebrile from the *Cinchona officinalis,* gathered by the Peruvian *Cazadores de Quina.* This very bitter bark is valued in making apéritifs; it is also used in exotic cooking, for example, among others, the mixing of spices and stimulants.

YOHIMBE BARK Containing dangerous alkaloids, it figures in the variations of African spices like *ras-el-hanout,* which are intended to have aphrodisiac properties. (*See* APHRODISIAC.)

Aromatic

A word of Greek origin, meaning, according to Littré,* "any vegetable substance that gives off a penetrating and agreeable odor." This rather vague definition is adequate for scented herbs of our gardens: dill, bay, chervil, basil, lovage, marjoram, rosemary, savory, thyme, etc. This definition is in apparent opposition to Littré's comment on spices: "Any aromatic or pungent drug that is used for seasoning." Without doubt, this would include the different peppers, cinnamon, cloves, cardamom . . . but what are coriander, turmeric, nutmeg, vanilla, etc.—spices or aromatics? The best authors disagree.

Let us merely say, in agreement with Dr. de Pomiane* and J. N. Escudier,* that the aromatics should be considered as gastronomic half tones, while the spices are violent harmonies, bordering on dissonance. The former bring out the original taste of food, and the second, imprudently used, take away all its personality.

The characteristic of the great schools of cooking, the South of France, Lyon, China, to mention only three, is to proscribe the bad notes in their taste harmonies. (*See* SEASONING, SPICES, *and* HERBS.)

* See APPENDIX.

Arquebuse

This explosive word does not mean, at least not the way we are using it, an antique gun, but an infusion or steeping of healing plants, also known as *arquebusade*. Some old recipes that combine several healing plants such as agrimony, gentian, and alpine mugwort, are still in favor in Savoy. Arquebuse liqueur (*Liqueur d'arquebuse*) is a slightly bitter tonic alcohol that a gourmet can appreciate during, or in the middle, of a meal devoted to *fondue savoyarde* or *reclette valaisanne*. (Trans. note: two rather hearty cheese dishes from Savoy.)

Arrowroot

An edible starch extracted from the rhizomes of a number of exotic plants of the *Marantas* (Antilles) or *turmeric* (India). Undoubtedly it is called arrowroot because of the healing properties people of the Orient attribute to it. Germans call arrowroot *Pfeilwurzmehl.*

Arrowroot, *sago* (the pith of a palm of Oceania), *salep* (flour of the tubers of Asiatic orchids), and *chuno* (semolina of South American Jerusalem artichokes) have pretty much the same use and taste. These rather bland vegetable products are used to prepare starchy soups and to thicken sauces and desserts. Anglo-Saxons dote on them.

Artichoke

(French, *Artichaut*) This leguminous plant, with a delicate taste and the Latin name *Cynara scolymus,* is a thistle that has been slowly improved by generations of gardeners. There is no point in mentioning familiar ways of preparing artichokes, only it should be said that the aroma of an artichoke is absolutely necessary in certain dishes, notably, the broth of Algerian *couscous, marga,* which has to include several vegetables, among them the artichoke or the cardoon. In the South of France, young artichokes, which are called *mourre de chat* (cat's snout), add a very distinct note to mutton stews and chicken sautés. Small artichokes in pepper sauce can be eaten *à la grecque* and become a sort of condiment.

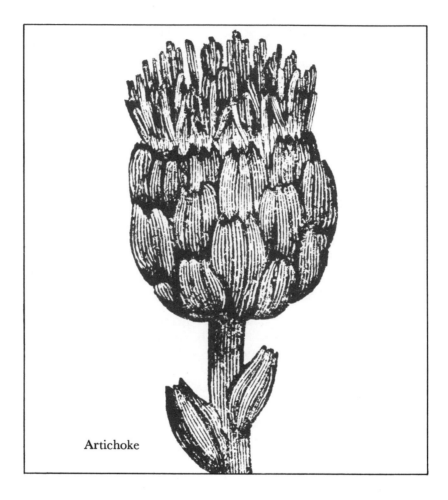

Artichoke

Asafoetida

A resin from an umbelliferous plant of the mountains of Asia Minor (Persian name, *Hingiséh*). Because of its antispasmodic properties, it has been used as a medicine since Dioscorides of ancient Greece. Despite its disagreeable garlicky smell, this resin, called *Laserpitium* by the ancients, was highly appreciated by the contemporaries of Augustine. The Orientals always call it "food fit for the gods." (*See* RESIN *and* SILPHION.)

Aspic

This culinary word refers principally to cold preparations covered with gelatin, but in old food books and even in modern recipes from the South of France, it is used as a synonym for lavender.

Atjars

An exotic spelling of the word achards. (*See* CHUTNEY.)

Aubaguier

This along with *abaquié, baquié,* and *lausié* are names used in the South of France and Languedoc for bay, symbol of triumph in sport and cooking. (*See* BAY.)

Avocado

(French, *Avocat;* Spanish, *Avocado*) This fleshy, agreeable fruit is also called *alligator pear.* It is produced by a pyramid-shaped tree (*Persea gratissima*) originally from Central America, but now found here and there throughout the tropics.

Both its nutlike taste and refreshing properties make this exotic pear enjoyable as a natural condiment.

In Mexico, avocado purée, livened up with oil, tabasco, and vinegar, becomes the famous *guacamole,* which goes especially well with roast game.

N.B. *The leaves of the avocado tree, steeped with sugar and lemon sections, become a refreshing African beverage called* babine *in the Congo.*

Azarole

(*Crataegus azarolus;* French, *Azarole*) A fruit of a small Mediterranean tree, *azerolier,* resembling a hawthorn; also called *Spanish pine* (*épine d'Espagne*). This little reddish medlar has an agreeable taste even if it is a little sharp. Compotes and preserves are made with it, and sometimes these are used like cranberry sauce.

Azarum

(*Asarum europaeum;* French, *Asaret;* German, *Haselwurz*) A small perennial plant growing in stony places or among damp brush, known by its leathery leaves and short, purple, blackish flowers. In France, it is popularly called *nard sauvage, oreille-d'homme, cabaret, gingembre sauvage.*

Its kidney-shaped leaves give off a peppery, lightly camphored smell. They are said to aid in controlling drunkenness. Dried and crushed, they are used in pastry making (on biscuits) or, in cooking, to season game, fish, roast pork *à l'ardennaise,* etc. This false ginger should not be overused as it has emetic properties.

Bacon

Whether it is salted or smoked, lean or fat (*gras*), or called pork breast, bacon, "bard," or ham fat (*poitrine de porc, bacon, barde, gras de jambon*), it is always the same fatty tissue from the same domestic pachyderm. The "king of unclean animals," as Grimod de la Reynière* called it, imposes his bacon on a thousand classic, regional, and foreign recipes.

Often bacon's use is more complex and more varied than one would imagine. The piece of bacon in a *coq au vin* or a *daube* can give them a flavor and a mellowness without objectionable tastes if it is first passed through boiling water. The aroma of smoked grease remains, but the sharpness is removed.

In Liguria, grated bacon, taken from the leanest part of the animal, is used as a condiment for a hot minestrone *à la génoise.* In Canada, it is cooked in a frying pan with caramelized sugar. In Scandinavia, grilled bacon, puffed by a hot fire, is a cocktail snack. In the United States, skewers of bacon squares and prunes steeped in port are cooked together. In the South of France, bacon squares and large mussels from Toulon are skewered and broiled. A dandelion salad or even lamb's lettuce can be stirred up in a warm salad bowl with bacon pieces crisped in a frying pan. (*See* CRACKLING, HAM, *and* LARD.)

* See APPENDIX.

Bagna Caudo

A sauce from Nice created to accompany light, bitter vegetables like cardoon, celery, and bulb fennel. It is prepared by slowly melting a large lump of butter with three chopped cloves of garlic, a sprig of parsley, and six or seven finely chopped anchovies. The anchovies must "dissolve" without the butter or the garlic browning.

Ballachan, Ballichong

Names given in Siam and Burma to nuöc-mam (which see).

Balm

This word generally refers to a highly scented resin [as well as to *baume styrax,* benzoin, and *baume de la Mecque* (balm of Gilead), extracted from *Amyris opbalsamum*]. These exquisite saps were mentioned in the Bible, and botanists of the last century wrote they were cosmetics highly appreciated by the sultans.

When Dumas and other old authors speak of the uses of balm in cuisine, they are usually referring to tansy, calamint, or domestic mint (*baume des jardins*), also known as garden balm, *melissa officinalis.*

Balm is also referred to as melissa (which see).

Bamboo

(*Bambusae*) A giant reed that grows in India and other hot countries. The young shoots are used widely in the food of the Far East. Fresh, they are eaten as a vegetable in China and Vietnam. The Indians pickle them in vinegar with pepper spices (*achards*), and the Japanese preserve them in rice spirits or saké.

In European and American groceries, excellent canned bamboo shoots are available. They taste something like artichokes. These sprouts should be sautéed in butter, then used with rice, mushrooms, fowl, etc. They can be blanched for twenty minutes in salt water, then finished in the oven, covered with béchamel sauce and grated parmesan. They are absolutely necessary in Chinese recipes. (The juice in which they are packed should be saved and used in other cooking.)

Banana

While everyone in the world is familiar with this nutritious fruit, which is seen in every market of Europe and America, its many uses as a vegetable and condiment are not so well known.

The plaintain (*Musa paradisiaca*), sold in stores that specialize in tropical products, is valued in Africa and South America (*Plátano*), boiled, baked, or fried, as a garnish for most meats.

The banana (*Musa sapientum*), which used to be called poetically Adam's fig (*figue d'Adam*), can be used as a condiment and is found in several interesting preparations: sweet mixed pickles, Mexican *cachitas* (snacks of grilled, salted bananas), suckling pig with *feï* (the banana oranges of the Pacific), and finally the famous Brazilian *feijoada* (black beans, pork, dried beef, hot sausages, in a spicy stew). To mollify the palate, a plate of sliced bananas and oranges is served on the side.

Barbarea

(*Barbarea vulgaris;* French, *julienne jaune* and *ronelle*) (*See* CRESS.)

Barbeque

Since the inception of Lyndon B. Johnson's receptions for foreign dignitaries at his ranch, barbecue has been a very popular expression. It is said that the word originated with the custom of the French in Louisiana to roast game with fur on; that is, with the *barbe*, or beard, colloquially. From the word *barbecuit*, literally, "cooked beard," came barbecue. A less dramatic etymology would have the word coming from the Mexican *barbacoa*, which means "broiling on a wood fire."

European grocers now stock a great many American sauces for barbecue as well as smoked salts for seasoning outdoor broiling meats. (*See* HICKORY.)

For those of our readers who wish to take some initiative in this matter—and we wish them luck—remember that *all aromatic herbs* can be used in this way. Even such rarely used aromatics as mint, wormwood, anchovy butter, *vin de Banyuls* (Trans. note: a French portlike wine), or ratafia, can be used to flavor meats before cooking. *Pastis* can be used on fish. Powdered juniper, *ras-el-hanout,* mustard, and tomato concentrate can also be used. Only hard liquor can not be used in soaking meats; this tends to harden the flesh. (*See* WOOD FIRES.)

Basil

(*Ocimum basilicum;* French, *Basilic;* German, *Basilienkraut*) A marvelously scented *Labiata* that the Hindus dedicate to Vishnu and the ancient Greek raised to the rank of "royal herb." While widespread on the periphery of the Mediterranean, it also grows in a number of other countries. It is excellent in the famous turtle soup, the succulent *soupe au pistou* from the South of France, in scrambled eggs, roast veal *à la génoise,* in duckling *à la niçoise,* in crawfish *à la nage,* and in all preparations containing fresh tomatoes. Delicious shrimp omelettes are made in Annam with fresh sage and basil.

There are several varieties of basil. Large-leaved curly basil is best for Italian minestrone soup and sauce; lemon basil, which tastes lemony, is better for summer salads.

An important reminder: do not boil basil for more than a few seconds, or it tends to lose its characteristic aroma. In the winter, dried basil is to be preferred to the very emasculated powdered basil. The tiny, hard stems should be removed from dried basil before soaking in water with a little lemon juice. Basil seeds, difficult to find in our groceries, are used as a spice in some Arab countries.

Some cookbooks improperly refer to the word *pistou,* in the dialect of the South of France, as synonymous with basil. Actually, it is really a *pommade* whose secret we will reveal under the word *Pistou.* (*See also* TURTLE HERBS.)

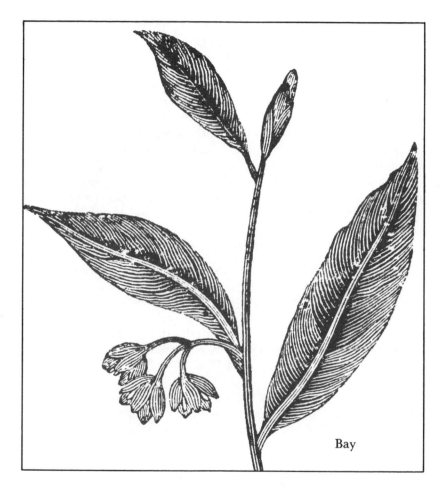

Bay

Bay

(*Laurel Bay, Bay leaves*) (French, *Laurier;* German, *Lorbeer*) Different trees and bushes have this name. Knowing how to distinguish them is a little like covering yourself with laurels before your friends. The little guide below is unknown to poets and sculptors but very useful for kitchen hands:

COMMON LAUREL (French, *Laurier-Sauce, Laurier d'Apollon, Laurier noble*) is called *Laurus nobilis* by botanists. The smooth, wavy leaves contain a very aromatic ether and are used as spices. The yellowish flowers, grouped in small bundles, and the black, somewhat fleshy fruits are medicinals. The ancients believed that the vegetable protected against lightning, so they covered their leader during storms with branches of laurel. A lovely legend explains this practice: the nymph Daphne, fleeing the embraces of Apollo (God of art and light) was changed into a laurel bush. The laurel rapidly became the symbol of glory and scholarly success. The word baccalaureate comes from *baccae laurae* (laurel berries).

CHERRY LAUREL (French, *Laurier-cerise, Laurier-aux-crèmes, Laurier-amandier*) is Linnaeus' *Prunus laurocerasus*. Its leaves are large, thick, and shiny, as though varnished. Its flowers are white and very small. The fruits look like wild cherries. They are first red and then blackish. The cherry-laurel is smaller than the common laurel and more decorative. Venetian merchants returning from Constantinople introduced it to Europe from its native Black Sea shores.

The leaves and the flowers of the cherry-laurel give off a strong odor of bitter almond. They contain hydrocyanic, or prussic acid. Nevertheless, they can be used cautiously for flavoring desserts (one leaf to a quart of milk). An essence used by liqueurmakers and bakers is extracted from the leaves.

OLEANDER OR ROSE-LAUREL (*Nerium oleander*) A uniquely decorative shrubby tree. Its leaves are pointed and gray, its rose flowers are very large and beautiful, and sometimes very light.

Because it originated in Persia or in India, the rose-laurel is the most susceptible of all laurels to cold. It is also the most dangerous because it contains a good dose of prussic acid. In 1812, in Spain, the army of Marshal Suchet was put out of action after having skewered and cooked mutton with rose-laurel.

COOKING USES: *Common bay, Apollo's laurel, now democratically reduced in rank, is one of the few native European spices. It has many uses, some better known than others.* The least experienced cooks know that this pretty leaf should be quivering in a pot-au-feu *and that it has a place in a great number of simmered dishes, almost all court-bouillons, and all marinades. Often the bay leaf is tied with thyme and parsley in a* bouquet garni. *Sometimes, it is reduced to a powder, as is the English custom.*

Bay goes particularly well in fish and crustacean preparations. It is important not to use too much bay as it hides a strong bitterness.

The common bay also bears a flavor of Greek and Latin civilization, according to Doctor Leclerc. *Some leaves impaled on the skewers of* chicke-kebab *or* chachlik *give these preparations a certain distinction that evokes the Bosphorus or Caucasus.*

In Spain, bay, paella, *and* puchero *are inseparable. In the U.S.S.R., it sets off the many formulas for bortsch and* stchi. *Swedes and Norwegians, to console themselves for their sad winter's sun, add some bay leaves to the hops in making* lageröl, *a light and thirst-quenching beverage. Licorice manufacturers use bay to flavor the essence of licorice, obtained by boiling and pressing.*

In the South of France, bay, called aubaguier, *is the most common and most useful of all aromatics. The cooks of Nice or Toulon manipulate its aroma with extreme adroitness. Bay figures notably in béchamel with olive oil;* raïto, *a roux of tomatoes moistened with red wine; octopus* en daube, *rabbit sautéed with olives, the famous* ratatouille niçoise, *as well as tomato soups, the slow cooking of lentils and chick peas, etc. But it never dominates the other tastes. Thus in bouillabaisse, one single leaf of bay mixes with the ardent saffron and the juices of rock fish. The sea perch grilled with fennel is simply dabbed with olive oil with a bundle of bay sprigs. (See* BOUQUET GARNI.)

Beer Cooking

An article recently appeared about the inauguration of a German beer museum in Einbeck, in Lower Saxony. This statistic also appeared in the press: the average Belgian consumes about 165 quarts of beer a year, and only 11 quarts of wine. These facts make the point, without further comment, that the German and Belgian cooks are inclined to add their favorite beverage to their dishes.

* See APPENDIX.

Let's mention a few: *soupe à la bière,* which Bismark enjoyed, *carbonades flamandes, goulasch à la munichoise, fricadelles de Cologne, coq à la bière, carpe à la bière.* They are always mellow, slightly sweet preparations, thickened with flour and seasoned with a little sugar, cinnamon, cloves, and even gingerbread crumbs.

The best beer for cooking is undoubtedly Belgian *lambic.* It is always improved by adding a few juniper beers and by being reduced without boiling (best accomplished in the oven). On the other hand, the English use ale, mixed with mustard and grated cheese, to cover a Welsh rabbit before putting it in the oven.

Beet Root (Garden Beets)

(*Beta vulgaris*; French, *Betterave rouge;* German, *Rote Rube*) This vegetable plant, with a tap root, sometimes plays the role of an aromatic, even a condiment, in foreign cuisines. Beet water, with a little sugar and vinegar, flavors and colors the famous Russian bortsch, the Polish equivalent *barszcs,* "red" horseradish, and the vinegar sauce for Swedish *sillsalad.*

In Hungary, it is the height of good taste to decorate the rice that accompanies the paprika stews with bits of beet soaked in sugar and vinegar. In Madagascar, the beet is fermented to make *betsabetsa,* a bitter alcoholic, slightly repulsive beverage.

In France, the beet adds a joyous and mellow note to a salad of lamb's lettuce or dandelion. The beet is also a refreshing garnish for roasted game and colors vegetable purées.

Bell Pepper

(French, *Poivron doux;* German, *Milde Paprikaschote;* Italian, *Peperone;* Spanish, *Pimiento*) Sweet, very fleshy variety of the *Capsicum annuun.* Horticulturists and market gardens offer the seeds or the fruits of a variety of peppers: sweet Spanish pepper, sweet American pepper, sweet square pepper, pepper-tomato (*doux d'Espagne, d'Amérique, carré-doux, poivron-tomate*). Succulent canned Spanish pimientos, truly stuffed full of sun, bright red, or orange, as well as dried, sweet pepper in jars are available.

COOKING USES: *This agreeable and very polite fruit cannot be refused the rank of a necessary condiment. A* paella *that is not garnished with strips of*

Bell pepper is not worthy of the name. In the South of France, it is mixed with filets of anchovy and black olives in many hors d'oeuvres. It is an element in the famous ratatouille niçoise *and in the not less worthy* pebronata, *a sort of Corsican goulash. The Basques find it perfect with the eggs in a* piperade. *The Guineans mix it with okra in* foutou, *their national stew. The Turks and the Balkan people prefer it filled with meat.*

Benzoin

A highly scented resinous sap, smelling something like vanilla, which is secreted by a plant growing in North Vietnam and Sumatra (*Styrax* or *Storax*). It was widely used in medicine in times past, and also in the incredible culinary preparations of the Goth cooks, who did not hesitate to add toilet water to certain foods.

FRENCH BENZOIN When old food writers speak of benzoin, they mean *benzoin-impératoire* (*Imperatoria Ostruthium*), an umbelliferous plant native to France. Even the Gauls added some well-crushed leaves and stems to their *oxygarum* (which see), one of their common condiments. Later, French benzoin was an element in *orviétan*, one of the electuaries (syrupy medicines), favored by the doctors of Molière's time.

The sweetest tasting French benzoin, something like angelica, is also an element in secret formulas of the monks who make liqueurs like Chartreuse. In Switzerland, more specifically in the canton of Glaris, it is used to flavor some dried paste cheeses. If one of our readers found himself in some Alpine pasture, he could dry this herb to use in pastry-making, or in making *ratafia* (which see). Its odor does not suit meat preparations.

Betel

The Hindu word that is synonymous with pepper. The botanist Linnaeus used the word freely to designate a single *Piperacea, Piper betle,* a vine whose seeds are ignored for the leaves that are pounded in a mortar, mixed with areca nuts and quicklime to become a chewing gum highly fancied on the shores of the Gangis and Brahmaputra.

It is also called long pepper (*poivre long*), which was mentioned by Taillevent* in his *Viandier* (1375) and sold formerly by Venetian merchants. Thereafter the round pepper became the preferred variety. Even vegetables are in competition in the open market, it seems.

Bicarbonate of Soda

An alkaline powder to which big eaters and dyspeptics need no introduction. It can also be used as a water softener for cooking carrots or dried vegetables. But this process should not be abused; it is scandalous when applied to the beans for a *cassoulet*! A single spoonful of vinegar is more effective in neutralizing hard water.

As for the less well-known uses of bicarbonate of soda in cooking, it replaces or reinforces chemical leavening in pastry for quiche, it is used in the ready-mixed pizza sold by the groceries, and it puffs little meat cakes, such as Rumanian *mititei.* In northern China, on the shores of the Yellow River, where not much rice is grown, it swells the little steamed breads made of corn flour.

The use of bicarbonate of soda to make a fondue of any style is a heresy. Generally, it destroys the vegetable's vitamins when used in cooking. (*See* LEAVENING.)

Bigarreaux au Vinaigre

(*See* CHERRIES.)

Birch Bark

In Norwegian Lapland and Alaska, the silver bark of the frail Arctic birch has an essential role in smoking salmon and salmon trout. Of all the woodsy essences, the *Betula nana* makes the lightest smoke and does not leave a resinous residue. (*See* SMOKING FISH.)

* See APPENDIX.

Bitter Orange

(*Citrus Bigardia;* French, *Bigarade;* German, *Pomeranze*) A sort of yellow orange that is too bitter to be eaten raw. The English use it for orange marmalades, and the skin is used in the manufacture of curaçao. The flowers are used to make oil of neroli, which is widely used in making perfumes and candies.

The bitter orange justly finds a place in the many preparations termed *à l'orange,* notably those with duckling or veal. Orange pieces, reinforced by lemon and grapefruit peel, can be used as a substitute. (*See* CURAÇAO.)

Black Africa

This part of the world, rich in flora and fauna, in natural splendors and in folklore, is unhappily much less wealthy as far as food is concerned. Aside from the *couscous* invented by the North Africans, and the *foutou,* a pleasant fish stew from the Ivory Coast that is consumed throughout Western Africa, there is no great African dish.

Each tribe, if not each clan, has its own customs, but most often they are disappointments for the gourmet. It is the typical cuisine of a hot country, much too spicy for our tastes and limited by local taboos. The best memories of old jungle hands, like the safari fans, generally revolve around excellent game roasted in the open, and delicious fruits consumed at their peak. Elephant foot, filet of wart hog, leg of gazelle, and ostrich eggs are not yet available in Europe.

Only Senegal and its neighbors have any kind of a culinary tradition. The best recipes contain rice, excellent fish, tasty vegetables, hearts of palm, and fowl. As for unusual spices and flavors, we might mention grated coconut, which figures in all the sauces, crushed roasted peanuts, the seeds of the cabbage palm, papaya purée, the skin of the tamarind and the *limon,* small, highly perfumed African lemons.

Oil of palm and peanut oil and Karite butter are the most common cooking fats. (*See* BUTTER TREE.)

Blatjang

A synonym of chutney (which see).

Blood

Well before Lycurgus* (he forced a single dish on the La-cedemonians—the famous *brouet*, primitive ancestor of the blood sausage of Auvergne) animal blood had figured in a number of recipes. The people of cold countries have always doted on this substantial but digestible food. Eskimos and Laplanders consume reindeer blood, frozen or clotted, during the long Arctic winter's night, to combat the anemia of the far north.

The Swedish prepare the more refined *svartsoppa*, or "black soup," with goose blood as soon as the first snow falls. The delicate Chinese cuisine also includes soups and stews with chicken blood, but cooking with blood is largely a French practice.

The people of Périgord, Auvergne, and Lyon are past masters in the art of making stews thickened with blood, often called *civets* (although etymologically this word designates a meat cooked in a sauce with chives). There are *civets* of hare, rabbit of Garenne, young boar, roe deer, sucking pig, eel, *langouste*, etc. (The *civets* of crustaceans have usurped the name, as they do not include a blood liaison.) Sometimes the word blood, in French, *sang*, appears on the menu: *canard au sang, coq au sang,* etc.

It should be noted that only hare's blood and young boar's blood give more than a dark color and a mellowness to the various *civets.* They contribute an animal smell, hot and intense, to the thickening of stew. They are set off with a little wild thyme *(serpolet)* and bay, as well as marc, or Armagnac. Chicken blood or that of domestic rabbit is rather bland and can take nutmeg, juniper, or a whisper of powdered cloves. All these thickening operations obey the following rules:

Save the blood and the chopped or pounded liver of the animal; moisten it with a little vinegar and a spoonful of red wine. Add to the sauce at the end of cooking, taking care not to boil the preparation or the blood will clot; thicken the sauce with blood, with an egg yolk, or a spoonful of acidulated cream *(crème fraîche),* or a little starch or arrowroot. It is possible, of course, to use one blood for another, that is, to thicken a *civet* of hare with the blood of a rabbit, a chicken, or even a pig. If no blood is available, it is possible to thicken the sauce of a *civet* with blood sausage, poached

* See APPENDIX.

42

in acidulated water or dried, then passed through a food mill; but this is a rather shoddy dodge.

We have mentioned *civet* of eels, and lamprey. This kind of marine animal has a blood that resembles that of land animals. On the other hand, the ink of octopus and cuttlefish is not blood but a liquid dispersed in the sea as a protective screen by these careful cephalopods.

Borage

(Borago officinalis; French, *Bourrache;* German, *Borretsch)* A pretty plant with a hairy stem, fleshy, wrinkled leaves, blue or red flowers in the form of a five-sided star. It grows wild in plowed fields, on slopes, and is often cultivated, especially in Germany. Its diuretic and sudorific properties were known to the Moors in Spain who gave it the name *abourach* (father of sweat).

Borage (as well as bugloss) is an edible herb unjustly depreciated. The young shoots have a fine taste of cucumber. The leaves can be eaten stewed in butter or pickled in vinegar; the stems must be avoided as too hairy. German cooks find borage quite pleasant and mix it, dried or fresh, with dill to heighten the taste of *potées au chou,* omelettes, soups, and court-bouillons. The English used to use borage to prepare red wine and other beverages with herbs, undoubtedly inspired by the Spanish *sangría.*

The star-shaped flowers are quite attractive in a seasonal salad, especially if they are mixed with nasturtium flowers.

Bortsch

The current etymology notwithstanding, bortsch water *(eau de bortsch)* used by the Rumanian and Balkan cooks is very different from the cabbage and beet broth of Russian bortsch. This fermented water, flavored with lovage, is indispensable in the preparation of the sourish soups that have made the restaurants of Bucharest, the best in all Central Europe, famous. In this area, bortsch water is sold in grocery stores, just as new potatoes can be bought in our stores.

Bouquet Garni

A sacred and simplistic formula by which hurried authors designate the thyme, bay, and parsley, tied in little bundles, that are used in *pot-au-feu*, stews, etc. The goal of this book is precisely to help beginning cooks to escape the monotony of their *bouquets garnis.*

According to traditional French lexicographers, there is also an aromatic bunch *(bouquet aromatique)* containing rosemary, savory, etc. But where is the cook who knows cooking shorthand up to this point?

Boutargue

(*See* POUTARGUE.)

Bowle

A term that refers to the refreshing German alcoholic beverage known also as *Maïtrank* (May wine). It is flavored with young shoots of woodruff.

Brines

Salt solutions in which meats and fish are soaked in order to preserve them. There are also dry brines that simply contain sea salt crystals. The liquid brines are saturated with salt, saltpeter, brown sugar, and flavored with a number of herbs and spices.

The small cuts of meat (tongues, hams, etc.) can be salted without special equipment. The large cuts are treated by professionals with proper pumps to inject the saline solution and with ceramic or slate brine vats.

Broccio, Bruccio

A delicious Corsican cheese made with goat's or cow's milk and cooked cream. It is something like *brousse* of the South of France and Italian *ricotta.* Broccio is eaten fresh from March to November, and dried during the winter months. The Corsicans put a little broccio in all dishes: omelettes, canelloni, partridge stuffed with raisins and broccio, *flans, tartelles* with broccio or *fiadoni,* etc.

Anybody but a Corsican may substitute white cheese flavored with aromatic herbs in recipes that call for it. Dry broccio can be grated like Parmesan.

Brown Sugar

(French, *Cassonade;* German, *Rohzucker*) Called *cassonade brune* by French grocers, it is the first product obtained in the production of cane sugar once the molasses is removed. Sometimes it is called *moscouade.* Brown sugar is preferred by candy-makers and bakers because of its rumlike taste.

In cooking, brown sugar is valued as an element in sausage-makers' brines, but it can be used instead of white sugar in many recipes. The Germans season their sweet and sour dishes with a little brown sugar, notably red cabbage in lard. American cooks coat a ham with brown sugar before putting it in the oven. The Chinese add it, after refinement, as fuel in the smoking of fowl.

Bugloss

(Lycopsis arvensis, Anchusa Italica; French, *Buglosse;* German, *Ochsenzunge)* The little bugloss *(petite buglosse* or *lycopside)* and Italian bugloss are two closely related edible plants, resembling borage.

Another variety, wild bugloss or alkanet, known to botantists as *Anchusa officinalis,* has the same fresh taste of cucumber and can also be included in seasonal salads, but it is better known for the dyeing properties of its roots. The famous henna *(nails' flower)* with which the Orientals tint their fingers is extracted from it. It is one of the products authorized for coloring butter in France. (*See* FOOD COLORS.)

Burdock

(*Arctium lappa;* French, *Bardane;* German, *Grosse Klette*) A *Composite* that is large, with purplish-red flowers. It grows on slopes and in ruins and is also called in French *glouteron, herbe aux teigneux,* and *lampourde.*

Burdock is used in the South of France, the Scandinavian countries, and Japan. Its roots can be eaten like oyster plant. The young shoots and leaves are called *chou d'âne* (donkey-cabbage salad). The entire palm has a slightly bitter taste that puts it high in the esteem of gastronomes.

Butter Tree (Butter)

(*Beurre de Karité*) A sort of vegetable fat which looks like lard,' valued by the cooks of Senegal and Mali, it is extracted from the berry of the butter tree *(Butyrospermum parkii),* which looks like an oak and grows abundantly on the high African plateaus. It is thicker than coconut butter. It enhances the flat cakes made of manioc or corn flour and lubricates wart hog stews, compotes of okra, etc. It is nearly unobtainable in Europe.

Button Mushrooms

(French, *Mousseron*) This name, in French, is given to several varieties of small mushrooms growing in the moss, or in the fairy circles of marshes. Among them is the *Agaricus albellus,* or muscat mushroom, with a wide foot and a swollen base, and the *Agaricus tortillis,* or *faux mousseron,* yellow or reddish, appearing in the fall. It is recognized by its very frail pedicule.

The flesh of all the small mushrooms is somewhat hard, but very delicate. Their flavor is musky. They may be dried and preserved easily after threading them on a string. They are valued in omelettes and wine sauces. It would be a ·mistake to cook them with a lot of garlic or shallots like common mushrooms. The button mushrooms tolerate only chives, chervil, or dill. Acidulated cream and very dry sherry are their most beautiful shroud. (*See* MUSHROOMS *and* MOREL.)

Calabash

Originally the fruit of a tropical tree native to the Antilles *(Cucurbita lagenaria)*. It forms gourds with a yellow pulp and flat white seeds. The seeds are used to make *pepián,* a fragrant Mexican sauce. The pulp and seeds are also used to make a thirst-quenching syrup.

The name calabash has been extended to the fruits of the *baobab (Adansonia digitatao),* a typical African tree of gigantic height. The powdered leaves are the *lalo* of the Senegalese, a condiment mixed with various food, but especially *couscous.* The fresh fruit is called *monkey's bread* and has a sourish taste. The pulp can be used in experimenting with sauces to be used for making chicken in tropical styles.

Calamint

(Satureja calamintha) One of the *Labiatae,* also called mountain mint *(menthe des montagnes).* Its very subtle smell is close to that of *menthe glaciale.* It is used in herb medicine and more rarely in confection. Arquebuse water contains calamint. Calamint can be used, in small quantities, in marinating a large piece of game with tough flesh.

Calamus

(Acorus calamus; French, *Jonc odorant* or *Acore;* German, *Gewürzkalmus)* The famous reed of the ancient Egyptians that was used by the scribes as well as the cooks. Growing in the Nile Delta and other humid spots, notably China, it is in the same family as rum. Its threadlike shoots and its fleshy stems are strongly scented, similar to the odor of iris and violet. Calamus root preserved in sugar is still sold on the shores of the Bosphorus. In China, the fresh, tender leaves of *Chan-Po-Tzé* serve as seasoning under that name, which has been translated as scented reed *(jonc odorant).* In England calamus grows in the gardens of old colonial officers. It is mostly used by liqueur-makers.

Calvados

The alcoholic spirit made from cider, whose name is protected by French law. Good calvados is aged in casks of oak after it has been extracted from cider with a good alcohol and perfume. Sometimes it is cut with a little perry. This spirit, disdained by pseudogastronomes, gives an original taste to various preparations: *Caneton à la rouennaise, tripes à la mode de Caen,* partridges with cream, Norman fish stew, etc. It can also be used with cider in moistening sauces just before they are finished, with acidulated cream *(crème fraîche)* and spirits. Last, but not least, the famous *trou normand,* the Norman hole—a glass of calvados taken in the middle of a very copious meal—marks a joyous respite in the middle of a rustic banquet.

Camomile

(Matricaria chamomila; French, *Camomille;* German, *Kamille)* A small plant of the Compositae family, of which there are several cultivated and wild varieties: German camomile and Roman camomile. Their white flowers, which look like little daisies, are very aromatic and highly esteemed by herb doctors. They are also used in the cosmetic industry as shampooing decolorants. The gourmet is only concerned with camomile in that it is an element in the preparation of certain aperitif wines, notably vermouth.

Canada

The gastronomy of English-speaking Canada is too directly influenced by the Commonwealth of Mint Sauce and by proximity to Uncle Sam's can openers to merit special mention. Let's just say that we have eaten, in Montreal, excellent grills—necessarily washed down by soda pop—as well as marvelous pastries, due to the genius of Hungarian refugees.

On the other hand, the French *Canayens* of Quebec and Ontario know how to preserve old recipes from Poitou or Normandy and make them go with American products. Among other specialties are *cretons* (meat cakes), *chaudronnées* (fish stews), *talmousses* (cream cakes)—so many old French words that are more familiar to scholars than to Parisian chefs. Religious French-speaking communities have strongly contributed to the maintenance of this French standard.

Among typical aromas of the New France are caribou marrow, dried bear meat, honeys, maple syrup, a number of well-fleshed and refreshing berries, like the cranberry, *attoca* that the Indians make into a sort of cider, and the *gourganes* (swamp limas).

Incidentally, and this is not well enough known, despite its rigorous climate, Canada produces good red wines. These permit the French Canadian gastronome, threatened by an Anglo-Saxon encirclement, to keep up his morale as well as his traditions. Quebec, and a good number of smaller cities, remain in the forefront of French cuisine.

Caper

(French, *Capre;* German, *Kaper*) This common condiment, of somewhat mysterious origin, is neither a fruit nor a seed. It is the flower bud of the caper bush or *Capparis spinosa*, a spiny bush abundant in Mediterranean countries. The best capers come from Roquevaire in the South of France, which is the world capital of this delicate article. There the flower buds that have not blossomed are gradually gathered, and salted or soaked in vinegar.

The smallest are called *non-pareilles,* the largest *capotes.* The half-blossomed bud and the flower are not as highly valued. Some frauds attempt to sell elderberries as capers, but they are easily recognized by their long, smooth appearance.

In the Middle Ages, the caper was considered an excellent medication against the plague. Dumas, who did not care much for it, said quite prettily, "It suits old people and melancholy people in cold weather!" Today, universally esteemed, capers generally combine their flavor with white sauces, black butter, and the sundry preparations of crustaceans. Capers, filets of anchovies, and sun-filled vegetables like the eggplant go well together. In Austria, they are used to flavor *Liptauer*, a fresh cheese. It would be a gastronomic sin to consign these tender buds only to fish and sea food. The caper can, on occasion, underline the personality of domestic rabbit, prepared as in the South of France, tripe with anchovies, cold meats with vinaigrette sauce, veal's head, *steak tartare,* etc.

Caponata

A vegetable stew set off by capers. It is a distant cousin of the French (Nice) *ratatouille.*

Caramel

In addition to its many uses in baking, confections, etc., liquid caramelized sugar is used to color many foods: consommés, sauces, aspics. Carême* and Dumas*, in speaking of caramel, use the expressions "monkey juice" and "monkeying with a sauce." This practice, which Prosper Montagné* thought unorthodox, is more legitimate in the great Chinese cuisine, because it is used to prepare dishes like glazed pork, where the caramel plays the role of a true aromatic (with soy, monosodium glutamate, nuöc-man, etc.). Certain cold countries that look for calories, like Canada or Sweden, impose caramel in unexpected ways, for example: to set off bacon and eggs that are then gratinated in the oven. Caramel also figures in chutney, pickles, etc. (*See* SUGAR.)

* See APPENDIX.

Caraway

(*Carum carvi;* French, *Carvi*; German, *Kuemmel*) An umbelliferous plant of distant Asian origin that is highly esteemed, particularly in Central and Northern Europe. If you do not know of its existence, it is because of the silly habit of calling it meadow cumin (*Cumin des prés*) confusing it with true Oriental or Mediterranean cumin (which see.)

Its flowers are white or light pink, its root is rather thick, and the plant is intensively cultivated in Holland and Central Europe. The seed is blackish, narrow, and curved like a moon crescent. It has only one carpel. The taste is less peppery than that of true cumin, and its more subtle perfume is a lot like anise. The ancients, notably Julius Caesar, called caraway *chara*, the Arabs, *krawya*, a word that sometimes becomes *cravilla* in Oriental groceries.

Caraway is rather a culinary half tone. It is made for cooking fish and crustaceans. These elongated, finely perfumed seeds are found in *choucroute*, as well as Irish stew, Alsatian green beans, and Hungarian goulash (in very small amounts). Its aroma goes well with smooth paste cheese, especially Muenster. Sometimes this mixing has been done by the cheese-maker: Géromé of the Vosges, Gjetost of Norway.

Cardamom

(French, *Cardamome;* German, *Kardamom*) A spice that occupies a place to itself on the shelves of specialized Western groceries. It is abundant, but few buy it. Nevertheless, it is highly valued in India, and every cook calls on cardamom when using curry or *ras-el-hanout.*

The cardamom seeds are small, brown, and irregular, numbering ten, twelve, or sixteen, in yellow capsules about three-eighths of an inch in diameter. They are the dried fruits of *Elettaria cardamomum*, a large bushy plant of the *Zingiberaceae* family, native to Malabar and Ceylon. Cardamom is sold whole or as powdered seed. The aroma is peppery, bitter, highly aromatic and in all honesty a little pharmaceutical. What are they good for? With the exception of the mixed spices cited above, cardamom requires

Caraway

certain circumspection. The Chinese themselves prefer to class this spice among the medicinal drugs.

In Syria and Egypt, powdered cardamom is used to flavor buffalo stew, Turkish coffee, and some sherbets. Two European countries are at the head of the worldwide consumers: Finland and Sweden. They use cardamom, as well as anise, to perk up the taste of baked products. To be perfect, gingerbread and spice bread require a whisper of powder of *elletaria* (the Malayan name for cardamom). It goes well with sundry bitter liquors, such as Italian bitters and English ginger ale. To our mind, pure cardamom presents a sole, indisputable advantage: it neutralizes the smell of garlic. At the end of a meal in which your guests have eaten the most powerful *aïolis,* make each chew a single seed of cardamom. The pariah spice is a marvelous deodorant and an aid to digestion. (*See* ABAHAN, AMONOM, CURRY, RAS-EL-HANOUT.)

Cashew Nut

(*Anacardium occidentale;* French, *Noix d'acajou;* German, *Walnuss*) Several tropical trees have the name cashew-mahogany, popularized by the cabinetmakers. The anacard, or the cashew apple, is the only one to have a place in cooking.

Its fruit is the cashew apple, amusing but sourish. The Brazilians make a thirst-quenching drink, a valuable vinegar, as well as preserves from it. This apple, by quirk of nature, is lengthened by a seed called a cashew nut, a kidney-shaped almond with a sweet, agreeable flavor. The inhabitants of India are quite enamored of the cashew. For four centuries, they have cultivated the cashew tree in the lagoons of Kérala and elsewhere to be able to have this nut for their recipes. The Indian cashew industry presently employs more than 100,000 workers and does a yearly volume of 50,000 tons. The American nut has been given over to the Asian specialists.

The cashew nut is a true exotic condiment. In the Antilles, the natives eat it roasted in coals. In Brazil, it is an element in variations of the famous *feijoada* of Rio or São Paulo, but the Indians prize it more than all the others. They grate it finely and add it whole to skillful compositions of chutney, curry (which see), etc. They also fry it with various spices to make snacks. They coat fowl or asparagus destined to be glazed with cashew. This nut goes well

53

with all cheese preparations, in various breadings, in chicken or lettuce salads, and in chocolate and banana desserts. In French cuisine, cashew nuts, when finely grated, are generally reserved for use in an avocado salad.

Caterpillars of Milk Vetch

Certain pods of the plants of the *Leguminosae* are fine, white, and curved like worms. For a long time, this resemblance has permitted jocular *maîtres d'hôtel* to play on the naïveté of guests: they add this vegetable "caterpillar" in twisted shapes to their salads. The reactions are quick to come.

The "caterpillars" taste like dwarf butter beans that come from three comestible plants: milk vetch *(Astragalus hamosus)*, scorpius *(Scorpiurus vermiculatuso)*, and coiled lupulin *(Medicago turbinata)*. The pod of lucerne grass, which is tougher, can be used as a substitute.

Cayenne Pepper

(French, *Poivre de cayenne;* German, *Cayenne Pfeffer*) It is not a pepper but a very little capsicum, generally reduced to a yellow-orange powder. It comes from *Capsicum frutescens minimum,* cultivated in French Guiana and the Antilles. The pods are not longer than three-quarters of an inch. Their odor is bitter, animal-like, and their taste is volcanic. The powder, sold in the grocery store as cayenne pepper, resembles very fine bread crumbs under an eyeglass. It is sometimes adulterated with dried and broken tomato pulp and seeds. More frequently, it is mixed with sea salt to preserve it.

Cayenne pepper is very useful in cooking. Unlike ordinary pepper, it should never leave the kitchen for the table. Its taste is hotter than that of gray pepper, burning, and not spicy. The dried pods can be bought and broken up between the fingers when needed. Do not rub your eyes with these same fingers. Cayenne pepper in powder is quite adequate, because it is used with extreme moderation.

USES: *This spice is welcome in the preparation of crustaceans such as crayfish cullis,* homard à l'américaine, *crab salad, and sundry bisques. It goes particularly well with saffron and tomato and is also found in recipes for fish soups,* risotto, *and even* paella. *A knife point of cayenne is enough! It is better to season these dishes before the cooking is finished so that the fine crumbs of pepper can blow up in the cooking steam. Cayenne can also season white sauce, omelettes, and dried or green vegetables, especially cauliflower au gratin. It goes well in all the preparations containing cheese that are baked, even in cheese-spread bread. A whisper of cayenne gives a high flavor to certain sugared dishes like fried bananas, and even to creole punch.*

Cedrat (Citron-Tree)

(Citrus medica; French, *Cedrat;* German, *Zedrat-zitrone)* Fruit of the Persian variety of the lemon tree, widespread in the Orient and on the periphery of the Mediterranean. It is the shape of a large quince, with a thick peel used in preserves, and a sweetish, mildly agreeable pulp. It used to be called *aigre de cèdre.*

In Corsica, the citron is used to make an agreeable liqueur, *cedratine.* In South America, it perks up refreshing beverages. In Morocco, where it is called *Laranj* (this Arab word is the origin of *orange*), pressed citron is used to acidify canned preserved olives. It can be used like a bitter orange to give an amusing touch to the cooking of duck, but it is recommended to soak its peel three days in salt water, then rinse it, to tone down its bitterness. (*See* BITTER ORANGE *and* LEMON.)

Celery

(Apium graveolens; French, *Celeri;* German, *Sellerie)* A vegetable plant highly valued in cooking for its stems, tubers, and even its leaves. Several varieties are cultivated, responding to a variety of culinary needs. Its botanical name of "scented smallage" *(ache odorante)* indicates that all parts of the umbelliferous plant can play an aromatic role in the cooking pot.

Most concentrates sold in the groceries as *pot-au-feu* are strongly set off by celery. The celery stem, finely cut in julienne, is indispensable in *soupe au pistou* from the South of France, Italian minestrone, and even the true Italian tomato sauce.

A related plant, lovage or perennial celery, plays a like role in the sourish soups of the Balkans and the vegetable creams of

Switzerland and the Teutonic countries. (*See* LOVAGE.)

Celery seed and celery powder are available as well as the famous celery salt that both barmen and cooks use. (It agreeably accents tomato juice as well as a soup.) Celery seed can be used like fennel seed to liven up a baked fish, a *potée aux choux,* a cheese soufflé, a cauliflower au gratin, a duck with red cabbage, etc. Celery in all its forms is employed to flavor the chestnut purée that accompanies some game.

Cèpe

(*Boletus edulis;* French, *Cèpe;* German, *Steinpilzo*) The cèpe is a large edible mushroom, a variety of *Boletus.* It is also called *tête de nègre* when it is young and its cap has not yet turned ocher. Dumas remarked, "The cèpe is sought after in the South of France as a seasoning." Its very delicate odor and its characteristic taste are enhanced by garlic, paprika, *fines herbes,* and Madeira wine. Reciprocally, finely sliced fresh or dried cèpe gives a high flavor to the most common sauce.

Chakchouka

A pleasant Tunisian specialty made of tomatoes, onions, sweet peppers, and eggplants fried in oil (à *ratatouille niçoise* without squash). Originally chakchouka was eaten as is, accompanied by *merquez* (mutton sausages) and fried eggs.

Champagne

Celebrated the world over, champagne is at once a combination of juices from black and white grapes and a knowing mixture of growths. It is not identified by territory, but by commercial brands. It is shaken, dosed, and manipulated before being sold, marked *brut, extra-dry, dry sec,* and *demi-sec* on the label. *Blanc de Blanc* is champagne *nature* made from white Pinot-Chardonnay grapes.

USES: *Cooking with champagne is a luxury that is rarely justified. It is more enticing on the menu than on the table. Once boiled, this prestigious wine loses its particular qualities. Its light bubbles and fine foam are not made for the pot. The lightness and spice of champagne is only found in sauces made by rapidly swishing a frying pan. Filets of sole with champagne are worthwhile. Champagne also keeps a certain character in jellies and aspics.*

What about chicken with champagne, or pike braised in champagne? They do not surpass, in our opinion, preparations with Chablis or Pouilly, and are much more expensive. One thing for sure, it is better to cook a chicken in the most ordinary Muscadet than in a sweetish champagne of doubtful origin. On the other hand, it is perhaps interesting during cooking to moisten a pâté, a fowl terrine, or a godiveau with champagne. The carbon dioxide gas given off by the wine makes these dishes lighter. In Troyes, where very juicy andouillette are preferred, the sausage is scored and at the last minute a half-glass of champagne is poured over it.

One amusing use for champagne is "moistening" onion soup. Prepare it as usual, with a small amount of broth, then moisten it with a half bottle of brut *champagne at the end of cooking. Shut off the heat before boiling starts. (See* WINE.)

Chanterelle

(*Agaricus cantharellus;* French, *Girolle;* German, *Pfefferling*) Faithful victim of the mycophagist, it appears in spring and only dies under the dead leaves of fall. The chanterelle, also called *jaunet* and *chevret,* is a very agreeable condiment. Its rustic, simple flavor adapts especially well to the omelette or the frying pan, in the company of garlic and aromatic herbs. It does not attempt to equal the cèpe and the morel, which are the king and queen of edible mushrooms. (The truffle is a god.)

The chanterelle, when sold "fresh," or rather in a state of decomposition, is improved by being cleaned, threaded on a cord, and dried. If it looks as if the mushroom had been attacked by larva and insects, it is sufficient to place it above a pot of boiling water for ten minutes before drying it completely. (*For its uses, see* MUSH-ROOMS.)

Charcoal

Wood charcoal and even animal charcoal were widely used in the time when refrigerators existed only in the imagination of inventors! The power of adsorption of charcoal to rapidly reduce putrefication gas was known long ago. In the old days, fresh-killed game was cleaned and then filled with wood charcoal to keep it several days. Today, fragments of charcoal can be tied in a cloth and dipped in a broth gone sourish to get rid of the odor of fermentation. This process also works to clear a liqueur. A hot coal in tired oil clarifies it.

Otherwise, powdered charcoal is used in the United States as an aromatic for the barbecue. The jars of powdered charcoal of aromatic woods, carbonized and pulverized, are used to give grills cooked at home the flavor of barbecued meat. The Germans call this unexpected aromatic *Holzkohlenaroma*.

Chatni

A synonym of CHUTNEY.

Chayote

(*Sechium edule*) A little cucurbit native to Mexico, but also cultivated in Spain and North Africa. Chayotes can be found in a number of grocery stores that specialize in exotic products. The white pulp of these fruits, valued in the Antilles as *chistophines* or *briones*, is rather delicate and resembles that of the cardoon. They can be prepared as garnish for a *poulet créole*, or used as an ingredient in *couscous*.

Chenopodiaceae

(*Chenopodium;* German, *Gaensefussgewaechse*) The *Chenopodiaceae*, or goosefoot, are herbaceous plants with palmate leaves. The best-known comestible *Chenopodiaceae* are spinach and beets, but there are other varieties known to cooks: Bon Henri goosefoot and white goosefoot, or pigweed (French, *Ansérine Bon Henri* or *Ansérine blanche; C. bonus henricus* and *C. album*) wild or cultivated, can replace spinach or be used to liven up rustic salads.

MEXICAN TEA (*Chenopodium ambrosioides;* French; *ambroisie ansé-*

rine) Highly scented, it grows in the Western Hemisphere. It livens up exotic sauces and is used as an infusion.

PIGWEED (*Chenopode-quinoa C. quinoa*) A comestible herb very popular in Peru and neighboring countries. Its farinaceous seed was one of the favorite foods of the Incas. It is still eaten in cakes, groats, meat, seasoning, etc. It is also fermented with millet or roasted and is made into beverages like beer or coffee. The dark-green or reddish leaves are spicy and tasty. The cultivation of pigweed in the last century was undertaken by French gardeners, but unfortunately abandoned.

N.B.   There are many other *Chenopodiaceae*, for the most part edible and close to orache, or spinach.

Cherry

(*Prunus avium;* French, *Cerise;* German *Kirsche*) The cherry tree as a member of the *Rosaceae-Amygdalaceae* is supposed to have been imported from Asia Minor by Lucullus. It is said that its fleshy drupes have been part of the pleasures of the table for a long time. In addition to its many uses in making desserts and other sweets, and the numerous alcohols and liquors—*kirsch* of Alsace, *Kirsch-wasser* of Germany and Berne, cherry brandy from Denmark or France, *wichniovka* from Moscow, and *ratafia de cerises* of the South of France—cherries, bigaroons, and morello cherries are used as a condiment. Duck with cherries is well known; cherry soup, which made Dumas on one of his bad days grimace; pickled cherries, another German formula that can be used as a pickle either with roast fowls or somewhat insipid meats.

N.B.   The leaves of the black cherry tree (*cerisier-mahaleb*), also called *Bois-de-Sainte-Lucie,* are very highly scented and can be used to liven up cooking in Alsace and Germany.

Chervil

(*Anthriscus cerefolium;* French, *Cerfeuil;* German, *Kerbel*) An umbelliferous plant that has a great role in the botany of gastronomy. It is an annual plant that grows wild in Central Europe and on

59

some Mediterranean shores. Its leaves are always tripinnate and a pretty green, and its white flowers are always in umbels. Several regions and the gardener's art have encouraged the growth of different varieties: common chervil, sold in French markets; curly chervil, most decorative; and bulb chervil, which is valued for its roots.

Several adventitious varieties little known to cooks also exist: sweet cicely (*cerfeuil musqué*), as large as a fern, growing in mountains and strongly scented; wild chervil or *sylvestre,* whose greenery gives off a strong, somewhat bitter aroma, should be approached carefully because it resembles hemlock.

Chervil, a fresh, anise-scented, natty herb, takes its name from the Greek *kaïréphyllon,* which means "herb of joy." Its green leaves, cut in "tufts" with scissors, go well with soups and salads and as an accompaniment for roasted meats. It is an ingredient in cream of leek soup, chicken cream soup, chervil soup—a Dutch specialty, and the famous *gazpacho* of Spain. As for meats, the piquant taste of chervil seems created for the young goat, rabbit, and young fowls. It also has an important role in combinations of *fines herbes* to flavor an omelette, a white wine sauce, etc.

It is important to avoid the slightest boiling of chervil, which takes away all its aromatic properties, and to avoid any delay in using it after it is finely cut; its aroma is particularly volatile.

Cheshire (Cheese)

The famous English cheese, which has at least three varieties: *white* (mild), *pink* (artifically colored), and *blue* (full of veins of mold). Its spicy taste is exploited by cooks to perk up an onion soup, a celery salad, or mushroom salad. In Nordic countries, Cheshire cheese is used as hors d'oeuvres surrounded by radishes. This cheese is an element in the English Welsh rarebit.

Chestnuts

(Fruits of *Castanea vulgaris;* French, *Châtaignes;* German, *Kastanien*) The chestnut is one of the *Copuliferae,* a quick-growing, long-lasting tree. Its fruits, chestnuts, have played a great role in feeding the poor population in Sardinia, Corsica, and the Massif

Central of France for a long time. Improved by cultivation and grafts, the chestnut tree can bear large nuts without inside partitions, which makes candy-makers very happy.

Corsican cuisine makes special preparations with a base of chestnut purée: *polenta de châtaignes, brilloli au lait, farinana à l'huile, amojata,* chestnut tart, etc. Formal French cuisine has adopted chestnut purée to accompany roast game. The flavor of chestnut goes particularly well with celery, star anise, and lemon peel. It is also a delicious ingredient in stuffing recipes.

N.B.   In the southern United States and in Mexico, exotic chestnuts are often threaded on a skewer with chicken livers or veal kidneys. The same can be done with European chestnuts if one has parboiled and dried them a half hour before grilling. They should not be peeled, but split with a knife.

In France, chestnuts are called *marrons* rather than *châtaignes* when referring to fruit of a chestnut tree that has been improved by graft and cultivation to have only one fleshy kernel.

The horse chestnut (*marron d'Inde*), is produced by a tree of the same family (*Aesculus hippocastanum*), planted in public gardens and avenues. Its bitter and disagreeable taste makes it unsuited for human consumption, but horses and cattle eat it; it is toxic for fowl. Mutton fed horse chestnuts is said to have tender flesh and a pleasing taste.

Chicha

An alcoholic beverage highly prized in Central America, Bolivia, and Peru. It is made of a must of fermented corn, seasoned with pineapple pulp and molasses. Chicha, depending on the crop, resembles a cider, marc, or a fortified cooked wine. In Latin American cooking, it is often used to swish a pan in which a tender meat, such as kid, or fowl has been cooked.

Chicory

(*Cichorium intybus;* French, *Chicorée;* German, *Zichorie*) A perennial plant of the *Compositae,* whose leaves and roots, under different names, are neighbors in the food stores.

Wild chicory has a slightly bitter taste. The young shoots can be added to assorted salads. Among the cultivated varieties are curly chicory, escarole, endive, and a German variety, Madgebourg chicory, whose root is dried and roasted as a substitute for coffee. Curly chicory is prepared with lard, creamed meat juices, or béchamel sauce. As a garnish, it is too often forgotten. Its bitter flavor agreeably underlines starches, lentils, chick peas, etc. In Poitou and Gascogne, well-stewed fresh *flageolets* and *mogettes* are eaten with leaves of chicory, moistened with acidulated cream or nut oil.

Chile, Chili, Chilli

A Mexican pepper. Preserved chiles, *piquines verdes* or *rojos* (small strong red or green peppers), *chiles jalapeños* (large pepper, hotter than our peppers), and *chiles relleños* (stuffed chiles) are found in many groceries.

The English make chilli or chili from *chillitos*, very little, hot peppers. The name as well as the fiery tastes are found in red chili sauce and in jars of green chili. The green chilis are small and, by looks alone, could pass for capers. In Europe they often come from Hong Kong because of a healthy spirit of copying that exists between Chinese and Mexican grocers.(Trans. note: Chili powder of the American Southwest is a blend of chili peppers and several spices.)

China

One has to be not only a gourmet but a poet, sociologist, and economist to speak knowingly of this prestigious mother cuisine. The Chinese culinary art has influenced all the gastronomy of the Far East (Japan, Vietnam, Thailand, Indonesia). In China itself, there are several schools: northern, the roughest; southern, which tends to abuse fats and spicy seasoning; and central, admirably subtle and balanced.

This entire book would not be enough to give a precise idea of Peking and its 10,000 recipes. Regrettably, we have to limit ourselves to sending the reader to specialized works and to citing the key ingredients and words of this science, all of which are becoming more and more accessible: star anise, cinnamon, powdered five mushrooms, Chinese mushrooms, monosodium glutamate, kumquats, litchis, lotus, lily flowers, sesame oil, soy, as well as bamboo shoots and nuöc-mam, the latter especially important in Vietnam. It is interesting to note that our aromatic herbs and our comestible plants are well known to Chinese and Vietnamese cooks: watercress, cucumber, mint, sweet pepper, sage. Sometimes the gastronomy of the Chinese is astonishingly close to the Moslem's, for example in their use of honey, coriander, and ginger. Smoking and the use of spirits (yellow wine) brings the culinary preparations of this immense nation very close to those of France. (More information is contained in sections dealing with the words mentioned in this article.)

Chinese Mushrooms

In the country of sampans, paper lanterns, and the cultural revolution, edible cryptogams survive revolutions. Chinese mushrooms from Peking or Hong Kong are the same as those that the Emperors Tcheou Ming and Tsing ate. One does not have to be a Red Guard to distinguish between them.

PERFUMED MUSHROOM, called *nam-huong* in Vietnamese. It looks like the French *oreille de Juda*, a modest *Auricularia* with a concave cap that in French forests is found attached to the roots of the elder. A traitor that has escaped to French cuisine.

BLACK MUSHROOM or *moq-nhi* of Saigon, is not really a cryptogam. It is, in truth, a weed of the China Sea. This marine vegetable slides under the teeth and sideslips the tongue, leaving a light iodine taste.

Without extolling these mushrooms to the clouds, we would like to recognize the merits of these Chinese condiments. It is necessary to wash them very thoroughly in the case of the black mushroom and to let them swell in warm water for twenty minutes. The water in which the perfumed mushroom has soaked, once filtered, can moisten a sauce or stretch a soup.

Chives (Rushleek)

(*Allium schoenoprasum;* French, *Ciboule, Ciboulette;* German, *Lauchz-wiebel schnittlauch*) Belonging like the onion and garlic to the *Lilia-ceae* family, chives are slender perennial plants that grow in tufts. Their fleshy leaves are more esteemed than their scanty bulbs, with a taste that differs only slightly from onion's.

Chives and rushleek are very common in Europe, from Lapland to Sicily. The Swede Linnaeus, who was fond of poached eggs dusted with chives, gave it its Latin name. The Germans call it cutting leek, and the English, rushleek. Very decorative because of its pink flowers, it is often sold in the markets. It is interesting to dietitians because of its vitamin A and C content. All cooks know that chives, finely cut with scissors, pick up the taste of a salad, sauce, or omelette.

The late Léon Binet* reported in a recent book that it gives a very personal touch to potato tart from Brie, white cheese, vinaigrette used for cold meat, and other sauces of the same type, such as *gribiche alsacienne,* and *tartare.*

The *ciboule*, Welsh onion or stone leek, which is larger, more bitter and less widespread, is used by cheese-makers for an ingredient in some cheeses, notably Flemish Limburger.

Chocolate Sauces

In the article on cocoa, we will show that the pretty brown powder is used very lightly as a condiment. Many recipes of Latin-American inspiration use the toasted pods of the cocoa tree in cooking fowl and waterfowl. Dumas explained how to prepare a scooter duck with chocolate. (*See* COCOA.)

Chorizo

The famous Spanish sausage, originally from Estremadura, full of tomato and strongly spiced, is supposedly smoked on juniper twigs. It contains the meat and variety meats of half-savage pigs that run wild on moors. In France, two varieties are sold, more or

* See APPENDIX.

less spiced. *Chorizo* should always be cut in diagonal slices as long and thin as possible.

 Chorizo is an element in *paella, olla podrida* (the Madrid *pot-au-feu*), sundry rustic soups of Galicia and Aragon, and as a garnish for scrambled eggs Spanish-style, or modest chick peas. It should not be boiled or frizzled but should simply be well reheated when added to other foods.

Chrysanthemum Flowers

In Japan, where floral art easily surpasses culinary art, these magnificent, fleshy flowers are eaten in a salad. Prosper Montagné* has also taught us that they can decorate a Francillon salad, composed of cooked, shelled mussels, grated celery root, and hot potatoes cut in slices and marinated in Chablis wine. (*See* FLOWERS.)

Chutney, Chatni

An Indian condiment highly favored by the Britons and by the people of South Africa who call it *blatjang*. Whether it is flavored with mango, tamarind, coconut, mint, or lemon, chutney is a sort of vegetable purée, spiced and sugared, containing onions, raisins, and fruit pulp marinated in vinegar.

 In the countries of the Commonwealth, the word chutney has become a synonym of a vegetable purée seasoned with peppery spices: chutney of tomatoes, eggplants, from Jamaica or Guiana. The different chutneys can be served with all the dishes of Indo-Malay cuisine having bland rice or a starch as an ingredient: with chicken *à la créole*, and with a light meal of cold meats, as the English do. In this case, it is amusing to serve ginger beer instead of wine.

Cider

The fermented juice of apples has occasionally played a role in culinary alchemy. It is used to moisten certain dishes in Norman-

* See APPENDIX.

style cooking (tripes, matelotes) before they receive the finishing touch of a glass of Calvados. Another by-product, apple-cider vinegar, prized by some doctors in the United States, has gained an interesting place in the preparation of salads and certain exotic specialties. (*See* CALVADOS *and* CIDER VINEGAR.)

Cinnamon

The bark or branches of several exotic laurels, either rust-colored or brownish, always very aromatic. This woody substance has been sought out from earliest times. Cinnamon is the *cinname* of the Song of Songs that the Queen of Sheba brought to the attention of Solomon. Nero burned cinnamon and incense, according to the legend, before the body of his wife, Poppaea, whom he had just slain with a knife. The Crusaders brought cinnamon back to flavor their favorite beverage, *hypocras.*

Botanists and cooks are in agreement when it comes to distinguishing between two varieties of cinnamon. Cinnamon de Ceylon comes from *Laurus cinnamomum.* It is light-colored and gives off a particularly agreeable perfume. Cinnamon of China, or bastard cinnamon (cassia) in sticks, is smaller and stockier. Its aroma is more subtle, a little bitter sometimes, and it smells like coriander. The Germans, who use and abuse this spice, call both varieties *Zimt.* There are also other cinnamon trees under other exotic skies, notably Guiana, Brazil, Africa, but their barks are much less valued.

USES: *It is hardly news to say that cinnamon is valuable in making desserts, sweets, confections, such as rice with milk, German compote,* chocolat à l'espagnole, *plum pudding, Viennese apple strudel, chocolate truffles,* café brûlot, *etc.*

Frenchmen depreciate the very subtle flavor of cinnamon. According to F.A.O. statistics, France is one of the Western nations that consumes the least cinnamon per capita (0.1 ounce a year, against 1.2 ounces in the U.S.). Without doubt the French are at once unjust and forgetful of the several merits of this spice. They should be reminded that if cinnamon does not figure among the four traditional French spices (even though it is among the Chinese "five perfumes"), it does not play a lesser role in celebrated preparations that have nothing to do with sweets: first of all, in couscous *(a whisper of cinnamon on the properly steamed and buttered semolina), then in* salmis

Cinnamon

*of wild duck (*col vert *wild water fowl), snail fricassee, as it used to be prepared in the east of France (nutmeg and cinnamon tempering the garlic and onion), mussel soups,* alycot Béarnais, *sundry roasts of pork, notably pork with cinnamon, a Portuguese specialty, many wine sauces, duck with cherries, Catalan rice with pimientos, and* pasta e fagioli, *a thick bean soup with macaroni made in Venice.*

In the area of beverages, the famous Spanish sangría *requires a touch of cinnamon. In Asian cuisine, cinnamon is inseparable from* abgoucht *(the traditional Iranian* pot-au-feu*), Ceylonese curry, and the whole gamut of Chinese recipes.*

Cinnamon Tree Flowers

(French, *Fleurs de cannelier*) are the flower buds of *Laurus cassia,* dried like cloves. The Orientals use them in combinations of soy sauce (Chinese, *tsiang-yeou*) to flavor fish stew, chicken with pineapple, etc.

Cistus

(*Cistus creticus;* French, *Ciste,* German, *Zistus*) A Mediterranean bush that gives off a gum resin, *ladanum,* which used to be used in medicine. Its persistent leaves and branches are sometimes used by Corsicans, Cretans, and Sicilian cooks like myrtle to flavor a court-bouillon or a charcoal grilling.

Clary

(*Salvia sclarea;* French, *Sauce sclarée;* German, *Muskat-salbei*) A variety of sage cultivated in Germany and England. It is also called *orvale* in French.

The leaves' subtle odor makes them too musky to be used otherwise than in pastry and making certain Italian vermouths. German wine-makers use clary like woodruff and nasturtium flow-

ers to season the must of *Gewürztraminer*. In Grasse it is highly
sought after in the perfume industry.

Cloves

(Eugenia caryophyllata; French, *Girofle;* German, *Gewuerznelke* and
Nelke; Italian, *Garofano)* A spice furnished by the clove tree, an
attractive tree with persistent leaves cultivated notably in Zanzibar, Madagascar, and Indonesia. In flowering season, it bears little
pink bells that undoubtedly tempted the Portuguese navigators of
the sixteenth century. Its native territory is the Indonesian island
of Banda in the Moluccas. The extention of its culture on the
shores of the Indian Ocean is due to Governor Poivre. This minis-
ter of Louis XV did not hesitate to strip several clove and nutmeg
trees on the island of Manila despite the close surveillance of the
Dutch, and then gave them to colonists on the island of Bourbon.

Four parts of the plant play roles as aromatics. Its shiny
leaves, which look like bay, have a very strong taste but are hardly
scented. Their use is limited to the growing regions. Its fruit,
called clove matrix or mother of cloves *(mère de girofle),* is an egg-
shaped seed, crowned by the teeth of persistent flower cups. Although its export is forbidden by local authorities, it is sometimes
found on the market, dried or macerated. Its flavor is agreeable
and sweet. It is a sort of preserved fruit. Its peduncle—the stems
of the flowers—are known as clove claws *(griffes de girofle)* or clove
tails *(queues de girofle).* Distillers use them in making the essence of
cloves, for medicine or perfumery. The perfume of this essence
resembles pink and vanilla and is restricted in its culinary merits.

Finally, the clove nails *(clous de girofle),* which are the dried
flower buds, are sometimes boiled and smoked. Their very strong
taste and scent made it second only to pepper in popularity with
early spice merchants.

The name of this spice comes from the Latin *Caryophyllum*
chosen by Pliny, who adapted the Oriental word *karumfel* (which
continues in Arabic). Appreciated for thirty centuries by the people of Southeast Asia, this flower bud has become a real part of the
gastronomy of the Oriental cuisines. In China, in the time of the
anccinent emperor Hans, the courtesans chewed a clove before
speaking to the sovereign. They were used eight centuries before

our era in spice mixes comparable to the "five perfumes" of today. Known to Europeans since antiquity, it remained, until the Renaissance and the voyages of the Portuguese, restricted to being a sailor's charm, a costly analgesic or anti-ophthalmic. Magellan's companions finally discovered the producing tree and were followed into Asiatic water by a quantity of vessels given over to a fruitful buying activity.

USES: *This culinary incense must be used skillfully. All the spice mixes, Western and Oriental, use only a small amount.*

The whole clove, which should be plump, dried, and provided with a friable button, is generally "nailed" in an onion and added to the very heart of sundry invigorating dishes: pot-au-feu, boeuf miroton, *chicken in the pot,* potée aux choux, *many game* civets, hure de sanglier, *etc. As for fish, only* matelote tourangelle *and the* meurrette Bourguignonne *(Trans. note: regional fish stew) with a red wine base, can take cloves. This restriction doesn't prohibit the taste of cloves in a court-bouillon used for cooking* au bleu. *A clove of garlic can also be studded with cloves and introduced in the knuckle of a leg of lamb, or the onion that simmers in a* blanquette *of veal.*

Reduced to a powder, the clove finds takers among delicatessen-makers and the pickle specialist, as well as certain cheese-makers. (Cloves are found in époisses *cheese and in many foreign cheeses.) Cloves are also used in making Irish stew, Alsatian hare or rice soup, or Teutonic peas, a pig's head* à la frisonne (balkenbrij) *as well as many German delicacies. The German people appreciate the combination of sugar and cloves, notably in little cakes with honey and almonds, in salads and compotes of fruit. This usage is found in France in the making of gingerbread.*

N.B. Different European plants give off a perfume resembling cloves, notably the gillyflower. This is not of interest except to horticulturists and herbalists. On the other hand, certain types of pink as well as the fibrous, brownish root of herb bennet *(Geum urbanum)* were formerly used as substitute cloves in rustic stews. The name *poivre-giroflée* is also given to allspice (which see).

Clove Matrix

Fruit of the clove tree (French, *Anthofle*), which used to be eaten as a heavily spiced preserve. The clove we know today is the bud of the same tree, dried and preserved after various treatments.

Cocoa

An aromatic powder taken from cocoa beans that are fermented, washed, dried, and roasted. The tree has pretty red flowers and belongs to the *Malvaceae* family. The Spaniards, who discovered it in Mexico, faithfully transcribed its Aztec name, *cacauatl* (*Theobroma cacao* for the botanist).

The Mexicans still hold the bean, which served as money for their ancestors, in high esteem. They consider cocoa, quite properly, a versatile spice, not reserved only for sugared dishes. They support this argument with excellent recipes, notably that of *el mole* sauce, combinations of pepper and cocoa, found in the famous *dinde au cacao*, turkey with cocoa.

Coconut

The coconut tree, or *Cocos nucifera*, a large tropical palm tree with a slender curved trunk is a rich economic and gastronomic resource. Its leaves and stems are made into textile fibers. The pith of its stem is edible *(sago)*. Its nut, gathered unripe or ripe, yields coconut pulp used in baking or in exotic cooking, and coconut milk is used to prepare fermented beverages and moisten curry sauces. Coconut oil and coconut butter are widely used by tropical cooks. The fermented sap is drunk as palm wine.

These sundry vegetable products are elements in a number of exotic recipes. The milk and the meat are used to fill out many sauces. In Indonesia, the pulp is often fried in palm oil and used to garnish a chicken dish. The young shoots of the coconut tree are used in making chutney (which see) in Indian, Ceylanese, or Malay cuisines. The *coco* from Polynesia is the fermented must of the coconut tree sap. Once distilled, this beverage makes a very strong alcohol, *manu coco.*

Cognac

The most aristocratic and most imitated spirit in the world has made the little Charente town where François I was born famous from the Tundra to the Far West. It is a name—alas—too freely used outside France, and becomes *konjakk* for the Vikings, *coñac* in

Patagonia. In the Charente dialect, it has a more pleasant name, *cougna.* A refined alcohol brought to perfection in the seventeenth century for Dutch and British merchants, only Cognac and Armagnac have the right to the *Adquit jaune d'or* given by *l'Institut National des Appelations d'Origine* (National Institute of Regional Names). It is also referred to by its cabalistic initial V.S.O.P. (very superior old pale). (Trans. note: The French use the initials of the English words with the exception of T.V.F.C., *très vielle fine champagne,* very old Cognac from the *fine champagne* region.)

Aged seven or eight years in oak casks, enriched by tannin and other subtle elements, Cognac is a careful hybrid of varied distilled products. The wines of Grande Champagne have nothing to do with the wines of the Champagne. (Trans. note: Both a tiny region in the Cognac district and the wine-growing region east of Paris have the same name.)

Cognac, like other more rustic alcohols, is used to flame a fowl or piece of meat, a sauce, an onion soup, an aspic, making a roux for *sauce Américaine,* or *sauce Bordelaise.* Its culinary uses are innumerable, but it is often preferable to use a less subtle spirit and keep the *fine champagne* for the meal's end, poured in a snifter to be heated lovingly in the palm of the hands.

Cominos

Greek name for cumin, seen on some packages to distinguish it from caraway.

Compound Butters

Compound butter, like garlic butter or spice butter, is a condiment prepared either by mixing blanched garlic that has been grated or pounded in a mortar, or pepper and nutmeg, with very fresh farm butter. The mixture must firm up in the refrigerator before being used in the form of small lumps to garnish grilled meat or poached fish.

Mackerel flesh, which is a little bland, can even use mustard butter. There are other compounds:

RUSSIAN BUTTER is made of one part black caviar and two parts of fresh butter and is used to spread on the slices of dark bread that will be covered with filets of trout or sturgeon.

RAVIGOTE BUTTER, including chives, tarragon, and parsley, all finely chopped, goes well with *tournedos* or other meat cooked "blue."

STRONG BUTTER or *beurre fort,* improperly called rancid butter *(beurre rance),* is preserved butter highly esteemed by North African cooks. *(See* SMEUN.)

Compound Spices

(French, *Épices composées*) A sacred expression often used by Carême, indicates a pulverized mixture of spices and aromatic herbs. Below are two apparently judicious formulas.

CLASSIC MIXTURE (according to the *Manuel du restaurateur*)

	Per cent
Thyme	10
Bay	10
Marjoram	6
Rosemary	6
Nutmeg	20
Cloves	20
Cayenne	6
White Pepper	12
Coriander	10

PROVENÇALE MIXTURE (according to J. N. Escudier*)

	Per cent
Thyme	12
Bay	15
Rosemary	12
Basil	12
Nutmeg	12.5
Clove	10
White Pepper	10
Coriander	5
Savory	10
Lavender	1.5

* See APPENDIX.

These mixtures, which can be made at home, are extremely handy to beef up hastily prepared dishes. It is suitable, nevertheless, according to the particularities of each recipe, to reinforce one or the other of their ingredients. An important recommendation: don't keep compound spices for too long. Some aromas are more unstable than the others, and the taste of the mixtures can vary to their detriment.

N.B.   Another aromatic mixture that is sometimes called turtle spices, which are especially suited to season true and mock turtle soup, is discussed under the heading of TURTLE HERBS.

Coppa

Salted, smoked pork shoulder flavored with garlic, which is the most celebrated specialty of Corsican curers. (*For uses in cooking*, *see* HAM.)

Coriander

(*Coriandum sativum;* French, *Coriandre;* German, *Koriander* and *Stinkdill*.) An umbelliferous aromatic of distant Armenian origin, cultivated in the Orient, Greece, North Africa, Holland, Thuringer and, very rarely, in France. Its lower leaves resemble angelica and its upper leaves chervil. This greenery is easily recognizable by the fetid odor it gives off—the name coriander comes from a Greek word signifying "stinking." In French, it is also called *punaise mâle*, energetic or virile stink.

The fruit of the coriander, a ten-sided globule marked by longitudinal sides, resembles a large, gray pepper seed. Once dried, it gives off the aroma of both anise and pepper, more intense once it is roasted. This seed is one of the few spices gathered in cold-weather countries.

USES: *Coriander seed, whole or pulverized, is used principally to heighten the taste of artichokes and mushrooms* à la grecque, *vinegar pickles, and sundry liqueurs, notably Basque* izarra, *some German* schnaps, *and melissa water. It is also used in certain cold cuts, particularly* longeoles from Vaud, and certain Swiss formulae for sauerkraut. It is very useful in the preparation of large game and gives flavor to marinades used for it. Pulverized coriander can be dusted on roasted meats that will be eaten cold, as a cold cut platter. The Portuguese heighten their caldeirada, a fish stew, with coriander seed.

In North Africa coriander has a large role. The whole seed is an element in the spice mixture called ras-el-hanout. Kosbor, as it is called, flavors meat balls. In Egypt, where it is called kosbara, it flavors tamia-falafel, balls of starchy vegetables. The Moslems, like the Chinese, use the fine leaves of fresh coriander in meat broths—Tunisian cherbah, Vietnamese phô.

This spice, which loses its unpleasant smell in cooking, is sometimes known in France as persil arabe, cerfeuil chinois, or Tunisian tabel.

Cornes Grecques

(*See* OKRA.)

Coumarin

The scented element contained in the seeds and essences of many vegetables, notably sweet clover, woodruff, fenugreek, and vernal grass (*flouve*). It is identified as an anhyrdride of *orthocoumaric acid*. It is commercially extracted for the perfume industry from the Tonka bean. Coumarin has a role in certain aromatic German beverages, *Zubrowka* in vodka, and in Oriental or rustic foods through the intermediary of the vegetables that contain it.

Court Bouillon

A strongly aromatic and spiced infusion in which fish are poached or crustaceans cooked. Rarely, vegetables to be used for hors d'oeuvre are cooked in a courtbouillon. The qualification *court*, or short, does not refer to the quantity of liquid, but the brevity of the preparation. Sea water is used, without seasoning, for shrimp and crustaceans, while vinegar court-bouillon is used for *truite au bleu,* white wine for salmon, trout, red mullet; red wine for carp, perch, pike; and milk for sole, haddock, turbot.

Couscous

This Arab food is so much in vogue in Europe today that we will merely mention its dominant flavors. *Marga,* the broth in which mutton pieces or chicken is cooked, contains a cardoon (lacking a cardoon, a small artichoke), green beans, chick peas, and fresh beans. It is lightly salted, peppered by a tiny spoonful of *harissa* (purée of red pepper and garlic), and seasoned with *kermoun* (real cumin).

The semolina, generally hard wheat, but sometimes millet, is buttered with *smeun* in mid-cooking, while for kosher cooking, a little olive oil is added instead. It is served separately from the broth (only the broth's steam has touched it), and can be decorated with little bits of artichoke bottoms, Corinth raisins boiled in milk, and stewed chick peas.

This fashion of serving semolina is encountered only in Morocco. In Algeria, it must be presented without any decoration, simply flavored with a little touch of powdered cinnamon.

In Algeria, the meat is cooked in the broth, or roasted on a spit (*méchoui* or *brochettes*). In Morocco, it is preferred prepared on the side as a *tagine,* a delicious stew simmered with raisins. The famous Arab spice, *ras-el-hanout,* is necessary in *tagine.* In Tunisia, the same stew is flavored with rose petals, or *chachiouard.*

Jewish Tunisian cooking has a number of variations on the traditional *couscous,* meat balls flavored with *kosbor* (coriander), chicken soufflés, little meat pies surrounding pieces of beef, a veal's foot, even a fresh gilthead (a small fish).

Sometimes saffron is used to slightly flavor the semolina of *couscous,* while mint can flavor the *méchoui* as it turns on the spit. Even a Tunisian meat sausage and eggs can sit on the semolina. (*See* CUMIN, HARISSA, RAS-EL-HANOUT, SMEUN.)

Crackling

The skin of pork more or less scraped and cleaned of bristles. Very tough, it is eaten only in head cheese and is used in cooking only as a fatty, protective bed between a meat and the walls of a braising pan. Its aroma, rather strong, is nevertheless appreciated in making some rustic recipes (*daube provençale,* braised leg of lamb, *à la auvergnate,* etc.).

For the Vietnamese, puffed crackling, or *bi-bong,* is a delicate treat. Dried in the sun on hot sand, it is stewed, cleaned of hair, then cut in thongs. *Bi-bong* can be found in Chinese groceries.

Cran and Cranson

(*See* HORSERADISH.)

Cranberries

Several dwarf bushes of the *Ericaceae,* which abound in the underbrush of cold and mountainous regions, bear red or purplish-blue edible berries. These are cranberries, whortleberries, bilberries, lingon berries.

While the huckleberry is used for desserts or confections, the bilberry, which is very acid, is in reality a condiment. Preparations of these berries are used and abused in Teutonic, Nordic, and Anglo-Saxon countries. (*Preiselbeere* in German; *lingon* in Swedish). Another highly flavored variety, the American cranberry or swamp whortleberry, is sold either whole or as jelly.

The author, while against the abuse of sweet condiments, admits to having regaled himself in Norwegian Lapland with a braised reindeer filet surrounded by a compote of whortleberries. This berry compote can be served with highly spiced meat: wild-boar ham, leg of moose, etc.

Cream

The Littré* Dictionary defines cream as "an oily substance, agreeable to the taste, that rises to the surface of untreated milk." Although it is less digestible than its by-product, butter, cream plays an important role in a number of culinary preparations:

ACIDULATED CREAM, (*crème fraîche*) Top cream, enriched by numerous fat molecules captured by modern cream separators, is called double cream—*crème double.*

Acidulated cream is the inspiration of Norman cuisine, seasoning mussels, shrimp, fish, and eggs, as well as fowl, or veal cutlets. Even game does not escape this tasty tyranny. Cream can be used in place of meat juice in the dripping pan of a spit for basting. Let's not forget soups and stuffings. A tomato soup thickened with cream loses its acidity. A white sauce made into a *sauce normande* with the addition of a spoonful of cream admirably coats a white meat or an omelette. A salad seasoned with fresh cream and aromatic herbs is delicious. In summation, Norman gastronomy is well worth your indulgence if your liver can take it.

SOUR CREAM of Russian or Balkan cuisine is called *smetana* in Moscow and *smuntana* in Bucharest. It is more digestible than double cream of Norman recipes, and the dishes in which it is an element are not any less delicious: bortsch of Moscow or the Ukraines, *tchiorba* of Rumania.

This sour cream is made from top cream combined with buttermilk, a pinch of starch, and a trickle of lemon juice to complete it. Then the mixture is made homogenous. (Trans. note: French *crème fraîche* is the approximate equivalent of our heavy cream, acidulated, and slightly clabbered.)

Other foods of Central Europe at the moment they go to the table are splashed with a spoonful or two of sour cream: beef or veal goulash, stuffed cabbage, etc.

Cress

(French, *Cresson;* German, *Kresse*) Name given to several edible plants with fleshy rounded leaves.

* See APPENDIX.

WATERCRESS (*Nasturtium officinale*) Watercress is an excellent salad ingredient, crisp, crackling and spicy. Cress is cultivated in beds that are severely regulated because of the dangers of contamination with spearwort parasite.

Cresson de fontaine, as it is also called, is the ideal accompaniment for a mutton chop or any other grills. If seasoning is wanted, nut oil, or sunflower oil seasoned with lemon juice should be chosen. This salad should be mixed at the last moment. In Germany, slices of black bread and white cheese are garnished with chopped cress. In France, chopped cress is added to some mayonnaise for cold fish. Cress can also be cooked, sweated in butter, or meat juice after it has been blanched. It gives an original taste to different soups mixed with chervil and parsley. The Chinese also use cress as an element in chicken soups, chop suey, etc.

GARDEN CRESS (*Lepidium sativum;* French, *Cress alenois*) This plant is bigger, with more elongated leaves. There are also dwarf and curly varieties. Its taste is undoubtedly more pronounced, but its uses are practically identical. Dumas calls it the "most healthy of all *fines herbes.*" The people of Provence add chopped garden cress to the stuffing for tomatoes.

In France, the name cress (*cresson*) is given to a number of salad plants: pepperwort (*passerage*), lady's smock (*cardamine*) or bitter cress (*cresson amer*), horse cress (*véronique beccabonque* or *cresson de cheval*), wartcress (*corne de cerf*), yellow rocket (*barbarée* or *julienne jaune*). These herbs are all less tasty than common cress.

In the tropics, there are plants with like uses, notably the *breda mafana* of Madagascar, which gives high flavor to *roumazava*, the national stew.

Cretan Carrot

(*Athamanta cretensis* and *libanotis*) A large umbelliferous plant found on the periphery of the eastern Mediterranean in flinty Alpine areas. Now and then it is called white mountain parsley (*persil blanc de montagne*). Its aromatic seeds are used rarely in cooking, like fennel seeds.

Cubebs

(French, *Cubebes;* German, *Kubebeno*) Little black berries with a fragment of stem extending. They are borne by a vine of the Sunda Islands, *Piper cubeba.*

Cubebs have a taste less frank and more bitter than black pepper. Dumas has told us that the Hindus marinate these dried berries in the wedding wine when the groom is older than forty. In spite of this useful note, *poivre à queue* (pepper with a tail) as it used to be called, has been abandoned for other fruits of the *Piperaceae.*

Cullis

(French, *Coulis*) In old cookbooks, cullis refers to a preparation of animal or vegetable juices sieved or strained and kept for finishing dishes such as crayfish cullis. Today this word is generally reserved for tomato cullis.

Cumberland Sauce

It is named in memory of Ernest-Auguste, Duke of Cumberland and Brunswick, who doted on this sweet-sour sauce containing orange and lemon peel, dissolved in white wine, flavored by port, ginger, and gooseberry jelly. It is suitable for game, cold leg of lamb, etc.

Cumin

(Cuminum cyminum) is a large umbelliferous plant with a purple flower and a slender root, cultivated in the Arab countries, Greece, Sicily, and more rarely in the South of France. Its seed is yellowish, oblong, ribbed, and a little larger than an anise seed. It gives off a strong, unique peppery taste when crushed. If it is cut with a dull knife, it separates into twin carpels. This is the famous Arab *kemoun,* Greek *cominos,* ancient Hebrew *kamon* and German, *Pfeffertummel.* Cumin is a hot note in cooking and enters "at full

efficiency" in North African and Greek dishes (roast lamb, *couscous* broth, the Moroccan stew *tagine*). Cumin is present in curry, *ras-el-hanout,* and other Oriental spice cocktails.

Nothing prevents us from seasoning a *choucroute* with real cumin or spicing an Irish stew with the marvelous Turkish powdered *demoun.* On the other hand, it is not at all suited to German-style rolls, biscuits, and dried cakes. In some cases, compromises are acceptable: half cumin, half caraway, or preferrably two-thirds caraway and one-third cumin. This solution was whispered to us by old recipes for Jümmel, the most famous of German liqueurs.

OIL OF CUMIN is a bit of Alsatian cooks' cunning. It is made of caraway, boiled in sweet oil for twenty minutes. The oil is filtered, then chilled. It is used in the cooking or the stuffing of a somewhat tough fowl, or sprinkled on baked fish.

Curaçao

A liqueur prepared from the skin of bitter oranges (which see) taking its name from one of the Dutch Leeward Islands of the Caribbean. There are several brands of curaçao which all go well with desserts and sweets such as orange soufflé, fruit salad, melon in sugar, etc. This liqueur also lends its flavor to more substantial foods: a drop of curaçao agreeably seasons a crayfish cullis, as well as a mousseline stuffing for a delicate-tasting fish.

In addition, curaçao is indispensable in bigarade sauce, which is the most aristocratic envelope for serving Nantais duck. It allows cooks to forsake bitter oranges for common ones. (*See* BITTER ORANGE, ORANGE.)

Currant Sauce

The green or dark burgundy-colored fruit of the spiny currant bush (*Ribes uva-crispa*) is rich in citric and malic acids. Its sour taste lends itself traditionally to culinary preparations reserved for tough meats. This currant jelly, flavored with cherry brandy, transforms a *sauce poivrade,* thickened with game blood, into *sauce venaison.*

81

The common name of the fleshy berry, mackerel currant, (*groseille à maquereau*) indicates its principal culinary use.

N.B. Fresh currant juice, without sugar, gives an acid note to Hamburg eel soup.

Curry

The most famous and the most popular of Oriental spice mixtures. A citizen of both Madras and Bombay, it changes its identity according to the region, the caste, or simply the personality of the turbaned cook.

An orthodox grocer makes a distinction between *curry*, pulverized cooking spice made of turmeric, coriander, Oriental cumin, black pepper and red pepper, and *masala* or *garam masala*, the table seasoning made of a powder or a paste of cardamom, cloves, and cinnamon. A strict semantic definition would separate the traditional sauce dish, *kadhi* (an exotic transcription of the native word) from *masala*, the spice mix that seasons them in the kitchen or on the table, but the merchants have imposed their jargon, and curry has become the synonym of almost all Indian spice mixes. (*See* MASALA.)

This article is limited to the mixes sold and used in the West. They are compromises between one and another formula enriched by a weak supply of powdered, scented herbs. They pretend, in addition, to be mild, hot, very hot—but it's merely a question of their dose of hot substances.

Below is the composition of a very honest mild export curry, according to the confidences of a gourmet from Pondicherry:

	Per cent
Turmeric	25
Coriander	20
Real Cumin	10
Nepalese Pepper	10
Cloves	5
Cardamom	5
White Ginger	5
Pepper (cayenne)	5
Mace and Areca	5
Dried Herbs	10

All these ingredients are finely pulverized or milled before being stored in chests of scented wood. They can be seasoned with a little powdered vanilla, fennel seeds, caraway, ajowan, black mustard, nigella, ginseng root, zedoary, etc. The herbs in these formulas are generally *Labiatae* to which the basil of Provence and wild marjoram of Greece belong. In Réunion and Zanzibar, particularly hot versions of curry reign, with predominantly cayenne and turmeric as ingredients.

USES: *In India and Pakistan, curry seasons a number of vegetarian dishes and preparations of meat and fish, such as curried* kefta, *Indian mutton meatballs served in sauce, and* Hussaini, *a curried Oriental variation of lamb à la grecque, accompanied by tomatoed rice with curry. These meats are generally eaten with* chapatti, *softish flat cakes of wheat that strolling merchants sell; often they are stuffed with sautéed vegetables in curry. Finally, the* kichedri *rice is a sort of pilaf flavored with fried onions and Smyrna raisons cooked in coconut milk with curry and grated cashew nuts. All these preparations are enriched by very tasty vegetables, such as* karela *(bitter squash),* dal *(a kind of lentil), and* vaalor *(Indian beans).*

The wise Western cook will buy a curry or masala *only of known origin.*

Curry, used sparingly, can season a tomato soup, cold rice with mushrooms, sea-food pilaf, crab bisque, a lentil stew (Madras fashion, garnished with hard egg), a fish mayonnaise, etc. Pounded with white cheese, it is excellent for canapés. Curry underlines bland vegetables such as sweet potatoes, manioc root, etc. These vegetables are stewed, then sautéed, while dusting them with curry (for sweet potatoes, Djakarta-style). In the United States, curry sometimes is used to dust a grapefruit salad served as an hors d'oeuvre. (See RAS-EL-HANOUT.)

Daisy

(*Bellis perennis;* French, *Paquerette;* German *Gänseblumchen;* Italian, *Margheritina*) A little flower of the *Compositae* family that abounds on the lawns of public gardens. The daisy is generally considered a good-luck charm (except for pilots, for whom it evokes forced landings). Its spatula-shaped leaves are enjoyed by sheep, and is said to give an agreeable taste to their flesh.

Daisy flowers, gathered as buds, and well washed, can set off a composed salad. The young, tender leaves were eaten like cress by our ancestors. Both leaves and flowers should be used with moderation because the plant is slightly laxative. The daisy is scentless, but has a spicy, light, salt taste.

Dandelion

(*Taraxcum dens-leonis;* French, *Pissenlit,* German, *Lowenzahn*) A sort of naughty herb that belongs to the *Compositae,* also called *dent de lion, laitue de chien, salade de taupe,* etc. The young shoots, sometimes improved by cultivation, make a slightly bitter but healthy and appetizing salad. Generally eaten with crisped bacon, served on very hot plates, they can be chopped and used to garnish a stuffing or a meat browned in its own juice. The goat and the cow, like man, are very fond of dandelions.

Dandelion

The roasted roots of dandelion formerly were used as a substitute for chicory and coffee. Its yellow flowers, large single capitulum, sometimes called monk's crowns (*couronnes de moines*), are used by Anglo-Saxons to liven up and color wine.

From the medical point of view, dandelion is a depurative and diuretic as its name in French sufficiently indicates. It contains manganese in such quantity that its leaves are less rich in chlorophyll. Also, plant medicine prefers the very green wild dandelion to star dandelion, which is yellow like endive (Doctor Léon Binet*). Dandelion, sold in markets, is a hybrid sort much like chicory.

Dashi

A Japanese word meaning a broth of fish and algaes containing soda. In Vietnan, it is call *katsuo,* but it is imported canned from Japan. The fish is *bonita,* a variety of tuna, that the Orientals dry in the sun, then grate finely.

Dashi-katsuo, flavors fish soups, *quenelles,* and naturally the national Japanese dish, the famous sukiyaki (a stew of sliced beef, onion, bamboo shoots, watercress, mushrooms etc., prepared in chafing dishes before the diners).

Dill

(*Anethum graveolens;* French, *Aneth;* German, *Dill*) A large umbelliferous plant close to fennel and green anise. The medieval pharmacopaeia prescribed dried dill compresses for insomnia.

While relatively unknown in France, dill is famous among the Germans, Anglo-Saxons, and Russians (who call it *oukrob*). Its extremely fine and aromatic greenery gives a unique flavor to poached fish Swedish-style, marinated fish, eel and crayfish cooked German- or Austrian-style, and cold Russian soups.

IMPORTANT ADVICE: *This "bastard fennel"* (fenouil bâtard), *as it is sometimes known, loses its anise taste after boiling. Dust the boiled potatoes accompanying a fish dish with a fistful of dill, finely cut with scissors.*

Dried dill, or even the dill seed that is found in specialized grocers,

* See APPENDIX.

can be used in fish and sea-food soups and sauces, as well as in making bortsch.

SWEET DILL (French, *Aneth doux*) Common fennel.

Dittany of Crete

An aromatic plant celebrated by the ancients, cited occasionally in old cookbooks. It is undoubtedly *Origanum dictamnus,* a wild variety of marjoram. This name (*Dictame de Crète*) is improperly used for rye or related plants. (*See* MARJORAM *and* RUE.)

Doha, Doka

A mixed spice favored by poor people in Arab countries. It is a mixture of crushed and toasted red sesame seed, coriander, cumin, and nigella; sometimes it contains crushed nuts, jillet flour, or even dried cheese.

Doka is dusted on the flat bread, *baladi,* that the Egyptian *fellah* eats in the fields.

Dressings

An English word that has invaded a lot of countries and now timidly tries to seduce the French. It is synonymous with seasoning or cold sauce and means a syrupy product something like mayonnaise, with a somewhat strange taste. The best known, French dressing, claims a French heritage, even though it is notorious for containing sugar and paprika! Cocktail dressing contains grated horseradish, tomato ketchup, and Worcestershire sauce. Russian dressing is particularly sweet, combining sugar, onion and celery. These lubricants are highly valued by some Americans for green salads, crustaceans and cold meats.

Dripping

Another English word which jealously hides its meaning. Enlightened polylingual cooks know it because it means the roast fat used in making cakes, as well as the celebrated Christmas Pudding.

Eggplant

The fruit of *Solanum esculentum,* whose French name (*aubergine*) comes from the Arab *al-babindjan.* It is known to cooks prepared as Egyptian *baba-hanous* or Rumanian *vinete tocate,* as a delicious caviar. It is both an hors d'oeuvre or a condiment for cold meats.

Egypt

Egyptian cuisine, like that of Syria and Lebanon, is a very pleasant gastronomic compromise. Antique customs are found in it, notably the abuse of garlic and onion, mentioned by Herodotus, as well as the influences of the Arabs, kings of the spice trade until the fifteenth century, and the Turks. The Turks gathered a culinary science in the alleys of Constantinople and gave it to all the countries of the Ottoman Empire.

The basic food of the Nile Valley people is the *foul,* a tasty bean that is eaten after long stewing. It is seasoned with oil and lemon, garnished by hard-cooked eggs and chopped salad. Fine-grained rice, called *rozzette,* and *gamousse* (buffalo meat) are a *fellah's* luxury foods reserved for the feast days. On these occasions, the Egyptians eat thick stew seasoned with a great quantity of garlic, tomatoes, and powdered cardamom thickened with a drop of *mastika* (mastic tree resin). The condiments are *tahina* (a mayonnaise of sesame seeds) and *mokhale* (raw vegetables in vinegar), *tarchi* (pickled turnips), and the local cress. Another specialty highly appreciated in Cairo and neighboring capitals, is chicken broth seasoned with chopped *molokheia,* an Oriental herblike burnet. Cumin (*kamoun*) and coriander (*kosbara*) are frequently used to make the stringy flesh of the *gamousse* (donkey and camel) passable. When he has nothing else to eat, the Egyptian, a philosopher, eats a flat bread without leavening dusted with *doha* (powdered nigella, mixed with other spices). (*See* ABAHAN, CORIANDER, CUMIN, MOLOKHEIA, TAHINA, TARCHI.)

Elder Bush

(*Sambucus nigra;* French, *Sureau;* German, *Schwarzer Holunder*) A high, shrubby tree with white flowers and red berries that turn black. A friend to man, it grows near homes, in debris and recently cleared places. In French, it is also called *sambequier, suyer, smillet,* and *seur.* The branches of the elder are hollow and contain a large diameter of pith. Children make flutes and pea shooters from them. The pith is used by the watch industry for polishing very fine pieces.

Elder is a smelly plant. Its stems and leaves give off a noxious odor. But the dried flowers have an agreeable smell. They should be gathered just bloomed and dehydrated, in a shady, dry place. They are used in herb medicine as an emollient and a sudorific, and were once used to care for tuberculosis.

USES: *The flowers of the elder are valued by wine-makers who mix them with the grape must to give it a muscat taste, imitating Frontignan or Sauterne wine. In the southern Netherlands, they are used to perk up the taste of some ciders. They are always welcome in home-style vinegar or* surard. *Fresh, soaked a half hour in Chartreuse, they can be made into fritters.*

Elderberries, gathered completely green, are sometimes used to imitate capers after being macerated in vinegar. Their flavor is quite mediocre. Ripe, when black and full of dark-red sap, they are the grana actes *of the ancient pharmacopoeia, used as a purgative. In Brittany and in Flanders, elder leaves sautéed in butter or crushed with honey, used to be used as a laxative.*

Finally the pith of elder, carefully extracted from the branches and stem, can be eaten deep fried or in vinegar sauce. This substance has a delicate consistency but little aromatic value.

Elder Bush

Escabeche

A Spanish marinade in which fish heads are cooked. After reduction, the fish are left to macerate several days. Sardines *à l'escabeche* are prepared with vinegar, olive oil, chopped onion, garlic, capers, and *pimenton*. This dish, always eaten cold, is popular with the French returned from Algeria, Peruvians, and Chileans. In Murcia and Malaga, a tasty speciality, partridge *à l'escabeche,* is prepared.

Essences

This little old-fashioned word (in French, *fumets*) refers to home reductions, rarely to industrial reductions, such as game, mushroom, fish, truffle, essences. Crustacean oil (*huile de crustacés*) and anchovies essence (*essence d'anchois*) are used when an essence preserved in a fat or in a decoction of white wine reinforced with vinegar is needed. (*See* GARLIC, MUSHROOM, *and* CRUSTACEANS.)

Farigoule

The name in the dialect of the Provence for thyme, or wild thyme (*serpolet*). (*See* THYME.)

Fennel

(*Foeniculum;* French, *Fenouil;* German, *Fenchel*) A biennial umbellif erous plant native to southern Europe, but also found in Germany and England. There are several varieties:

SWEET FENNEL, or dwarf fennel of Florence, is a comestible plant well-known in France. The fleshy petiole, leaf stalk, improp erly called the head, on the bulb, is eaten with pepper sauce, au gratin with meat juice, as a garnish for fish or crustaceans, with many kinds of cheese, etc. The Italians dote on *finocchio,* and jok ing, use this name to signify some effeminate men (the vegetable fennel is a female fennel plant). Dumas complained about "the immoderate taste of the Neapolitans for fennel."

SHARP OR PEPPER FENNEL (French, *Fenouil acre* or *poivré*), half wild, has smooth-skinned stems and greenish seeds that are aro matics. The stems, dried and tied in little bundles, are used to flavor grilled fish, such as the famous Mediterranean sea perch or gilthead. The Chinese use it with brown sugar to smoke duck. The seeds, gathered before they are fully ripe, are always welcome in a marinade, a crayfish cullis, or a baked fish.

SYLVAN FENNEL OR BLACK FENNEL (French, *Fenouil sylvestre, Fenouil noir,* or *Fenouillet*) An entirely wild species, their unpleasant taste, their resemblance to poisonous great hemlock, sometimes called wild fennel, makes it wise to avoid them. Hemlock is recognized by its unpleasant smell of cat's urine.

DILL AND CARAWAY, very worthy related *Umbelliferae,* they are sometimes confused with pepper fennel, but their seeds are smaller or more curved.

These botanical notes are necessarily a summary. Naturalists have devoted considerable research to fennel without agreeing. Gastronomes will remember that the fennels of Provence are more sweet. The fine capillary extensions that are the leaves of this plant can on occasion replace fresh dill, although their taste is less, pleasant.

Good groceries have whole or powdered fennel seeds. They can enhance a fish dish, a stuffing, a blood sausage, or a cold meat salad, and make cabbage beans and lima beans more digestible.

Fenugreek

(*Trigonella foenum-graecum;* French *Fenugrec;* German, *Bockshornk-lee*) A *Papilonaceae* that somewhat resembles a clover, which is why the Germans call it *goat's horn club.* It is rather widespread on the periphery of the Mediterranean and is often cultivated as forage. Its fruit pods contain several brownish-yellow, oblong, bumpy seeds. Their aroma is agreeable, slightly sweet, like sweet clover or Tonka bean. All these plants contain coumarin (which see).

The Indians dote on fenugreek, which they call *helbét.* The dried, pounded seed is used in many condiment formulas (curry, chutney, etc.). They export it as well under the name of *ground methi.* The Arabs eat the germinated seeds and the young sprouts of fenugreek, which are reported to be quite fortifying. In the United States, an aromatic oil is extracted from them and used as a substitute for maple essence in making ice creams.

In the West, this aromatic (often imported from Morocco) is not highly valued. It only flavors the vinegar used for making

Fenugreek

pickles. The sole meat to which it is suited is the domestic rabbit, in a *gibelotte,* with many garlic cloves and a point of cardamom to counterbalance the sweetness of fenugreek. (*See* PASTRAMI.)

Fig

(*Ficus carica;* French, *Figue;* German, *Feige*) The delicious fruit of an Asiatic tree was introduced to France by the Phoenicians. It is generally violet, more rarely green, or creamy-white. Very rich in calories, it has an important role in the Arab diet. The *bellona, barnisote,* violet figs of Bargemont, and the yellow figs of Smyrna, are among the most valued varieties. The best dried figs come from Asia Minor. With the raisin, the jujube, and the date, the fig used to be part of the cough syrup and paste called *four fruits.*

In Greece and North Africa, a heavy wine and a worthy alcohol are extracted from the fig by fermentation. The juice of the fig, pasteurized and extensively refined, makes a delicious syrup. Fig leaves resemble grape leaves, but are more denticulate and fleshy. They are used in Oriental cooking to wrap stuffings with a rice or mutton base.

Fines Herbes

A trite expression that cookbooks use and abuse. Prosper Montagné* felt that *fines herbes* often refers to finely chopped parsley alone. But there is no more a universal herb in cooking than there is a panacea in medicine. It is more proper to return to ancient customs and to translate this expression as a mixture of at least three perfumed *herbes* reduced to "tufts" and capable of giving *cachet* to a seasoning. Dumas in his *Grand Dictionnaire de Cuisine,* cites a good twenty *fines herbes.* If a count is taken of regional and foreign uses, there are a lot more. The list below is far from exhaustive.

CLASSIC FINES HERBES: Chervil, parsley, tarragon, chives, rushleek, fresh thyme.

* See APPENDIX.

Fig

COUNTRY FINES HERBES: Garden savory, lemon thyme, garden cress, sage, vervain, burnet, hyssop, tansy, purslane, orach, marjoram, celery, lamb's lettuce, fennel, chicory, hop shoots, nasturtium or borage flowers.

REGIONAL FINES HERBES: Basil (South of France, Italy), lovage (Balkans, Germany), dill (Russia, Scandinavia, Germany) mint (Corsica, Spain, Greece, North Africa), samphire (South of France, Brittany), soybeans (Far East), mugwort (Germany, Poland).

It is also necessary to mention in this article some herbs appreciated by ancient cooks: alliaria, orach, azarum, star anise, borage, art-cress, sweet clover, horse parsley, wild marjoram, St. Johnswort, purslane, white stonecrop.

We don't suggest possessing or procuring all these herbs. On the other hand, it is always possible to grow two or three in pots on a window sill. Fresh herbs keep a long time in the refrigerator if they are wrapped in metal foil. Dried herbs are somewhat restored if they are soaked for several seconds in lemon water.

NOTE: The herbs listed above are all treated separately elsewhere in this book. (*See also* HERBS.)

Fish Bones

The skeleton trimmings of fish, once the filets are removed, are not necessarily wasted as culinary aromatics. If they are boiled with some aromatics and a little white wine, a concentrated broth, called fish essence (*fumet de poisson*) is produced, which will moisten a sauce or swish a cooking dish.

Five Spices (Five Powdered Perfumes)

A completely prepared mix very well known in all Southeast Asia, as *Hong-Lu* (and also *Ngou-Vi-Houong* in Vietnam). It is found in Chinese groceries. It contains star anise, clove, fennel seed, cassia, and Chinese pepper (*Zanthoxylum piperitum;* French, *poivre clavalier*). Notably, it is used to flavor the soy sauce used to lacquer duck.

Flowers

The language of flowers has always been familar to cooks. Many delicate corollas coming either from small plants or trees can be eaten. Nasturtium flowers can decorate a salad (particularly beet or red cabbage). On the shores of the Rhine, these are used to give pungency to the must of excellent wine, such as the *Gewürztraminer.* On the other hand, woodruff flower is found in European (particularly French and Rhineland German) glasses when the delicious May wine is served.

Lacking nasturtium flowers, use blue star-shaped flowers of borage or the fleshy petals of the chysanthemum blossom to transform lettuce salad into an impressionist masterpiece! Exotic chefs also have an artist's eye: jasmine, hibiscus, rose, and magnolia flowers bedeck their fowl and even some fish.

Other flowers are eaten in fritters: acacia, squash, lily, jasmine, violet, elder, etc. The marsh marigold has a slightly bitter taste and is, according to Dumas, made to be cooked, finely chopped in vegetable soups.

Flowers can also serve as aromatics: sweet marjoram, wild thyme, savory, especially lavender, even when they are not true spices or condiments (caper, clove, and cinnamon flower are dried or marinated buds). In China and Vietnam, the flower of the yellow lily, or *kim cham,* is as valued as vanilla. In Tunisia, fuzzy *chachiouard* rose petals season the sauce in mutton stew. Finally, *oeillet-ratafia* (a variety of carnation from Africa) has an aroma very close to cloves and is used by liquor-makers.

Food Colors

Many times it is important to give thought to color in food preparation. The true cook limits himself to making color harmonies, using the food products at his disposal. But this rule has several exceptions. Here are the secrets of his palate.

DARKENING A roux can always be made darker, that is browner, by using flour toasted in an oven, or caramel (Dumas called it *singer,* monkeying). A consommé can be colored with small onions darkened in a frying pan and placed in a cheese cloth to facilitate removal before serving.

GREEN The green products are well known: spinach leaves, or green wheat, pounded, blanched, and sieved. It is particularly good for use in mayonnaise and other cold sauces.

YELLOW This color may be supplied by aromatics such as turmeric or saffron. There are also some "home seasonings," especially in Marseilles, that will yellow a *paella* or bouillabaisse. Their composition is not certain, but undoubtedly they contain yellow naphthol, a mineral coloring for the French food industry, or even *Carthamus tinctorius,* an ersatz saffron.

OCHER Wild bugloss or dyer's bugloss roots contain henna, a well-known pigment. The vegetable product is also used to color butter and other food products manufactured on a commercial scale in France.

PINK Beets are often used to pick up vegetable garnishes.

VIOLET Tincture or simply blueberry jelly.

ORANGE Mixture of egg yolk and paprika or urchin roe for fish sauce. Combination of saffron and cochineal for other preparations.

RED COCHINEAL Known for a long time, it is not a seed as the ancient authors believed, but a little hemipterous insect that is a parasite on certain African cactus. It gives a very lively red, much used by French pastry- and liquor-makers. Spanish and South American cuisine widely uses this bright coloring— (*chupes,* Peruvian and Chilean stews, etc.). Cochineal has replaced logwood, which was formerly in vogue.

RED ORCHIL A violet-red paste extracted from a lichen, which delicatessen cooks use to color pickled tongues.

Four Spice Mixture

A typically French spice mixture (*quatre-épices*), literally translated in German as *Viegewuerzmischung.* The formula varies according to grocers and cooks, but generally it contains:

Ground Pepper	50 per cent
Grated nutmeg	25 per cent
Powdered cloves	15 per cent
Powdered ginger	10 per cent

The aromatic cocktail may contain allspice or cinnamon, as well. It is used only for long-simmered meats—stews, *civets,* wine sauces, pâtés, and *terrines salpicons.* It is also used by delicatessen-makers. Very much in vogue thirty years ago, today it is strongly challenged by mixtures of herbs and spices. (*See* COMPOUND SPICES *and* TURTLE HERBS.)

French Antilles

In the opinion of the travelers who take their appetites to the shores of the Caribbean, the food of the French Antilles is the most delicate and tasty of the region. Doubtless cayenne pepper and red pepper are a little abused, but this is the inevitable spice *ransom* of the subtropical climate. Martinique and Guadeloupe furnish their inhabitants with an abundance of fish and edible vegetables of all sorts. With the exception of pork and fowl, meat is rare there. Plantain, rice and beans are eaten, as well as a good deal of cod and sweet potatoes. Most of the dishes are stews, such as *calalou, matoutou, bloff,* and *poulet à la créole.* If people of the Antilles know well some of our aromatics, principally thyme, bay and saffron, they also know how to season their food with the local products: coconut meat, white rum, grated cashew nuts, and the bitter orange (which see).

Furze

(*Genista scoparia;* French, *Genêt;* German, *Ginster*) A shrubby tree, which, like the spiny gorse and other *Papilionacae,* has a reputation as an excellent fuel. It burns happily in the bakers' great fireplaces and ovens. It flavors a *cassoulet,* cooked on coals, or grilled blood sausages, but is a little too sweet to be used for cooking fish. The saffron-yellow flowers, when barely opened, are often preserved like capers. (*See* CAPER *and* WOOD FIRES.)

Galingale

The rhizome of *Kaempferia galanga*, an amonum of the *Zingiberaceae* grown in Indonesia. Generally reddish, it gives off a strong aromatic odor something like cardamom and a little like ginger. Its hot, somewhat brutal flavor enchants the inhabitants of Bali. Along with mango vinegar and acid tamarind, galingale figures among the condiments and physiological stimulants appreciated by these island people. The women of Bali find that little pieces of this root are a pleasant addition to chicken soups and acidulated stews.

Galingale, which has the reputation of aiding victims of sea-sickness, has appeared on the tables of Dutch and British steamers for a long time. It cannot be used except in exotic preparations, at the most, in a *gibelotte* or a fricassee (Trans. note: types of French stews) to make them interesting.

(Trans. note: *Cyperus esculentus*; French, *Souchet*; Spanish, *Chufa*; Italian, *Cipero* are also called galingale in English. The term is also generally extended in English to any *Cyperus*, especially *C. longus, C. diandrus*.)

A perennial herb with a running edible stock, in French it is also called *souchet-sultan* and *amande de terre*. It grows wild in hot and temperate countries. Its small tubers, the size of hazelnuts, are used by Southern French cooks and café-keepers. The taste resembles the filbert or chestnut, but is more aromatic.

103

The ground almonds are very tasty in stuffing for fowl, in a rabbit terrine, etc. They are blanched in milk after being washed and scraped. In Morocco, a variety of galingale native to the Sudan is called tafa soudania. *It is an element in mixtures of spices for cooking fowl. In Spain, galingale is indispensable in the preparation of* horchata, *an iced beverage similar to orgeat. All these uses are very old, a reference to* shbin, *the ancient name of* Cyperus esculentus *having been found in ancient hieroglyphics.*

Garlic

"Everybody is familiar with garlic, especially army recruits who use it to obtain a medical discharge. Its volatile caustic juice rubbed on the skin reddens and scourges it." (Alexander Dumas, 1873.) The bulb, which has been abandoned to the "inferior classes," belongs to the same botanical family, however, as the lilies of the kings of France. Linnaeus himself has granted this identity.

ALLIUM SATIVUM *(Liliaceae)* Called *Ail blanc* or *Ail commun* by the French, *Knoblauch* by the Germans, *Tcheknok* by the Russians, *Soum* or *Tsoum* by the Arabs. Its white cloves have long ago spread around the world.

HISTORY: *Garlic, native to Djungarie in Central Asia, has been known and appreciated since the earliest times. Galen called it a country* theriaca, *an electuary (medicine) of the poor. The builders of the great pyramids and the Olympic athletes ate great quantities of garlic to regain their strength. Ulysses is said to have chewed a garlic bud before exorcising Circe. Virgil, Pliny, and the prophet Mohammed celebrated its merits. Only the well-born Greeks scorned it. Entrance to the sacred temples of Cybele was refused to those whose breath smelled from the "stinking rose."*

In the Middle Ages, garlic disappeared from most home gardens, but it came back strongly during the mingling of the population caused by the Crusades. Nevertheless, Alphonso, King of Castille, banished from his court those knights who had eaten it. Garlic had to await the birth of the child who was to become Henry IV (whose lips were rubbed with garlic and wine from Jurançon) to gain noble credentials.

THERAPY: *Briefly, garlic was prescribed as an emmenagogue, a febrifuge, a disinfectant, and a vermifuge by the ancients. Today it is generally admitted that garlic has properties that regulate circulation troubles. Professor Vir-*

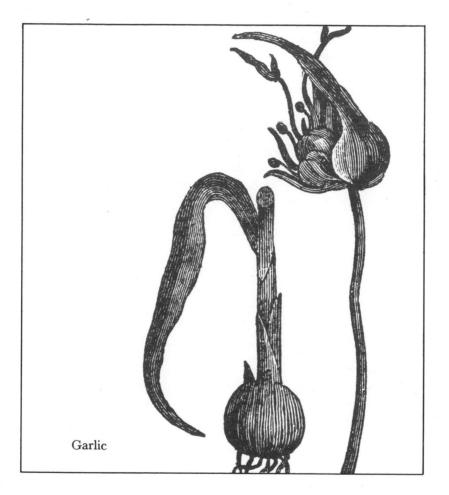

Garlic

tanen of Helsinki, a Nobel Prize winner in medicine, and some German dietitians consider it an excellent natural antibiotic. Still, American medicine seems reticent to accept claims.

PRINCIPLES OF USE: *First, it is necessary to know how to use garlic without abusing it. Contrary to a too widely held opinion, it is the Nordic male and female cooks who use it too much. Secondly, it should never be forgotten that garlic that "simmers" until it blackens gives off an odious smell. Whether the garlic is whole or sliced, it is better to fry it in olive oil and then remove it from the pan. Third, in certain Italian recipes, notably* poulet frit de la vieille Romagne, *a favorite food of Mussolini, the cook is instructed to fry the quarters of fowl on a "bed" of garlic and sprigs of rosemary. In all similar cases, cloves of garlic should be put in the pan* without *peeling them, simply half-crush them by mashing the garlic against the kitchen table! This trick is infallible. Fourth, rather than slicing cloves of garlic into little pieces with a kitchen knife, it is better to pound the pulp.*

The use of a mortar is, unhappily, not widespread; we suggest that the same results can be achieved by using a very fine grater or a garlic press, both of which are very inexpensive.

GARLIC IN THE FOOD OF PROVENCE First, let us say that the garlic that grows south of the Loire River is finer and more scented than that cultivated in regions without a great deal of sun. The latter is sometimes bitter, its pulp is fibrous, and the cloves are not as fleshy, containing less aromatic oil and more sulphides. According to two excellent authors:

> *Garlic is not at all the brutal, incivil condiment that in Northern countries strengthens the breath of common people. Garlic in cooking of Southern France does not impose the least displeasing acidity. It is delicate and pure like Mistral's verse. It is eaten without effort and without aftereffects at night. Better yet: it gives dreams of oleander and silver olive trees.—Jean Noël Escudier**
>
> *If olive oil in different quantities is used in all Provençal cooking, it is not exactly the same with garlic. It is not to be used without discretion, except in some dishes to which it gives the keynote . . . its taste should never dominate and extinguish the other tastes, but rather strengthen and heighten them.—Joseph d'Arbaud: La Provence.*

* See APPENDIX.

CHOICE OF GARLIC The largest buds of garlic are to be preferred because they profited most from the sun. A certain "growth" can also be chosen, and sought, thanks to the producer's labels in the little cellophane bags, found in France and elsewhere.

PINK GARLIC, improperly called red garlic *(ail rouge)*, is an excellent variety of white garlic sold in fall and winter. It is an early plant, very fragrant, planted in fall. [It should not be confused with red garlic *(ail rouge)*.] (*See* ROCAMBOLE.)

FRESH GARLIC *en branche* is unheard of in the markets, but is called for in numerous country recipes: kid with green garlic (*chevreau à l'ail vert*, etc.).

POWDERED GARLIC is now being sold in all good groceries. There are several excellent English and even Dutch preparations (*knoflookpoeder*) as well as American brands. It can be made at home by drying a large quantity of finely grated garlic in the oven and sieving it through a fine strainer. It is used in making the powder for aromatics necessary for some Oriental recipes or as a substitute to be kept in reserve for fresh garlic.

GARLIC ESSENCE is a practically forgotten preparation, also used to replace fresh garlic or to flavor certain vinegar sauces. Grated or powdered garlic can be steeped in boiling white wine. To keep it a long time, add several drops of vinegar. (*See* AÏOLI *or* AÏLLOLI.)

Garum

Also called *liquamen.* It was the most valued condiment of ancient Rome. It takes its name from *garus,* a small anchovylike fish. Garum was made from fish entrails, dried in the sun, like the Vietnamese nuöc-mam (which see.) (*See also* PISSALAT.)

Gelatin

Transparent and tasty, the culinary gels are certain protein juices obtained by heating, then gelled by chilling. Classically, they are made by the long boiling, reduction, and filtering of broths of beef, fowl, calf's foot, or fish bones and trimmings, with certain vegetables and aromatics. There are also vegetable gels which combine the natural sugar and pectin of certain fruits (currant, quince, quince seeds, etc.).

Formerly, the gelatins for aspic were obtained by boiling for a long time animal horns of various sorts. Today it is obtained from collagen in bones and skin stock by hydrolysis. It is tasteless but it may be seasoned with meat juice, Madeira wine, Cognac, caramel, or browned onion. It is in good taste to decorate the mold into which the gelatin is poured with tarragon or chervil. (*See* AGAR-AGAR *and* KOMBOU.)

Gherkins

(French, *Cornichons;* German, *Gurken*) The botanist's cucumber *Cucumis sativus* is an annual climbing plant native to Nepal. It has been cultivated in Europe since antiquity. Hippocrates made a great case for its fruits as a laxative.

There are several varieties known to gardeners: the yellow or white cucumber, and the green or gherkin *(concombre jaune* or *blanc, concombre vert* or *cornichon).* The second is smaller, studded with rough spots and hard-fleshed. They are sold raw in the market, but more often are offered already preserved in vinegars (sometimes made artificially green with copper salt, which is revealed when the pickle is speared with a fork, for the metal tines are immediately covered with traces of sulphate).

The use of gherkins to accompany boiled meats, terrines, pâtés, grills, etc., has become universal among the white peoples. Only the way they are prepared and flavored varies a little. Sweet gherkins are placed in sweetish Anglo-Saxon marinades. *Citriuoli nell'aceto* possesses as much temperament as Italian women. Russian *agoursis,* juicy and delicate, are called *kastravetsi* in Rumania and the Balkans.

In some countries, the seeds of the cucumber or gherkin are prepared as a substitute for orgeat syrup. As for the cucumber skin, it is a bitter aromatic sometimes used in English cocktails (Pimms, etc.).

Ginger

(*Zingiber officinale;* French, *Gingembre;* German *Ingwer.*) The rhizome of a plant that resembles the gladiolus corm, takes its name from the Gingi district, east of Pondicherry. Ginger is cultivated in India, Vietnam, and China, as well as in Tahiti, the Antilles, and Africa.

The peppery, biting taste of ginger has been appreciated from the most ancient times. The Romans, through Egyptian merchants, procured these rhizomes, and Pliny, a little astonished by their flavor, attributes this vegetable to the country of the Troglodytes. Later, the merchants of Venice toward the end of the Middle Ages were active importers of this spice, then still of mysterious origin. One of them, named Marco Polo, was the first European to admire its pretty yellow flower spikes in the East. Ginger was in the pharmacopoeia of the Arabs and also of doctors of Rabelais' time. Today its exciting, stomachic, and carminative property is not highly valued. According to Doctor Henri Leclerc,* it is especially known to horse dealers who use its powder as a rectal specific to force horses to raise their tails proudly.

VARIETIES The spice-lover easily finds powdered ginger, crystalized (sugared) ginger, and preserved ginger in syrup, in most good groceries. He knows that best "growth" comes from India and Jamaica. The first-quality Indian is called three finger (*trois doigts*). *Ratoon* is the last-quality Jamaican, the least commendable.

These are the white gingers, that are peeled, as opposed to the unpeeled gray ginger of China or Africa. The latter has a more violent and also more acid taste. It is necessary to select hard, compact ginger free from damage by larva and insects when buying from some importers.

Praised by Taillevent*, chef to Charles VII and also the first Frenchman to write a cooking tract, *mesche* was white Indian ginger, sold by the Venetians as *micchino,* while *colombino* was gray ginger coming from Samarkand. Happily for India's economy, this poorest country in the world produces annually 16,000 tons of this precious food.

* See APPENDIX.

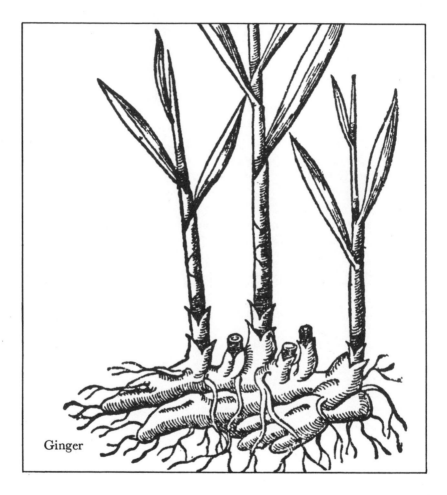

Ginger

USES: *The white spice* (épice blanche), *as it was prettily called in the time of Louis XI, is hardly in favor any more with French cooks. This is not the case in England. The Anglo-Saxons add ginger to a number of beverages: ginger ale, ginger beer, Jamaican ginger, ginger brandy, and ginger wine. They dote on the spicy taste of ginger in many different sweets: Christmas pudding, ginger nuts, ginger marmalade, etc. They sprinkle melon with powdered ginger.*

Ginger can be used in European cuisines—as opposed to Oriental—in stews, such as chicken stew, to garnish a vol-au-vent, *in wild duck sauce, in barbecue aromatics used for a white meat, and for renewing the aroma of a chicken curry. It may also be used (more orthodoxly) to introduce it to the timid in the many exotic foods that contain ginger: Moroccan chicken with ginger, Cantonese pork with ginger and soy sauce, Indonesian or Dutch goose with ginger, Bombay fish balls with ginger. It is interesting to note that ginger is also an element in most of the compound Oriental spices: curry, ras-el-hanout, etc.*

It is useless to stock fresh ginger roots because they quickly lose their aroma. Ginger should be used like garlic, in small quantities, sliced and sautéed in a pan with coarse salt. Powdered ginger can be added during or at the end of cooking. For some gourmets who follow a strict diet, ginger is useful, like tarragon, as a salt substitute.

Gingerbread

(French, *Pain d'épice;* German, *Pfefferkuchen.*) A pastry preparation that belongs to a very old tradition. In France, the gingerbreads of Dijon and Reims are the most appreciated; in Flanders, it may be called *cougue* and is modeled in the form of an individual or animal. Made of rye flour, boiling reddish honey—and most often molasses syrup—gingerbread is flavored with ginger, cinnamon, and candied fruits are often added. For a long time, Nordic cooks have been interested in it, for crumbled gingerbread is found in a number of beer sauces. (*See* BEER.) In Central Europe and Austria, soaked gingerbread, passed through a strainer, is used to thicken sauces, stuffings, etc. Finally, dried gingerbread, reduced to fine crumbs, can be used to bread small cuts of meat.

Ginseng

(Panax schinseng) A small plant grown in Soviet Asia and China. Some wild varieties are also found in Canada and the United States. Its whitish root has a weak odor of fennel and a sugary bitter taste. In China, ginseng is used as a popular panacea. The Western doctors who used it in the eighteenth century as "Chinese mandrake" seem to have forgotten it. Only its slightly aphrodisiac and tonic properties are recognized. A number of Chinese recipes employ ginseng in the same way as ginger.

Glutamate

(See MONOSODIUM GLUTAMATE.)

Gombo, Gumbo

(See OKRA.)

Goose Fat (Graisse d'Oie)

Sociologists have observed that France is divided into five culinary regions, according to the way the inhabitants use butter, olive oil, acidulated cream, lard, or goose fat. No other gastronomic domain is as well defined as that of cooking with goose fat. It includes most of the southwestern region of France. The goose, formerly dedicated to Juno, finds its fatty tissue master there, hardly challenged by lard and peanut oil. Outside France, few cooks use goose fat consistently. The Danes, Hungarians, and Balkan people know it well, but reserve it for well-defined uses. The merit of goose fat is precisely that it does not smell of fat. Of all animal fats, if one eliminates duck and turkey, it has the most *olein*. Often it may be adulterated with cotton oil for cooking, which is not very agreeable. The fluidity and lightness of goose fat allows it to be mixed, better than lard, with Banyuls or other sweet wines. In *garbure,* the stewlike soup of Gascogne, or in the *elzekaria,* the thick Basque soup, it has a role like that of olive oil in minestrone or *soupe au pistou.*(*See* LARD.)

Grains of Paradise

(French, *Malaguette* or *Maniguette*) "Pepper, ivory and large monkeys," is how the Portuguese sailors of the Renaissance described the riches of the coast of Malaguette, at present called Sierra Leone. The name *Malaguette,* is popularly pronounced *maniguette* by analogy to the cook's *manigances* or tricks. The name Grains of Paradise designates a large, highly scented grayish seed.

In 1245, in Lyon, the apothecaries were in dangerous competition with the pepper merchants in selling these smooth black seeds with the acrid taste. Today, the malaguette, or Grains of Paradise, is not much used, but the Tunisian Arabs have them brought by caravans from Timbuktu. Malaguette is scorned in the West. It is the fruit of *Aframomum meleguetta,* an amomum, a group of aromatic plants. Several bushes of the same family give similar products: *habzeli* or *zélim* of Ethiopia, *xylopie* of South America, etc. Today, red pepper is more popular than Grains of Paradise. (*See* RED PEPPER.)

Granadilla

Granadilla is a tropical fruit, also called *passiflore, barbadine, maracuja, passion fruit* and, botanically, *Passiflora edulis.* Egg-shaped, orange or red, it is grown in tropical America, Australia, etc. Its sourish pulp is highly scented, delicious in marmalades; it is also an element in some creole recipes.

Grated Cheese

The use of cheese crumbs in cooking is a very old tradition among the people of Provence. In the sixteenth century at the latest, it became current in Paris under the influence exercised over the gastrononomy by Catherine de Medici's Florentine cooks. In Franche-Comté, in Savoy, and in the Valais, Switzerland, it is the ruler of certain culinary preparations: *fondue, raclette valaisanne,* fried *escalope de fromage,* and the curiously named "cheese steak," *bifteck au fromage* in Lausanne.

Grated cheese, sprinkled with discretion on a dish of macaroni or on a dish to be browned under the broiler, gives a very distinctive, mellow taste. Without exaggeration, it can be called an aromatic, which is why the choice of grated cheese should be considered a matter of great importance by cooks. Here is our advice on the subject:

GRUYERE and its French equivalents are especially suited to *gratins* of potatoes, or cheese omelettes, but used routinely they quickly become monotonous.

PARMESAN Called in Italy *formaggio di grana,* it is without a doubt the best cheese of all to grate, because it is ripened for several years in cellars. Preferably, it should be bought in pieces in an Italian grocery and grated at home,where it can also be mixed with another kind of cheese. (See below.)

The rind of Parmesan should not be neglected. Cleaned of its ashen covering, it can be cooked in a minestrone or a *soupe au pistou,* which it flavors very agreeably. This is one of the secrets of the cuisine of Liguria.

Many other cheeses are excellent for grating—notably Swiss *sbrinz* (called *spalen* in the United States), and *emmenthal* even though it is a little fat; also Corsican broccio, Italian *cacciocavallo,* and Dutch Edam, once they are well dried.

Very soft cheeses, such as Gorgonzola or Camembert, mashed with a fork, can liven up many a culinary preparation. A piece of Gorgonzola chosen from the veined part has a place in Italian-style vegetable cream. As for Camembert, the gastronome Gaston Derys liked putting it in onion soup moistened with champagne. (*See* BROCCIO, MOZZARELLA, *and* YOGHURT.)

The old cooks of Provence are certainly the most skillful in the choice and use of grated cheese. Although their teachings are often contradictory, one can attempt to summarize them: for macaroni, etc., use half Parmesan, half Gruyère (freshly grated with a fine grater and not cut in long, tough fibers); for vegetable soups, (*pistous,* etc.) use half Dutch, half Parmesan; for fish soups, use Parmesan alone; for omelettes, use pieces of Gruyère, goat or ewe cheeses, beaten if they are fresh, crumbled if they

114

are dry (brousse, broccio, etc.). They should be seasoned with aromatic herbs: chives, basil, mint, etc. (*See* CHESHIRE *or* PARMESAN.)

Guava

The fruit of the guava (*Psidium periferum*), also called the Antilles pear (*poirier des Antilles*). This exotic yellowish or pinkish fruit comes in various sizes and is not very tasty raw. Once cooked, it becomes exquisite, making fine compotes, preserves, pastes, and jellies. The guava also exists in China, where it is purplish in color. Soaked in wine or in corn alcohol and seasoned with red pepper slices, it sometimes is offered as a condiment.

Ham

"The pig, along with the rabbit, is the most prolific animal in the world." Vauban, a military engineer and an excellent mathematician, devoted himself to a treatise called *Ma Cochonnerie* (the word *cochon* is "pig" in French). He calculated that, after twelve years of farrowing, the issue of a sow would be 6,434,838 pigs.

This picturesque bit of teaching was offered by Dumas in his *Grand Dictionnaire de Cuisine.* He permits us to state without preamble that pork, fresh, smoked, salted, or fried, is a food so widespread in the world that it is often called upon to play the role of a condiment.

Ham, more particularly that of Parma, Bayonne (that is to say d'Orthez), York, Prague, Asturia, Auvergne, Mayence, Westphalia, Bastogne, or simply of Paris, contributes its flavor to the most unexpected dishes. Melon is often eaten in Italy with *prosciutto di Parma,* cut in fine slices. *Escalopes de veau en papillotes* owe their interest to a mixture of chopped herbs and mushrooms as well as to the slice of York ham that covers them.

Finely chopped salted ham is an element in the delectable Cantonese rice and Indonesian stuffed fowl. The chopped ham of Paris or Mayence is found in Bavarian cheese sausages, ham soufflés, omelettes, pastry shells, stuffings, etc. There are also recipes for consommés using ham and Madeira wine, crepes stuffed with ham, rolls of tuna in ham, pheasant with ham and

117

sauerkraut, Spanish-style trout larded with ham. No other meat offers itself as freely to the imagination of the chef.

As for other parts of pork, the shoulder is made into Corsican *coppa;* the filet, smoked as bacon; and other meats, such as *boeuf boucané* of Grisons, or *Bundenfleisch,* Oriental *pastrami,* and Corsican *miscicia* from goat or mutton, can be used as an element in culinary preparations. (*See* COPPA, CRACKLING, BACON, *and* PASTRAMI.)

Hardhay (St. Johnswort)

(*Hypericum perforatum;* French, *Millepertius;* German, *Johanniskraut*) A perennial Hypericum that grows in dry places, common in Southern France where it is called *truscalan.* Its common name comes from the numerous bladders that resemble perforations sprinkled on its somewhat sticky leaves. The pretty star-shaped yellow flowers keep their color after being dried. In Scandinavia, they were once used to color grain alcohols.

Hardhays, which had an antidiabolic reputation, were occasionally used in certain rustic recipes for liqueurs, healing aromatic spirits, marinades, etc. The heads give off a bitter odor if they are rubbed, and their taste is resinous and a little acrid.

Harissa, Arissa

This favorite condiment of the North Africans is most often a red, very spicy purée—rarely a powder—darker than paprika. According to tradition, this condiment must be prepared with little hot peppers, garlic, and tomato pulp, all well crushed in a mortar.

Moistened with two spoonfuls of bouillon, a large lump of harissa forms the red sauce that replaces mustard next to all North African dishes. Although it has a little too much tomato taste for this use, harissa may figure in a Chinese or Vietnamese meal. Canned harissa, generally imported from Tunisia, is especially useful to season a cold sauce; for example, the Provençal *rouille,* squid *à l'américaine* or a Spanish *poulet au piment.* It can also be mixed with paprika in a Hungarian dish.

In Morocco, harissa yields its place to three varieties of powdered pepper: *felfla loua* (a sort of sweet paprika), *felfla soudania* (very strong), *felfla harra* (a mixture of peppers and red peppers, bitter and aromatic).

Hay

A mixture of dried vegetation that is very useful in curing some small cheeses such as *pithiviers,* in keeping apples, etc. Its smell, so much more marked if it is cut in the mountains, lightly imbues these foods. Its costliness today as animal feed explains why beef has lost the flavor it used to have.

Hazelnut (Filbert)

(*Corylus Avellana;* French, *Noisette;* German, *Haselnuss*) Fruit of the hazel tree (*coudrier* or *noisetier*). This species has given way to a number of cultivated varieties in Italy and elsewhere, whose fruits are called filberts (*avelines*).

Hazelnuts make very agreeable dessert fruits, eaten fresh or dried and they also furnish an agreeable oil. (*See* OIL.) Grated or, more rarely, pounded, they are used as a condiment in Mediterranean countries: *Morue à la biscayenne* (cod) dusted with crumbled hazelnuts and almonds; *truite aux noisettes à la pyrénéenne,* or sprinkled on minestrone *à la génoise,* etc. We shall skip the innumerable uses of hazelnuts and filberts in pastry and confections.

Herbs

According to the excellent lexicographer Claude Augé,* the word herb (*herbe*) applies to a "soft plant whose aerial parts, including the stem, die each year." Among the many plants within this definition, ancient authors distinguish three catagories of cooking herbs:

EDIBLE HERBS: sorrel, Spanish lettuce, beets, purslane, etc.

* See APPENDIX.

SEASONING HERBS: Chervil, parsley, tarragon, chives, cultivated savory, fennel, basil, burnet, etc.

SALAD HERBS: Include most seasoning herbs as well as celery leaves, leaf stalks of fennel, plaintain, tansy.

This clever categorization is hardly useful any longer. At least two hundred herbs—without counting the many varieties—are found to be excellent in the cooking of our modest planet. We wager that very appetizing aromatic plants exist on distant stars. (H. G. Wells in the *War of the Worlds* made a large place for an extraterrestrial herb.)

Mixtures of dried herbs are studied in our articles on Compound Spices. (*See also* FINES HERBES.)

N.B. Many different aromatic vegetable plants used in cuisine are called *herbe* in common language. Below is a brief glossary:

COMMON NAME	ENGLISH (LITERAL)	ENGLISH
Herbe amère	Bitter herb	Tansy
Herbe à l'âne	Donkey Herb	Savory
Herbe aux anges	Angels' Herb	Angelica
Herbeaux couronnes	Crown Herb	Rosemary
Herbe aux cuillers	Spoon Herb	Wild Cress, Wild Horseradish
Herbe à maquereau	Mackerel Herb	Green Mint or Peppermint
Herbe royale	Royal Herb	Basil
Herbe sacrée	Sacred Herb	Sage, Hylsop
Herbe de grâce	Herb of Grace	Rue
Herbe aux vers	Worm's Herb	Wormwood
Herbe de feu	Fire Herb	Mugwort
Herbe à l'agneau	Lamb's Herb	Pennyroyal
Herbe au citron	Lemon Herb	Melissa
Herbe à la poudre de Chypre	Herb of the Powder of Cyprus	Musked Mallow
Herbe aux teigneux	Pesty Herb	Burdock
Herbe des Juifs	Jew's Herb	Jew's Mallow

(*Also see* TURTLE HERBS, COMPOUND SPICES, *and* VENETIAN HERBS.)

Hickory

(*Carya ovata*) An American variety of the white walnut, bearing pointed leaves and fragile-shelled nuts. Its very hard wood is used by ski- and musical-instrument-makers.

Hickory salt, very popular in the United States, is either sea salt smoked for a long time over hickory wood coals, or a mixture of monosodium glutamate and hickory ash, also smoked. This cooking aromatic received its inspiration from an old Balkan tradition in which walnut ash was frequently used in cooking. In our opinion, hickory salt is very valuable for flavoring a grilled trout or seasoning home-style grills of pork and veal. Its first use is to bring the aroma of a true barbecue to an electric broiler. It is not well suited to small cuts of beef. For a steak or a sirloin nothing surpasses the herbs of Provence. (*See* CHARCOAL, WOOD FIRE, *and* SMOKE.)

N.B. Americans make use of hickory dishes or plain boards to hold roasts cooked in the oven, in order to give them a characteristic taste.

Holly

(*Ilex aquifolium;* French, *Houx;* German, *Stechpalme*) A little tree, with spiny, persistent, and decorative leaves. Bird lime, dear to fowlers, is made by boiling its bark. Its red, globelike fruit contains sour little nuts that formerly were dried, grilled, and powdered to make a bitter purgative beverage something like coffee. The leaves of Paraguayan holly contain an alkaloid close to *theine* and are prepared as a tea called *maté*.

BUTCHER'S BROOM (*Ruscus aculeatus;* French, *Petit-houx* or *fragon*) A very different bush bearing little leaves like those of boxwood, but spicy. The acid red fruit, which ripens in winter, tastes a little like wild cherry. The berry can be used like a cranberry, while the nuts can be employed as a substitute for coffee, as the Corsicans do. The young shoots have a piquant taste, slightly like turpentine. According to Roques, a botanist of the nineteenth century, the young shoots of butcher's broom are the "sweet of the farmer, the shepherd and the poacher." They can take the place of asparagus points and *fines herbes* in an omelette.

Honey

"Syrupy substance that the bees gather on the flowers. For a long time honey took the place of sugar" said Alexander Dumas. He reminds us that honey is nothing more than a variety of sugar. In this role, it has figured in many country recipes. Today, it seems to be scorned by cooks, wrongly, we feel. Why should we use the morsel of sugar to flavor some sauces and avoid this vegetable aromatic gathered by those hard-working insects?

Cul-de-veau au miel (calf with honey) made our ancestors rejoice. Well before that, the Romans appreciated suckling pig with honey, presented to the guest who rested softly on the *triclinium*. Honey is always in favor in Italy. It perks up sweet and sour sauces and seasons *aceto dolce* (which see) of the same order. In China, gourmets use honey and brown sugar in the delicate smoking of fowl and in marinating shellfish. In Fez, the patrician city of Morocco, saddle of lamb is always covered with honey, quince, and cinnamon. It is delicious! The Turks of Istanbul add a little spoonful of honey to *patlican salatasi*, an eggplant "caviar" seasoned by lemon juice. In the United States, many worthy housewives consider that ham is its most delicate if it is cooked in the oven with honey and hickory salt! A drop of honey is enough to flavor a dish. Dissolved by the cooking steam, caramelized on the walls of the casserole, it spreads a sweet vegetal aroma. There are acacia, heather, chestnut, lavender, apple, thyme, and sainfoin-flavored honeys. (Sainfoin is an Old World, cloverlike, blossoming legume.)

Hong-Lu, Hung-Liu

Chinese name of five spices (which see).

Hops

(*Humulus lupulus;* French, *Houblon;* German, *Hopfen*) A climbing perennial plant, undoubtedly native to Russia, but cultivated in Western Europe for a thousand years. This vegetable hermaphrodite simultaneously bears insignificant male flowers and female infloresences or *strobil.* Gathered in the month of September, these conelike strobils are dried or dehydrated, then shaken to rid them of a resinous yellowish dust, the *lupilin*. Its distinctive alliaceous odor and bitter flavor are used by brewers to flavor barley must in making beer. For a long time, doctors have maintained that lupilin is a powerful sedative and an aphrodisiac, exactly the opposite of stimulants in the cuisine of gallantry. This characteristic, similar to that of the poppy, is very rare among the food aromatics. Lupilin also gives a characteristic flavor to the honey of bees who have visited hop plantations.

In German and Flemish cuisine, the young hop sprouts (called in French, *jets de houblon*) are used. Gathered even before they show above the ground, they have an agreeable taste that resembles asparagus. Sautéed in butter or with cream, they provide the stuffing in the very excellent *poularde à l'anversoise*.

Horse Parsley

(*Smyrnium olusatrum*) A large biennial *Umbellifera* that used to be cultivated as *persil noir* (black parsley) or *ache large* (big smallage). It is found in the wild in shady, cool places. Its taste is strongly aromatic, though a little acrid, making it appreciated as a condiment. Horse parsley could not take the competition of true parsley and celery and has practically disappeared from French cooking. The root of the perfoliate horse parsley, nevertheless, has an agreeable taste. Wild horse parsley should be gathered with the greatest care, for it resembles poison hemlock.

Horseradish

(*Armoracia rusticana* or *lapathyfolia;* French, *Raifort;* German, *Meerrettich*) In France, both the black radish (*radis noir*) and the German horseradish (*raifort germanique*) are called *raifort,* but only the second interests us in this article. It is a wild or cultivated Crucifer with a spicy root, brownish on the outside, white on the inside. This condiment, which delights German people and Slavs, used to be called in France *moutarde des capucins, cran de Bretagne,* and *cranson.*

The root, grated or sliced in fine pieces, is one of the most valued boons of German gastronomy. It is similar to mustard,

Horseradish

although it has a prettier color and a less elaborate taste. Grated horseradish is preserved in vinegar. Sometimes it is also colored pink with red beet juice.

USES: *In Germany, this condiment is often mixed with egg yolk, sour cream, whipped cream, or sourish grated apples. Horseradish can also be cooked. It is very pleasant quickly cooked in black butter, in hollandaise sauce, or in a coulibiac (a Russian dough-covered preparation). In Bamberg, Lower Franconia, the world capital of horseradish, it is preferred stirred up in a remoulade or mayonnaise sauce, with chopped hard-cooked eggs, sliced cucumber or radishes. It also combines its spicy flavor well with herring or a fatty cheese. But of all these uses we would especially remember it accompanying bockwurst, the modest German sausage that is served smoking hot, with little crisp rolls, in the beer parlors of Germany. A frank and honest dish, it easily consoles us for the many pseudogastronomic preparations served in the same country.*

Hydromel

A fermented beverage, ancient as wine that might have been invented by Aristides, King of Arcadia. Called *melicraton* by the Greeks, *aqua mulsa* by the Romans, *chouchen* by the Gauls, and *miod* by the Vikings, hydromel made merry the love feasts of our ancestors. Although basically made of honey, hydromel may be flavored in a thousand and one ways: with vanilla, cinnamon, rose, jasmine, and many other pleasant flavors.

In our time, hydromel is not completely forgotten in France. Bee-keepers still know how to make *hydromel chablis, hydromel champagnisé, hydromel grenache,* etc. for a most discriminating clientele.

Hypocras

Another celebrated beverage of the Middle Ages is called *hypocras* because wines, soaked with aromatics and fruits, were passed through a Hippocrates' filter (*chausse d'Hippocrate*) used by apothecaries. Taillevent* has left a recipe for *hypocras aux épices,* flavored

* See APPENDIX.

with cinnamon, white ginger, and cloves, but today, Spanish *sangría* and the German *bowle* are preferred.

Hyssop

(*Hyssopus officinalis;* French, *Hysope;* German, *Ysop*) A large perennial of the *Labiatae* family, growing on slopes in temperate and southern European regions. Its name comes from the Hebrew *ezop* and it is mentioned in the Bible. The thin, dark, persistent leaves form a sort of transition between the needles of rosemary and the lanceolate leaves of tarragon. Its bitter flavor resembles lamb's lettuce, rosemary, and savory, with a slight scent of camphor.

Hyssop, well used in medieval cuisine, is still known to Germanic cooks. Dried hyssop can be bought in groceries and gourmet shops that sell a variety of aromatics. This bitter herb should be used with caution: finely chopped, it seasons potato salads, or lentils, stuffings, marinades, and roast veal. The blue, sometimes pink, flowers of the hyssop are used in some liquors. The ancient herbalists considered these an excellent remedy for chest ailments.

Ink

Lest anyone misunderstand, let us say quickly we refer to the black liquid spilled in the sea by some cephalopods—the little cuttlefish, *encornets, supions, chipirons,* etc. The cooks of both sides of the Basque country push refinement (or cruelty) to the point of simmering these kinds of animals in the ink that they put forth for marine evasions. The result is amusing, even if one considers that the ink's taste is weak; it should be enhanced by adding urchin roe.

Iris of Florence (Orris Root)

(*Iris florentina;* French, *Iris de Florence*) All iris rhizomes contain a volatile oil whose somewhat acrid perfume recalls that of violets. Florence iris, recognizable by its small size and white flowers, is especially aromatic. Its rootstock, cultivated in Tuscany and Provence, is used by perfumers, pharmacists, cosmeticians, and druggists to perfume various products. It occasionally enters into gastronomy by means of liquors (Izarra, of the Basque Country, for example, sherbet *à la violette,* pastries, and so on. In the time of Gothic cuisine, the iris and rose water flavored unimaginable preparations. This rhizome, eaten imprudently, is sternutatory and vomitive—in other words, it causes sneezing and vomiting.

Italy

French gourmets have a short memory if they forget that their ancestors, lovers of gallimaufries and other fat mouthfuls, were taught many culinary refinements by the Florentine cooks of both Catherine and Marie de Medici. In the sixteenth century, in France, only the people of Provence knew how to use spices and condiments with discernment. By contact with the Italians and Arabs, they had kept and continuously perfected the skills of the *vicarii supra coenas,* the culinary experts of ancient Rome.

The blue waves of the Mediterranean deserve to be emblazoned on the shield of the great Western cuisine. The Italian cuisine was itself strongly influenced by the gourmet traditions of ancient Greece and by the gastronomic subtleties taught at Byzantium and in Alexandria. Rich in thousands of specialties and incomparable agricultural products, the cuisine of Italy varies from the north to the south of the boot. But without a doubt it is synonymous everywhere with the judicious and instructive use of country aromas—savory vegetables chock full of sun, aromatic greens, sea foods, condiment cheeses, cooked wines, etc. This cuisine, although highly seasoned, rarely makes use of Asiatic spices. The F.A.O., installed in its palace on the banks of the Tiber, reveals in its statistics that the Italian consumes infinitely less of cloves, nutmeg, and pepper than does the Anglo-Saxon, the German, or the Frenchmen. The Italian harmony is made of half tones and accords of delicate tastes. (*See* ACETO DULCE, GARLIC, ANCHOVIES, BASIL, CAPONATA, FENNEL, HAM, MARSALA, MOZZARELLA, MYRTLE, OLIVES, MARJORAM, PARMESAN, PISTOU, ROSEMARY, SAGE, *and* TOMATO.)

Jasmine

(*Jasminum officinale;* French, *Jasmin*) A shrubby tree with smooth leaves and white, heavily scented flowers, grown in the Orient, on the periphery of the Mediterranean, and warm sections of America. The flowers have a large role in perfumery and are valued in homeopathic and allopathic medicine. A while ago, it was an infallible medication for fears and sundry agonies. In Turkey, jasmine wood is used to make the stems of pipes! The smooth, dried, and shriveled flowers are the palish leaves in Mandarin jasmine tea. Fresh, they garnish or decorate stewed Chinese or Indonesian chicken. In the Arab countries, guests are offered bracelets or necklaces made of jasmine flowers. Western confectioners sometimes try crystallizing them in sugar, but their perfume is fleeting.

Jujube

(*Rhamnus zizyphus;* French, *Jujubier*) The tough, scented, little fruit of the jujube tree grows widely in southern Europe and in Oriental countries. Some of this fruit that the Arabs call *nabka* is eaten like a date and is also prepared as sundry sorts of confections. In the Far East, fragments of jujube pulp decorate small rolls and pastries. In North Africa, a paste of honey and jujube is called *chichourle.*

Juniper

(*Juniperus communis;* French, *Genièvre;* German, *Wacholder;* Italian, *Ginepro*) The common name of the evergreen juniper. Often it designates the berries and the many alcohols that they flavor. This little conifer grows wild in the most varied climates, from the Tundra to Andalusia. Its fruit, first green then turning blackish, takes two years to ripen. It contains three minuscule seeds with a peppery taste, surrounded by a fine resinous, sweet pulp. The Nordic people use this berry to great advantage.

British gin, Dutch and Flemish *schiedam, pécquet* from Liege, *Wacholderschnaps* from Westphalia, and Danish *aquavit* are some of the grain alcohols distilled with juniper berries, sometimes mixed also with anise or cumin seeds. Juniper berries are also combined with hops in the brewing of some Scandinavian beers.

USES: *Juniper is inseparable from many preparations, particularly sauerkraut. In Europe, small birds, notably the thrush, Corsican blackbirds, and woodcock, roasted either on a spit or in an oven, in a casserole,* chaud-froid, *or in a pie, increase their subtlety if they are sprinkled with crushed juniper berries or stuffed with whole berries. In addition, this fruit is one of the classic ingredients of all marinades and all court bouillons.*

Juniper can also flavor barbecued white meats, the oily sauce of crayfish à l'ardennaise, *Danish braised duck with red cabbage, flaming* rognons de veau liegeoise, *indeed even the* pot-au-feu *of the Causses and the Basses-Alpes.*

Reduced to a powder (it can be ground in a pepper mill), a hint of juniper may flavor the crust of a quiche lorraine *or the sweet crust of an apple tart.*

Juniper is not only a Nordic aromatic. The Spanish blend it into chorizo—*smoked on twigs of juniper—and in other sausages. In Indonesia, the berry is still appreciated in alcohol, even though it is a vestige of Batavian colonialism. In Turkey, finally, leg of mutton is marinated with juniper and marjoram to give it the taste of venison. (See* AQUAVIT.)

Juvert

The pretty provincial name for parsley, which should not be confused with sour grape juice (*verjus*).

Juniper

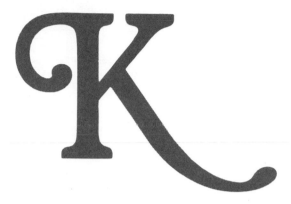

Kajou, Kajoo

(*See* CASHEW.)

Kasha

In the Russian language, this word is a synonym for groats. Found most in Russian restaurants it is steamed or boiled, resembling a blackish, lightly blown-up rice. Kasha is hulled and lightly grilled buckwheat seeds. Astonishing as it seems, it comes to us from Amsterdam, Lubeck, and Copenhagen. The Germans and the Danes use unmilled black wheat or rye groats to make the country bread called pumpernickel. The Vikings and the Cimbri knew only this kind of bread.

Kasha may be prepared with fat, like rice. It goes particularly well with *pojarsky katleti* (which are never veal chops, but beef or chicken chopped with onion), roast suckling pig, Caucasian *chachlik,* etc. Kasha can also be crushed and prepared with ewe's milk, with cheese like polenta, or as a pudding with milk, honey, raisins, etc.

Ketchup

Written ketchup, catchup or catsup, this is a condiment sauce on which Anglo-Saxons dote. It has its origins in the Hindu or Indonesian *Ketjap,* a kind of chutney that is more syrupy and contains mushroom purée. Today, ketchup is a mixture of tomato sauce, onions, vinegar, brown sugar, and spices—a tomato ketchup. To season spaghetti with tomato ketchup is a gastronomic impertinence. (*See* TOMATO.)

Kirsch

An excellent alcohol prepared in Alsace and in other French provinces with the must of a midseason cherry (the black heart cherry, *frontelle, ragotine, marchotte*). In Switzerland and Germany, it is called *Kirschwasser.* Aged from four to five years in ash-wood casks or in glass carboys covered with willow, this alcohol is dry and highly fragrant. It is used in several pastries and confections.

In cooking, kirsch plays a supporting role. It says its piece in *fondue valaisanne* (where it cuts the white wine); in escalopes of veal Strasbourg (where it flavors the envelope of smoked ham and grilled cheese). It can be used to swish dishes in which white meats were cooked and can combine with paprika.

Kola Nut

(*Cola acuminata;* French, *Noix de kola;* German, *Kolanuss*) Nut of the kola, a very large African tree resembling a chestnut, it has a bitter taste that does not become sweet except after mastication. The blacks of the Congo and Cameroons eat kola nuts daily, and it yellows their lips and saliva. This exotic nut figures especially in the code of pharmacists. It contains a stronger concentration of caffeine than the coffee bean, as well as other alkaloids that act rapidly on the nervous system.

Pulverized kola nut is more a physiological stimulant than a condiment. Nevertheless, it is found in some formulas for Moroccan *ras-el-hanout* and sundry tropical and equatorial African dishes: *mokoto* of the Cameroons (a stew of tripe and pigs' feet, seasoned with garlic, squash seeds, pili-pili, and kola), *couscous de manioc,* papaya purée, etc. In Western cuisine, it is used rarely to give unusual taste to a number of sweets, even to English biscuits. Its bitter aroma goes well with cinnamon, chocolate, and ginger.

For our part, we prefer to use kola nut in some refreshing beverage like Iberian *sangría,* so right for summer evenings.

N.B.   Kola nut is combined with an extract of the leaves of the South American bush, *Erytroxylon coca,* to prepare many soft drinks that associate the names of these two plants. To speak of this at length would be to venture out of gastronomy.

Kombou

An edible alga grown in Japan, also called *Iziki,* sold dried or marinated, and also powdered. From the botanists' point of view, it is a *Laminaria (Fucus digitatus),* close to other algae used as food in Iceland, etc.

The marine vegetable has an agreeable iodine taste that goes quite well with soy sauce. The Japanese use these algae in fish and crustacean soups, in stews, and infusions. It can also be used in compounding salads of a more Western inspiration. It is a simple condiment relegated to a discreet role. To eat algae is a gastronomic exoticism, and a dietetic effort. (*See* ALGAE.)

Kumquat, Cumquat

A tiny orange of the Far East, scarcely larger than an olive. It is borne by one of the *Rutaceae, Fortunella margarita,* which, by this name, commemorates the tribulations in China a century ago of the Scottish botanist, Robert Fortune. The Japanese call it *kunnkann.*

The flesh of the kumquat is highly scented; it is difficult to distinguish from the epicarp, which is also edible. It is offered widely by fruiterers.

USES: *This small, exquisite orange figures in the preparation of many Chinese sweets, notably, Eight Treasure Cake. It enhances marvelously a fruit salad or a melon compote. The kumquat lends itself, like the sour orange, to duck with orange sauce and, like the little African lemon, to marination in vinegar. (See* LEMON.)

Kvass, Kwass

A very light Russian barley beer made with many ingredients: *liébny kvass* with rye bread, *klioukvény kvass* with wild raspberries, or oak buds. This beverage is served with excellent cold soups.

Lacquer

(French, *Laque*) A sort of cooking varnish that is the glory of Chinese cooks who possess a certain high gloss of knowledge. It requires the use of a paint brush, as well as soy sauce, powdered sugar, and great patience. (*See* LACQUERED DUCK *under* SOY SAUCE.)

Lamb's Lettuce

(*Valerianella locusta;* French, *Mâche, Doucette, Boursette, Salade des moines;* German, *Ackersalat*) Originally a wild valerian, it has been improved by generations of gardeners. Lamb's lettuce has blue flowers and the size of the leaves depends on the variety. (The one called *mâche d'Italie,* or *tardive,* has large light-colored leaves).

The spicy, slightly bitter taste of these fine vegetable leaves is delicious served raw. It can be mixed with other salads, with *fines herbes,* added to a stuffing, mixed with stewed beans chopped and pounded with Roquefort cheese, or for garnishing a canapé spread. (*See* ROCKET.)

Lard

(French, *Saindoux;* German, *Schmalz;* Italian, *Strutto*) Melted, clarified pork grease. In pharmacy and perfumery, it is called *axonge* by the French.

Cooking with lard tends to be out of fashion. Animal greases are challenged today by peanut oil, margarine, etc., in addition to (according to modern medicine), cholesterolemia and arteriosclerosis. But this cuisine has its defenders who affirm that a meat cooked in lard is drier and less "oozy" than a food treated with vegetable butter or oil. Thus, in Vienna, the true *Wienerschnitzel* is always fried in lard. It is only on this condition that an elegant woman might sit on a breaded cutlet without staining her dress! In central Italy and in Rome, oil is reserved for frying fish, lard being preferred for *fritto misto, carciofi fritti,* etc. In Hungary, all the *gulyas* and *pörkölt,* and paprika stews, are prepared with lard. In central and eastern France, cooking with lard is popular but in the southwest it meets competition from goose fat. In a very general way, it can be said that there is an axis of lard-lovers that starts with the Massif Central and crosses the German and Slavic countries before ending in China. The Chinese use only lard for cooking. Their sesame oil is almost always consumed raw. They know how to fry the ginger in coarse salt and lard, or how to enhance a cabbage soup with lard, without which these foods become indigestible.

In Gascogne and Béarn, a large lump of lard formerly was used to thicken *garbure,* the thick southern soup, during cooking. The fat of a preserved goose or even olive oil is better than lard in the same role. In the old cuisine, lard (pork fat) was duly heated to season many salads.

To us, melted bacon fat seems more proper for this use, though condemned by the dietitians. The Anglo-Saxons themselves are skeptical in regard to lard; they prefer suet (beef kidney grease) and drippings.

Latin America

A cuisine of Spanish-Portuguese inspiration reigns from the southern border of California to Tierra del Fuego. It is very well adapted to the resources of the different territories and their very variable climates. Among the most widespread foods are manioc flour, sweet potatoes, small brown or red beans, plaintain, avocado, and the omnipresent cornmeal, as well as a multitude of very tasty fruits.

An explosive spice, chili, inspires most condiments, although rosemary, marjoram, and other local herbs that are similar to tansy, mint, or basil have a certain role. Some oddities: *cochayuyo,* an alga that thickens Chilean soups and sauces; sweetish flour of Peru; turtle lard—an Amazonian treat; *zapallos*—small Argentine gourds, *isote* flowers that the Guatemalans chop finely and mix into omelettes; and, finally, corn or cactus alcohols (*chica, pulque,* etc.) figure in some recipes. (*See* CHICHA, CHILI, PULQUE.)

Lavender

(Lavandula vera; French, *Lavande;* German, *Lavendel)* One of the large *Labiatae* with a woody stock and small violet flowers clustering along the stem. The Romans used these flower heads to perfume their baths, and the name of the plant comes from the word *laver,* to wash. Lavender is extensively cultivated in France and Italy for the perfume industry's use. It also has a place in flower gardens. Its role in cooking is episodic. The pulverized heads are elements in some Provençal compound spices, and also under the Moroccan name *khzame* in *ras-el-hanout* (which see). There is a risk of the sweetish aroma of lavender corrupting the taste of the dish. Nevertheless, very old French recipes make mention of *aspic* or *spic,* the name of a particularly fragrant variety, *Lavandula spica.*

N.B. Two or three twigs of lavender very prettily decorate the immaculate napkin on which certain dishes such as *terrine* or *pâté en croute* are placed.

Leaven

Many kinds of leavens are used in baking and pastry-making to raise the doughs. They contain either microorganisms or substances which free carbon dioxide gases. Everybody knows bakers' leaven which is the sour dough and also yeast; beer leaven, a microscopic mushroom, *Saccharomyces cerevisiae,* whose action is energetic and rapid; and, finally, chemical leavening containing sodium carbonates or sodium ammoniacs.

Occasionally, these products are useful to the cook in preparing pastry dough *(pâte à foncer),* pizza, or *quiche.* More rarely, they can be used to make chopped meat or *godiveau* more spongy. The

Balkan people add leaven or bicarbonate to *boulettes, bitokes, mititeï.* (*See* BICARBONATE OF SODA.)

Leaves

A great many leaves have a large role in cooking, ranging from the very fine tripinnate leaves of chervil to the wide classic leaf of lettuce. A goodly number among them are used as envelopes for the main dish—for example, stuffed cabbage, or Haitian suckling pig wrapped in banana leaves and cooked in coals. Without a doubt, this packaging gives an aroma to meats and fish, even to the chopped stuffings, but we prefer to devote this article to the leaves of trees whose culinary function is not evident.

The vine leaf is the traditional envelope of Turkish or Oriental *yalantzi dolmas.* It is prepared in brine as in Alsatian sauerkraut. Vine leaves are available in cans in gourmet food shops.

The oak leaf or cherry leaf is used as an aromatic in Central Europe for marinating gherkins (which see). The linden tree leaf, duly chopped, is used for stuffing some roasted game in Russia. The leaves of the myrtle give a lift to fish soups in Corsica. The bay leaf is the best known. These protective, lightly aromatic leaves are particularly suited to the excellent cheeses of France. The chestnut leaf, notably, covers the *banons* made in Dauphine; Cantal is molded in beech leaves; goat cheeses of Rouergue are covered with black currant or walnut leaves; soft paste cheese are cured between two walnut leaves, *jonchée* cheeses from Languedoc are cured in wattles of green reeds.

Leek

(*Allium porrum;* French, *Poireau;* German, *Lauch*) The leek (also called *porreau* in French), related to garlic, has been cultivated for thousands of years. Its bulb is less biting than garlic and onion. Its long pipelike leaves have a pleasantly spicy taste. In Provence, the leek is called *asperge du pégot,* that is, shoemaker's asparagus. In Paris, as elsewhere in France, the leek and potato soup is a favorite of everybody—the midinette as well as the gourmet. The leek has a reputation for its tonic action on the vocal cords. Nero gorged himself on leek broth before seizing his lyre and declaiming.

PREPARATION: *The leek is prepared hot or cold, notably with cream, béchamel, breaded, glazed, marinated like an artichoke* à la grecque, *etc. On occasion, in Lorraine and in the north of France, it garnishes* quiches *and* flamiques. *In Provence, stuffed leeks are a favorite, with some very tasty recipes resulting. In central China, where garlic is less favored, the leek substitutes for it in many fried dishes—breasts of fowl sautéed in coarse salt, etc. In Tuscany, sliced leek is sautéed with celery stems and a little garlic, before adding the tomato paste to make* salsa di pomodoro.

Lemon

(*Citrus medica;* French, *Citron;* German, *Zitrone*) Native, like so many vegetable aromatics, to tropical Asia, the lemon tree *(citronnier* or *limonier)* is a medium-sized tree of the Hesperides family. Acclaimed in Asia Minor well before our time, it was lyrically mentioned by Virgil. Forgotten for several centuries, the "Median apple" was rediscovered by the Crusaders who sucked its acid pulp to protect themselves from the fevers of the Orient. Intensively cultivated in Italy, Spain, and Africa, the lemon produces fruits of an unequal quality. A first-class lemon is recognized by its smell, its tight peel, and its weight. The best of all is undoubtedly the little Oriental lemon, also called *citron gallet,* which has a smooth, fine skin.

Modern medicine has confirmed the tradition that the lemon, a veritable concentration of vitamin C, is a powerful remedy for scurvy, and even an antiseptic. (It contributes to the neutralization of amoeba and bacteria.)

USES: *The uses are varied. Its juice can replace vinegar in most salad dressings, particularly those of raw vegetables—grated carrots, etc. It also flavors shellfish, mayonnaise, and some white sauces. Its zest (grated peel) is preferred to the juice when it is used in a mixture containing milk or cream that might curdle. In Greece, giltheads (fish) are baked on a bed of onion and lemon slices. In South America, in the Antilles, and especially on the Pacific coast, some filets of fish are prepared by letting them soak several hours in lemon juice, which is equivalent to actual cooking. In India,* nimbopani *is a lime juice that is mixed with ginger and cardamom. In Egypt, salted and marinated, lemon is a condiment.*

Lemon

N.B.   Lemons are made juicier by soaking them ten minutes in hot water.

Lentisk

(Pistacia lentiscus; French, *Lentisque;* German, *Pistazie)* A variety of pistachio tree cultivated in Greece and in the Levant for its fruit —a reddish stone fruit—known as the *bottom* in the souks of Asia Minor, that gives a slightly strong oil.

For a long time, its wood has been used to make toothpicks, an industry that today seems to be in jeopardy. It is the resin that especially interests us. Under the name *mastika,* it is celebrated throughout the western periphery of the Mediterranean.

Letcho

(French, *Letcho hongrois;* Hungarian, *Lecso)* A Hungarian condiment exported in cans. It is a tomato paste, seasoned with green pepper, onion, smoked bacon, paprika, salt, and marjoram. It also accompanies all the *pörkölt, gulyas,* etc.

Lichens

(French, *Lichen;* German, *Flechte)* Very small vegetable organisms containing algae and mushrooms, or combining these two species in symbiosis. Lichen attach themselves to rocks or tree trunks, preferably in humid places. Abounding in the tundra, they also exist up to the edge of the Sahara Desert.

From the most ancient times, man has used lichens in his food. Their bitter and disagreeable elements generally disappear after washing. In cooking, they give off viscous material from which a vegetable gel can be made. Reindeer lichen gives to the flesh of these semidomestic animals a very characteristic taste. In periods of famine, the Laplanders formerly ate flat cakes of lichen and Arctic pine bark. In Iceland and in the mountainous regions of Greece, the *Cetraria islandica* or cetrariam is used in medicine and for the clarification of beer. Nomad people of the Sahara used lichen *(lichen de chêne)* with mugwort and certain resins to embellish mutton recipes or young camel dishes. Dyers' moss, a coloring used by delicatessen-makers, is taken from an algae-lichen *Parmelia saxatilis,* which is grown on the rocks of the Mediterranean. Gathering lichens is a difficult and rather unprofitable operation and has had to cede its place to marine algae in the food gel industry.

Licorice

(Glycyrrhiza glabra; French, *Réglisse;* German, *Süssholzwurzel)* Licorice wood is the dried root of the licorice tree of the perennial *Leguminosae* family native to the Caucasus, and grown in all Mediterranean countries. By repeated boiling and pressure, licorice is extracted. The taste of the root is both acrid and sugary, that of the purified licorice more flavored and sweet. The black, shiny, rubbery essence so loved by children is one of many uses of this flavoring agent.

In North Africa and in the Levant, licorice root ranks among the important of culinary aromatics. Scraped, dried, and pulverized, it is an element in some compound spices, notably *ras-el-hanout.* Called *arpsous,* it can also season snails or cuttlefish, following the ancestral recipes that the veiled women of Fez and Agadir have handed down.

Licorice, traditionally associated with green anise, reinforces many refreshing beverages—the infusions called coco, *pastis,* etc. It is precisely by means of this well-loved apéritif that the root of the licorice enters very discreetly into bouillabaisse and other dishes of the South of France. (*See* PASTIS.)

Lily Flowers (Daylily)

The cooks of the Far East appreciate the corollas of flowers as decorative elements, sometimes as fritterlike magnolia petals; but the perianth of the yellow daylily *(Hemerocallis flava)* is a true cooking condiment. They reach Hong Kong and Saigon as *kimcham,* resembling thin saffroned dried beans. Their taste, like that of a highly scented mushroom, goes particularly well with exotic soups containing celery, fennel, common mushrooms, pork, and chicken. Count on four or five flowers per guest. Soak them one-half hour, and then stew them about ten minutes.

Lily flowers can be easily mixed into Western recipes—omelettes with *fines herbes,* duck with French peas, or compound salads. Their aroma combines very well with cheese, nuts, etc.

Liqueurs

Liqueurs are sugary alcoholic beverages aromatized and flavored in sundry ways. They are much less valuable to the cook than raw alcohols. The only one among them that has an important role in cooking is curaçao (which see).

Nevertheless, certain preparations that are slightly exotic call for liqueurs such as Benedictine, Chartreuse, etc., notably, filets of sole with Benedictine, according to the recipe of the Countess of Perrégaux. In Denmark, red cabbage with sugar and vinegar is often flavored with a spoonful of cherry liqueur. With fresh water fish and crustaceans we prefer to use *kümmel.* It is delicately imbued with caraway and cumin and much more distinguished than "aquavit with cumin."

Litchi, Lychee

(Litchi chinensis; French, *Letchy* or *Lychee) A* large pearly cherry, with a slightly musk-tasting flesh, borne by an Oriental tree of the *Sapidnus* genus. Litchis are also gathered in Réunion and French Guiana.

This exotic fruit is sold peeled and preserved, or well conserved, in syrup. It can be an element in confections, in extreme cases in sweets, but it deserves to be mentioned in this book because its exquisite taste gives a final touch to a Chinese supper. The Chinese make a sweet beverage, *litchi* wine, from this berry. The longan and rambutan are similar Asiatic fruits with a less subtle aroma.

Lotus

Homer speaks warmly of a faraway country, the land of the lotus-eater, where travelers were struck by amnesia if they consumed a fruit called lotus. Today, Oriental food purveyors offer lotus seeds, and lotus root in syrup. By eating them, does one risk losing his memory?

There are several exotic *Nymphaea* that bear the name lotus. These plants resemble our charming water lily, *nénuphar,* but the flowers are prettier and the leaves are as large as dinner plates. Two varieties, the pink lotus, or *Nelumbo,* and the white Egyptian lotus, or *Nymphaea lotus,* used to interest temple priests as much as cooks. The mummy of Ramses II, discovered in 1881, was surrounded by pink lotus flowers. Vishnu, a Brahmin divinity, is always represented seated on a lotus leaf.

The pink lotus has disappeared from the shores of the Nile, probably as a result of a drought that was prolonged, but the Asians have carefully nurtured it, considering it a symbol of fertility. The starchy seeds of the lotus *(hat-sen),* have an almondlike taste, and in Vietnam are used in a sugared soup, thickened with arrowroot starch. In China, these seeds are elements in many sweets, notably "eight-treasure sweet." In Java, the petals of the pink lotus are used to decorate dishes or to season medicinal tea. The leaves are often filled with rice or shrimp. The roots are also eaten. The Chinese call them *nghô.* They are candied, then stuffed with a mixture of chopped meat, onion, ginger, and yellow wine. They prefer them cooked under coals. Made from water-lily roots for use in sweets, nenuphar flour is sometimes found in the West. In tropical America, the fruits and roots of the yellow lotus are eaten by the natives.

Both Western and Chinese medicine reveals that the seeds of lotus are sedative and soporific. They should not be consumed in too great a quantity. Homer was not entirely wrong.

Lovage

(Ligusticum levisticum; French, *Liveche;* German, *Liebstoeckel)* A large perennial *Umbellifera* of the smallage family known as mountain smallage or wild celery (in France, *ache de montagne, séséli des Alpes, sermontaise)* and improperly as perennial celery, *céleri vivace.* This plant resembles both angelica and celery, its flowers, its umbels, and its seeds closely resembling those of the related plants. They have little interest for us. On the other hand, the leaves and the root were well known in antiquity. The Etruscans used it as much

as the famous rosinweed (*silphium*). The Gauls used it in the *oléogarum*.

Today lovage is practically unknown to French cooks, which is to be deplored. Lovage especially interests the herbalists and phytotherapists.

LOVAGE SEEDS They have a slight turpentine flavor that limits their uses to liqueurs, marinades, and sundry macerations.

STEM AND ROOT These are dried and reduced to little chips, and sometimes smoked; they have a remarkable aroma that is more like dried mushrooms than celery root. The Germans, Austrians, and German-Swiss dote on it. They call lovage *Badkraut* (bath plant) and *Maggikraut.* This name (Maggi) is the source of a dehydrated soup mix and a celebrated brand.

LEAF The leaf has a marvelous fragrance reminiscent of that of celery, but sweeter and spicier. It is an element in cheese, notably *schabzigger* of Glarus, in many recipes of north Italy (where it is called *livistico*), and of the Balkan countries, too. It is used principally in soups, where it takes the place of tarragon or basil. More can be used, and it can be cooked longer. It goes perfectly well with all acid preparations, but can also be used to flavor baked unweaned lamb, chicken fricassee, herb omelette, herb butter, stuffed carp, etc.

Lupine

(*Lupinus albus;* French, *Lupin;* German, *Feigbohne*) An annual fodder plant, doubtless of Oriental origin, cultivated especially in Mediterranean regions. The fruit is a large brownish pod containing white compressed seeds, having a rather disagreeable taste that disappears when they are soaked in boiling water. Treated this way, then roasted, they are used in Brittany and Germany to produce an ersatz coffee. In Egypt, these seeds are eaten like dried beans. Their starchy, very insipid taste necessitates the use of garlic and spices to give flavor.

Mace

(French, *Macis;* German, *Muskat-bluete*) This is the fine envelope that forms a colored net around the kernel of nutmeg, also called *arille de muscadier* (nutmeg aril). This spice is generally sold as an orange powder, and more rarely in its original fibrous form.

Mace is highly scented, with a slightly sweeter flavor than the nut it covers. Their uses are identical. It is important to buy it in a good trustworthy shop, as it is often adulterated with wild mace, the insipid tegument of *Myristica malabarica*.

Madeira Wine

Of all the volcanic islands of the Atlantic Ocean, Madeira is the only one that deserves a place on the world map of the gastronome. For eight centuries, the Portuguese have raised celebrated grapes. They are *Malvasia, Sercial, Boal,* and *Verdelho.* Red or white, dry or sweet, Madeira offers a delicate taste of muscat or Malmsey. This last kind of grape, native to the Greek Island, lends itself to the preparation of dry, alcoholic aperitif wines.

In 1478, the Duke of Clarence was condemned to die by his brother Edward IV. He chose to drown himself in a cask of Malmsey, it is said. Some of the more discreet uses of this nectar include ham with Madeira, sautéed kidneys with Madeira, tournedos with

Madeira, and turtle and Périgueux sauces. A very sweet Madeira can be used to season a fruit salad or a small apricot tart. (*See* TURTLE HERBS.)

Maidenhair

(*Adiantum capillus veneris;* French, *Capillaire;* German, *Venushaar*) A variety of fern with little, finely-cut leaves containing an aromatic element. Not long ago *bavaroises au lait,* hot beverages for the chest, were consumed in Paris that contained boiled milk, egg yolks, sugar, kirsch, and maidenhair syrup. This same syrup is still used to prepare *capilé,* a soda pop very popular in Portugal.

N.B.   The young shoots of ferns, called *crosses-de-violons,* which are sometimes eaten like hop shoots, are not maidenhair, but male ferns or *Nephprodium* (or *Dryopteris*) *filixmas.*

Mallow

(*Malva sylvestris* or *M. moschata;* French, *Mauve;* German, *Moschus-Malve* and *Pappelkraut*) There are many varieties of edible *Malvaceae,* notably the common wild mallow and the musk mallow, with pink or purplish flowers and leaves very denticulated. Once dried, their leaves give off a light musky aroma; if cooked, they give off a viscous juice. In Roman times, these two mallows were highly appreciated as salads and condiments. In his correspondence, Cicero mentions having eaten too much of them. Today, they are used only to flavor certain cheeses, so they are called *herbe à fromage* or *fromageot* in France; in Germany, *Kaesepappel.*

Emollient and rather laxative, they can be disturbing to the lover of gastronomic curiosities. Another plant of the same family, the marshmallow (*Althea officinalis*), is uniquely medicinal. (*See* VEGETABLE MUSK.)

Manioc (Cassava)

(*Jatropha manihot*) A shrubby Mexican tree of the same family as *Euphorbia,* it was introduced, not native, to Africa and other subtropical regions. Its tuberous, fleshy root encloses food starch which takes the place of wheat flour for hundreds of millions of inhabitants of the planet. There is a difference between sweet and fresh manioc, *camagnoc,* or *juca dulce* (which can be eaten as a potato, boiled, cooked in coals), and bitter manioc or *mandioc.* The latter contains prussic acid and must be steeped or soaked in running water for several days before being used as food.

Manioc is eaten peeled, grated, and pulverized as a semolina and, as starch, sold under different names: *tapioca, cassava, couaque, moussache* or *cipipa, fofo, garry,* etc. But the only manioc that has a slightly interesting taste is that which has been steeped, then pounded in a stone mortar, and gathered in large balls to be fermented in the sun for eight days, as the people of the Cameroons do.

Maple Syrup

The maple is a majestic tree with an artistically-cut leaf that, while forgotten in statuary, has becoming the national emblem of Canada.

A variety of maple, *Acer saccharum,* native to North America, is called the sugar maple. Its sap, concentrated by boiling, has an aroma that is compared to honey and mocha cream, becoming the famous maple syrup which children and adults of North America adore. Passed through a centrifuge, it becomes maple butter. Distilled, it is the maple essence that flavors ice cream and desserts. Concentrated again, it becomes a sort of sugar candy. The sap, when allowed to ferment and then aged, becomes a light, maple-scented vinegar.

The syrup and butter are curiously used in Canada to prepare baked eggs to be used as a dessert. As caramel, they play a role in other original preparations: bacon and caramel, for instance. Why not follow this example, perhaps substituting a small spoonful of maple syrup for the two lumps of sugar called for in a *sauce bigarade? (See also* HONEY.)

Marc (Eau-de-vie de marc)

An alcohol extracted from the residue of wine-making. There are marcs made from both white and red grapes; the latter are more rich in alcohol because they have steeped longer with the wine.

The quality of the marc depends on the growth and the harvest; the best years for wine are the best years for marc.

This country alcohol is highly esteemed as a postprandial brandy or even as a cooking ingredient. Dumas noted in his time that *marc de Bourgogne,* which has a taste similar to empyreuma, has very zealous partisans. *Marc de Provence,* sold commercially, is well wrought and distilled.

Good quality marc, which has a bouquet of the sole products of the vine, advantageously replaces Cognac in flaming fowl and even less robust preparations—hare *civet*, eel stew, crayfish *barbouillade,* onion soup, and so on.

Marigold

(*Calendula arvensis;* French, *Souci;* German, *Ringelblume*) An annual of the *Compositae* family with hairy leaves and bright-yellow flowers. Its name comes from Low Latin *solsequia* (that which follows the sun). There are many splendid improved horticultural varieties. The oval leaves are not very interesting, but the flowers are valued by German and even North African cooks. Their taste is bitter and pronounced but it is called "the herb for all soups." Dumas added this yellow flower head to *potage aux herbes à la Dauphine*—a vegetable cream, seasoned with finely chopped spinach, orach, chervil, as well as marigold. It is recommended that the petals be separated from the rest of the flower, which is very acrid. This soup, Dumas also says, should be garnished with the white bread without the crust, as the taste of croutons will alter this fine and simple vegetable combination. In some northern European countries, marigold petals are used to season omelettes and are also mixed with *fines herbes.*

The marigold flower also has coloring properties. It was formerly used to yellow butter and to restore watered milk to its natural color.

The marsh marigold is a very different plant, belonging to the *Ranunculaceae* family. It has shiny leaves and bright-yellow flowers, with no husks. Its botanical name in French is *Populage* (the *Caltha palustries* of Linnaeus), and its flowers are also used to color butter. The leaves have a burning and disagreeable taste; but its flower buds, in many countries, are pickled in vinegar and used like capers. Their taste is both bitter and peppery.

Marinades

Marinating meat or fish, as a culinary procedure, has fallen a little into disuse. The widespread use of home refrigeration has supplanted marinade food-preserving procedures. The marinating of game remains, but public taste has also sustained certain changes. The necessity of soaking hare flesh in the same manner as winged game is strongly disputed by great French chefs. Nevertheless, marinating remains a very alluring art, where utility is joined to pleasurability. From time to time, despite the cost of venison, the amateur chef may encounter some game. The flesh of these red-meat animals is too tough to be eaten without being marinated.

Marjoram

(French, *Origan;* German, *Majoran;* Italian, *Origano*) There are more than twenty varieties of *Labiatae satureia,* answering to one name or another. These plant species are native to the shores of the Mediterranean, but are found in more limited numbers in the north of France, in England, and in Asia. From the point of view of culinary botany, it is especially suitable to choose Italian marjoram (*marjolaine italienne, Organum onites*), Cretan marjoram, (*origan de Crète,*) or the dittany (*dictame*) of the ancients, cultivated marjoram (*marjolaine cultivée*), *marjolaine à coquilles* whose flower spines recall hops, or wild Provençal marjoram (*origan sauvage*), a little plant with pinkish-white flowers instead of purple ones. All these varieties contain a more or less strong dose of a very aromatic essence related to thymol. It is preferable to use a marjoram that has been warmed by southern suns, since the dried plant keeps its full aromatic virtues.

Garden marjoram (*marjolaine de jardin*) is distinguished by its sweet smell, as opposed to wild marjoram (*origan sauvage*), which is more acrid, having an odor close to thyme. Marjorams of all types are highly appreciated in plant medicine, that is, in natural therapy (*phytothérapie*). Herb doctors recommend them as stomach tonics and antispasmodics.

Formerly, gay bachelors used to insert a sprig of marjoram in their boot tops before departing on their adventures. It is a lucky plant, always appreciated as a vegetable aromatic by cooks from the South of France and Naples, and admired today by *Les Compag-*

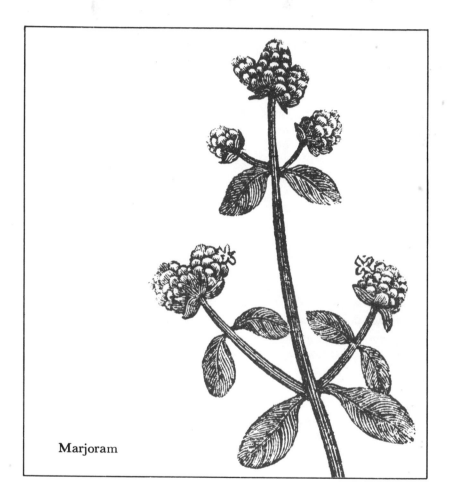

Marjoram

nous de la Marjolaine, the title of a group of journalists-gastronomes who emulate Marco Polo.

This delicious herb will soon become very familiar to cooks still intimidated by Mediterranean aromatics. There is little risk of committing blunders and it opens areas of new culinary creativeness for everyone. Dried, it keeps for a long time. It is sold in all good groceries.

USES: *Dried marjoram, either in powder (or better still) in flakes, is by far the aromatic most suited to Neapolitan pizza and other preparations of southern Italy (Roman* stuffatino, *a very thick stew, baked gilthead (a fish), etc.). Its scent, which is less intense than that of thyme, allows its use in* pot-au-feu *and in innumerable sauces. The Hungarians add a pinch of oregano to goulash, the Greeks to* suvlakia, *skewers of kid, and baked fish, the Poles to* zurek, *a sour soup. One of its jobs is to underline, discreetly, the flavor of tomato. All stuffings and delicatessen preparations are better with marjoram than with thyme or savory. It can also be substituted for these in water cooking of leguminous plants, in aromatic flavored vinegar sauces, and in all bouquets garnis. The fresh leaves of domestic marjoram can occasionally be considered as salad plants, and used like tarragon or garden savory, etc.*

Marrow of Beef

The soft, fatty substance contained in the medial cavity of an animal's long bones. Housewives frequently buy a marrow bone from their butcher which should not be confused with spinal marrow (*amourette*), which rather resembles the brain.

Beef marrow is a very fine food, known for its restorative properties. French cooks used it in many preparations, but most often it is spread on bread and eaten with salt and pepper. The most famous lover of marrow was Nicolo, the composer, author of *Rendez-vous Bourgeois,* who invented, perhaps for this kind of occasion, an ivory syringe for stuffing macaronis with poached and seasoned marrow!

The most classic use of beef marrow is in the garnish called *à la bordelaise,* reserved for small cuts of meat. It is better to remove the marrow raw from the bones and to cut it with a knife dipped in boiling water. Wrapped in a piece of muslin, it is poached for several minutes, in a very hot white wine or a court-bouillon seasoned with fennel. It is also embellished with truffle slices or an artichoke bottom (*garniture Masséna*). Beef marrow can also season certain soups and small stews as well as molded egg dishes.

Marsala

A very sweetish Italian wine coming from the growing district of the western point of Sicily, this is the product of muscat and malvoisie grapes. Marked by a territory that is both marine and volcanic, Marsala possesses an inimitable flavor. This dessert wine goes especially well with *cassata,* (molded ice cream filled with fruits), with *torrone,* a pistachio and almond nougat, and even in the confection of *sabayon* (Trans. note: pudding or sauce like English cream). However, it is equally delectable used to swish the pan after a white meat—particularly a veal scallop—has been sautéed. The cooks of Italy hold Marsala in high regard and take care never to corrupt it with garlic or onion, or to put it in contact with a very hot utensil. They combine it often with a julienne of mushroom and ham, and even with the white truffles of Mondovia or the true black truffles of Spoleto.

Masala

If you have a Brahman or a maharaja as a friend, you certainly know that "masala" is the native name for curry, while "curry" indicates the sauces the cook makes from it. Nevertheless, it will be sufficient for you to remember that Indian grocers and some importers retail curry paste under the name of masala. (*See* CURRY.)

Mastic

(French, *Mastika*) A word of Greek origin that in all the Middle East means lentisk resin, in the West formerly called Chio resin (*résine de Chio*). Mastic is sold as white, sometimes yellow, opaque drops. Their taste—hardly very pleasing—makes one think of pine tar with a little refreshing aftertaste.

    This resin has a considerable role in making *raki* (the Eastern anisette) and other aperitif beverages. It is also put in the candies that the visitor in the East is offered with a glass of iced water.

Mixed with paraffin, it becomes something to masticate and thus resumes its etymology.

Mastic of Lebanon and especially that of Egypt will accent cardamom and turmeric in certain stews and in *confits de moutons* (preserved mutton) with garlic. With greater profit, it is added to chocolate, pistachio, and orange-water sweets. (*See* LENTISK *and* RESIN.)

Mayonnaise

A sauce—and a word—that has gone around the world without being too distorted. On the other hand, it is in France that its spelling is hotly contested. Since the time of Carême* and Grimod de la Reynière,* gastronomes and purists have debated whether it is *mayonnaise, bayonnaise, mahonnaise, magnonaise, maillonnaise, moyeunaise*, or some other spelling. According to Prosper Montagné, it is a corruption of a very old French word, *moyeu* (egg yolk).

Mayonnaise is a "mother sauce" to which a quantity of ingredients or aromatics can be added. With parsley, chervil, tarragon, cress, it becomes a *sauce verte* (accompanying poached fish). Combined with whipped cream, it is called *sauce mousseline* (for cold fowl, asparagus, etc.). Fish eggs can be added (*sauce russe*), pounded anchovy filets (*sauce provençale*), stewed tomato and sweet peppers passed through a food mill (*sauce andalouse*), chopped pressed capers, gherkins, and chervil (*sauce tartare*) etc.

Mazavarro

A Mexican condiment made of a mixture of red peppers similar to the chili pepper, preserved in oil. (*See* CHILE *and* RED PEPPER.)

Meat Extracts

Invented in the last century by the German chemist Justus Von Liebeg who also discovered chloroform. They are very familiar in

* See APPENDIX.

the household. There are many brands of these formulas for beef tea and concentrated beef broths, or bouillons. These products are useful to cooks who want to avoid the chore of making brown stock, white chicken stock, or meat glacé.

Meat extracts, obtained by long boiling, concentration, and evaporation in a vacuum, are offered as little tablets that dissolve rapidly in hot water. They are often flavored with soy sauce, broiled onion, cloves, and other spices. In general terms, 70 pounds of meat and bones are required to make 2 pounds 2 ounces of extract; one-half ounce is enough to make a quart of water into an excellent meat broth.

USES: *While very useful to moisten a sauce or any other preparation, diluted meat extracts can also be used as a court-bouillon. They are indispensable in executing quick recipes. An odd note, these concentrated broths often come to us from the Argentine pampas where certain world-famous firms have built colossal factories on the edges of the pasture lands of the New World.*

Medlar

(*Mespilus germanica*) A round, navel-shaped, yellow fruit. If it is gathered when hard and sour, it is allowed to ripen on a bed of straw until soft, and acid. It has an agreeable wine flavor. The medlar is widely planted in Provence and Italy. It is prepared in a compote with red wine and sugar, it is introduced into sauces (goose with medlar), or even with the apples that accompany blood sausages, etc.

EXOTIC MEDLARS are the *sapotille* of the Antilles, the *sawo* of Manila, and the *bibasses* or *loquats* of Japan. Their scented tart flesh lends itself to the creation of culinary or condiment fantasies.

Mei-Kue-Lou

A Chinese rice alcohol, currently sold by exotic food shops in the West. This alcohol is not very widely used in Far East cooking, *houang-tsieou* (yellow wine) being preferred. (*See* YELLOW WINE.)

Melilot

(*Melilotus officinalis*) A rather large plant of the *Leguminosae* family related to clover. It is also called *trèfle de cheval, des mouches, des sorciers, mirlirot,* etc. Its flowers are generally yellow. When they are a pretty light blue, this plant is called *lotier ordorant, faux baume du Pérou,* in French. Its leaves and even its flowers give off a rather sweet intense odor when they are dried (in common with all plants that contain *coumarin*). In the country, bags of melilot are placed among clothes to perfume them and to protect them against moths. In Silesia, melilot is currently drunk like tea, and in Switzerland, in the canton of Glaris, some cheese and curds are seasoned with these blue flowers.

In cooking, melilot has a role that is a little neglected today. The botanist Valmon de Bomare recalls for us that formerly domestic rabbit, after entrails were removed, was filled with a large handful of melilot in flower to give it the taste of Garenne rabbit, before being hung and aged in the cellar. This aromatic plant can also figure in a marinade, in a refreshing beverage (used like woodruff), added to the dried herbs burned under a grill, etc. (*See* COUMARIN.)

Melissa (Balm)

(*Melissa officinalis;* French, *Mélisse;* German, *Bienenkraut*) The flowered tops of this plant of the *Labiatae* family with a fluted stem that grows naturally on the edges of southern European woods, are highly appreciated by the bees, hence its name. The Arabs make melissa into a cordial. Formerly it had an important role in medicine through the medium of *eau des carmes déchaussés* (water of the barefoot Carmelites), imperial water, chalybeate powder, etc.

Gathered during its first flowering, that is, toward May or June, melissa is a highly aromatic herb; at the end of the season it acquires a fetid color. German cuisine uses it pleasantly in small quantities in cooking fowl, mushrooms, soups, stuffings, etc. The Dutch prefer to combine it with mugwort in marinating fatty fish, which is why they name it *eel herb.* Because of its sweetish aroma it should be combined with a more acrid vegetable and used moderately. (*See* VERVAIN.)

Mesche

Ancient name of white ginger, coming from the Italian *micchino.* Guillaume Tirel, called Taillevent,* the oldest French food author, tells us in his famous *Viandier* written in 1373 that *mesche* is indispensable in *arbaleste de poissons,* in *potée de tétyne de vache,* and in *dodine de vert jus.* (*See* GINGER.)

Mesclun

A word in the dialect of Nice and Cannes that means a mixture of wild or cultivated greens served in the form of a salad. *Lou mesclun* brings its fresh, bitter-scented taste to accompany a grilled meat. It contains the young shoots of dandelion, shepherd's purse, rocket, groundsel, even burnet and purslane sometimes. Frédéric Mistral calls this mixture *cicoureiado ensalada champanello.*

Mignonnette

Formerly, the small sack of muslin, stuffed with pepper, cloves, and other spices that was steeped in a broth or sauce, was known as *mignonnette* to the French. Today mignonnette (for spice vendors and cooks) is coarsely crushed pepper, the granules being useful for preparing *steak au poivre, sauce Bercy,* and the shallot vinaigrette that accompanies oysters. These uses are generally reserved for white pepper, which has a more delicate aroma than gray. (*See* PEPPER.)

Milk, Concentrated

Concentrated whole milk without sugar is indispensable in preparating a great number of desserts, also many spicy dishes. A French brand recently based its advertising on these little-known

* See APPENDIX.

160

uses of this creamy liquid, mentioning that nonsugared concentrated milk is a very valuable ingredient in *béchamel* or *soubise* sauces.

This inexpensive, easy-to-keep product does wonders in other preparations: quenelles, stuffing and breading, eggs in condensed milk, slowly heated in a double boiler, ray (a kind of fish) with milk and cheese.

Concentrated milk can also replace cream. The Danes, today's Vikings crowned by whipped cream, offer a good example. In the dairies of Copenhagen, housewives continually ask for *floede* (heavy cream) of this or that concentration, to "cream" a white wine sauce or white sauce. Canned milk can be thought of as the lightest cream.

More digestible and less fragile than cream, concentrated milk runs the risk of curdling only on rare occasions (notably when vinegar or lemon juice is added or in the presence of certain vegetables like the artichoke). (*See* CREAM *and* YOGHURT.)

Milt

The white seminal substance that is found as a pocket on numerous male fish: carp, herring, mackerel, etc. Shad milt is one of the most appreciated. This "delicate, but very exciting food" (Dumas) can be used to pick up a poached or braised fish. This word (*laitance* in French) is improperly used for designating fish eggs, *kaviar* (*sic*) extracted from Baltic fishes, *poutargue*, etc. (*See* URCHIN ROE, *and* POUTARGUE.)

Mineral Water, Rain Water

All the waters said to be drinkable are not necessarily suited to the cooking of tasty foods. Naturally chalybeate or artificially chlorinated (by potassium chlorate or other bactericides) waters give the food a slightly disagreeable, stale taste.

In this domain, the baby is the model for the gourmet: all the neutral waters recommended for the preparation of bottles are excellent in cooking. A single hot-springs water can be used, to our knowledge, to soften a dish. We are speaking of the skillful marriage of carrots and Vichy water. Bicarbonate of soda can be used as a substitute to soften too-hard water, in which vegetables cook badly, but this custom is condemned by dietitians as it results in a veritable massacre of vitamins. (*See* BICARBONATE OF SODA.)

RAIN WATER was formerly widely used because of its softness to make French peas, lentils, etc., more mellow.

Mint

(French, *Menthe;* German, *Minze*) A genus of the *Labiatae* family containing several varieties. Their civil status was established on Olympus where Minthè was a girl friend of Pluto, king of Hell. When Proserpine, the legitimate wife of the god, dissolved the liaison, she transformed the pretty young girl into a modest plant. Where do these many mints that we know come from? From England, say the English; from China, reply the Chinese. From everywhere, answer the botanists prudently.

Among these perennial, strongly scented herbs, which plunge their roots in humid soil as well as far back in mythology, it is necessary to distinguish:

WATER MINT (in French, *menthe aquatique* or *menthe à grenouilles*) —large, reddish, rounded flower heads on top of the plant.

ROUND-LEAVED MINT (*menthe à feuilles rondes*) pink blooms in spikes.

PENNYROYAL (*menthe pouliot*) mauve flowers in little clusters at several levels.

GREEN MINT (*menthe verte* or *menthe cultivée*) official variety, has pink flower bouquets, fine lacy leaves.

PEPPERMINT (*menthe poivrée*) purplish flowers, smooth fragile leaves, doubtless the result of hybridization.

These many mints all have the Latin name of *Mentha* (the genus) followed by a qualifing variety or descriptive name: *aquatica rotundifolia, pulegium, viridis,* and *piperita.* There are also false mints, such as *menthe de montagne,* which belongs to the order of *Calamintha* (*Satureia alpina*), catnip (*menthe de chat, Nepeta cataria*), which only

162

the cat enjoys as it is acrid and harsh. (*See* CALAMINT *and* TANSY.)

All the true mints are valued for their digestive, tonic, and stimulating properties. Their leaves and their flowers contain more or less of a strong concentration of aromatic ether related to camphor. Peppermint is the one most often cultivated in England notably at Mitcham in Surrey. Mitcham mint has a large role in flavoring chewing gums, mint alcohols, mint caramels, peppermint candies, etc. The Germans call peppermint *Pfefferminze* and the Chinese *Lin-Tsao*. It is imprudent to grow several species of mint in small gardens, as they crowd out each other and may cross hybridize.

All of these sundry mints can play an interesting role in cooking. It is up to the cook to decide on the quantity to use, depending on whether it is wild or domestic mint and one's taste for mint as well as which is the more aromatic. Peppermint and pennyroyal— which latter the English call *pudding herb*—are generally the most esteemed. Today, especially in China, Greece, Corsica, Spain, and North Africa, mint is a food ingredient.

USES: *Fresh, finely chopped mint is today incontestably part of* fines herbes *and salad herbs, even though it was forgotten by Dumas. In Corsica, in the Balearics, and in Tuscany, it is often used to season omelettes, raviolis, and stuffings. In China and North Africa, it is an element in many soups:* phô, *the oriental* pot-au-feu, hariri, *and Moroccan mutton soup. The Italians occasionally introduce it into minestrone, mixing it with basil. Fresh mint is also suited to cooking green peas, mixed vegetables, or it can be discreetly spread on a beet salad, or added to some sauces like* béarnaise *and* paloise. *Let's not forget the delicious* sangría, *an Andalusian beverage of sliced fruits, herbs, and cinnamon, steeped in red wine.*

Dried mint, whether whole leaves, flakes, or—if need be—powder, can replace fresh mint in a stew, or a sauce. It has a judicious use on Oriental dishes: arnakhi psito, *Greek baked pascal lamb, North African* méchoui, *Turkish* chiche-kebab, *and also roast veal, baked rabbit, crayfish* à la nage, *or grilled gilthead (fish). A whisper of mint is enough.*

Dried peppermint is often mixed with green tea, according to a Chinese formula on which Moroccans dote; of course, leaves of fresh mint are better for this purpose. In Anglo-Saxon cooking, fresh or dried, mint lends itself to much more agreeable uses. London cooks add great quantities to stews, roast juices and gravies, puddings, etc. They dust mint flakes on aspics, even on boiled potatoes. Undoubtedly our readers have already discovered mint jelly, pineapple mint sauce, and chocolate mint sauce.

Molokheia

Also spelled *mouloukheia* and *meloukhié*. A cooking herb that is highly appreciated in Syria, Egypt, and Tunisia. Fresh, it smells like melon; dried, like cut hay.

This herb is nothing other than edible Jew's mallow, *corette*, for the botanist, corchorus olitorius, belonging to *Malvaceae*. In the last century in France it was called *mauve des Juifs* (Jew's mallow) or *guimauve potagère*. Arabs, North Africans, Jews, and Hindus consider *molokheia* a plant between cress and sorrel. It is eaten cooked, in green, slightly limy sauces, in chicken broth, even in the broth of Tunisian *couscous*. The gourmets on shore of the Nile's affirm that the smell is like that of snails! (*See* EGYPT.)

Monosodium Glutamate (MSG)

A vegetable salt that is highly prized in the Far East. Its chemical formula is $C_5H_8O_4Na$. Obtained by the decomposition of the gluten of beets and other protein substances, its flavor is more discreet than that of our table salt, which is of mineral origin. Mixed with calcium phosphate or sundry chlorides, it is used as a diet salt.

Monosodium glutamate is found in various forms in our specialized groceries: Japanese *ajinomoto*, the *ve'tsin* of Uncle Mao's socialist mills; in Vietnamese it is *mi-shin*. It is an element in aromatic mixtures such as seafood seasoning, and is a staple in Chinese restaurants.

Glutamate delicately seasons Oriental meats as well as sauces, and Western soups also profit by its use. (It is excellent in *soupe au pistou* and cream of asparagus soup.) Its claim of being able to bring out other flavors without smothering them also seems legitimate. (*See* SALT.)

Morel

(*Morchella esculenta;* French, *Morille*; German, *Morchel*) Round or pointed, frizzled or honeycombed, capped with yellow, gray, or more rarely white, the morel is one of the most noble edible mushrooms. It belongs, like the divine truffle, to the *Ascomyceteae* order.

This mushroom is, unfortunately, very rare. It grows only in spring, generally under elm trees, ash trees, and on slopes. Its flavor is generally so fine that it can be consumed immediately on gathering, cooked on the embers of an outdoor fire. It does not need highly seasoned accompaniments: garlic and shallot bully it. Stewing in butter, then thickening with cream (or a swishing with Madeira) are part of the consideration due it. A dish of morels dusted with bread crumbs and grated cheese can also be gratinated in the oven. The morel can bring an inestimable touch to sauces and stuffings, although it is not customary to give it a secondary role in culinary dramas. Nevertheless, used in a *coq au vin*, with a veal sweetbread dish, or in a simple omelette, it makes miracles.

Mozzarella

A southern Italian milk cheese. Neapolitan mozzarella and *provatura*, its Roman counterpart, are smooth paste cheeses that lend themselves particularly to cooking in the oven (pizza, etc.). They are traditionally combined with garlic, marjoram, capers, and anchovies.

Mugwort

(*Artemisia vulgaris;* French, *Armoise*; German, *Beifuss*) A large, very common member of the *Compositae* with reddish-yellow flower spikes, jagged leaves, and downy undersides. It is also called in France *herbe de la Saint-Jean.*

Highly prized by the sorcerers times past, it is still used by herbalists to make tonic infusions. Although generally ignored by French cooks, it is appreciated by the Germans and English. Its floral ends, gathered in culinary bouquets, are used to flavor duck and goose, even pork and eel. The flowers and leaves give off a scent recalling that of wormwood or tansy (which see). Mugwort can also be used judiciously in a marinade or a court-bouillon. In brief, an aromatic herb that is to be recommended for all moist cooking of goose and large fowl.

Mushroom Essence

Mushroom essence is found ready for use in good food shops. It can also be prepared at home by boiling mushroom trimmings for a long while, mixed with some pieces of cèpe or chanterelle, with a little wine. Reduce the broth, beat it with an electric mixer, then pass it through a fine sieve and add a drop of vinegar to assure its keeping well.

USES: *Mushroom essence can be used to flavor sauces, soups, some soufflés.*

Musk

(French, *Musc;* German, *Moschus, Bisam*) A strongly-scented substance taken from the glands of certain animals, various seeds and nuts. Muscat grapes, nutmeg *(noix de muscade)*, muscadelle pear, and even the muskrat received their names because of relatively similar smells.

Animal musk comes from the musk sac of the male Asian musk deer or the civet cat of Ethiopia. It is an organic compound classed among the *cycloheptadécanes.* It is employed as a fixative in high-quality perfumes.

Vegetable musk is generally obtained from the seed of musk-scented plants. *Hibiscus abelmoschus,* a plant related to okra, is cultivated in Africa and the Antilles as well as in America. Their gray seeds, the size of a millet seed, give off a rather pronounced odor, and it is used as perfume. The name *musc français* (French musk, *Malva moschata* and *M. sylvestris*) is also given to the seeds of the most common wild mallow. (*See* MAUVE.)

Like ambergris, it was used as an aromatic and aphrodisiac in medieval cuisine. Musk seeds, also called *herbe à la poudre de Chypre,* figured in savory stews. They are still used in certain African recipes, and like cardamom are used to enhance the flavor of Turkish coffee. Reduced to powder they can figure in *ras-el-hanout* (which see).

Animal musk and musk seed are violent, little-valued culinary aromatics which must be carefully used. In addition, they risk corrupting their neighbors on the spice shelf.

Mustard

A true cosmopolitan condiment, holder of innummerable identities: *Moutarde*, in French; *Senf* and *Mostrich*, in German; *Mostarda* and *Senape* in Italian; *Mostaza* in Spain and Latin America; *Senap* or *Sennep* in Scandinavia.

All these names reveal two etymologies: the Latin *Sinapis*, coming from a Celtic root. (It was the Gauls of Brennus who imported black mustard into Northern Italy.) The French *moutarde*, undoubtedly comes from *moût*, or must, that of the sour grape juice that is used in maceration, rather than the motto of the town of Dijon, *Moult me tarde* (a pleasant invention of the city councilors of the fourteenth century). Historians and botanists tell us that the Chinese cultivated several varieties of mustard 3,000 years ago.

From the point of view of natural history, it is necessary to distinguish:

BLACK MUSTARD *(moutarde noire or sénevé) Sinapsis nigra*, is the most widespread. An annual plant, about a yard high, with hairy stem and light-yellow flowers, its seeds are contained in a small brown siliqua, a pointed pod.

WHITE MUSTARD *(moutarde blanche) Sinapis alba* is the smallest. Its upper leaves are very denticulated; gathered while young, they have the taste of garden cress.

CHARLOCK *(moutarde sauvage) Sinapis arvensis*, also called *sanve*, is little valued. Its black, smooth seeds are sometimes used as counterfeit black mustard.

CHINESE MUSTARDS have spicy seeds; the leaves are used in Far East cooking. A number of other crucifers with strongly flavored seeds such as *Brassica juncea*, related to rocket, or Hesperis, which has acrid, sulphurous elements, also can be prepared as condiments.

Mustard has been enjoyed by Europeans for 2,000 years. Planted in Cisalpine Gaul before the third century B.C., the famous *garum* and *silphion* were preferred to it for a long time. Seemingly, the Greeks and the people of Levant were more easily conquered by it than the Romans. Christ himself used mustard seed as the subject of one of his parables. In the Middle Ages, mustard knew mixed fortunes. The kings of France and England were devoted to all the fashionable spices and the intense fragrances of the Orient. On the other hand, Pope John XXII appointed the first papal mustard supplier during his stay at Avignon. The town of Dijon was the first to profit by this action of the successor to St. Peter. The doctors also did a lot to insure the success of mustard, which they consider an excellent counterirritant poultice. Taken internally, it induces secretions of the pancreas.

The innumerable varieties of mustard presently on the market include principally

FRENCH MUSTARDS, which are preparations of both black and white mustard flours, boiled, then steeped with vinegar, sour grape juice, or must. Dijon, Meaux, Bordeaux, Rouen, and Reims are renowned in this area. Many spices (cloves, nutmeg, turmeric, etc.), salt, and a quantity of vegetable aromatics (tarragon, celery, chervil, parsley, chives), enter into their mixture. Certain formulas are particularly original: *moutarde à la ravigote* contains hot peppers and ginger; mustard with white wine, champagne, anchovies, lemon, or red fruits are all very tasty.

ENGLISH MUSTARD is generally sold as powder. It contains white mustard flower and *Brassica juncea* (from which an oil is extracted), turmeric, coriander, cardamom, etc. It is moistened with acidulated water as it is used.

FOREIGN MUSTARDS in sundry picturesque forms are pleasant: German Dusseldorf mustard, spiced or sweet, Italian mustard from Cremona with candied fruits, Tyrolian beer mustard, Mexican mustard with chile, etc. Tomatoes, mushrooms, horseradish, even maple sugar, are elements in some formulas.

USES: *The leaves of many mustard plants, if selected when young and tender, can be used like garden cress. The Chinese variety, called cabbage leaf mustard,* (moutarde à feuilles de chou) *is cooked like spinach.*

The whole seeds of white mustard play an aromatic role, along with cumin, in sauerkraut dishes, beef salad, cucumber salad, and in pickle marinades.

Mustard flour and also the pasty condiment are occasionally aromatics of great value: rabbit with mustard, whiting with mustard and lemon, and lobster thermidor. In Russia and Central Europe, mustard reinforces the creamy sauce that accompanies bitokes *and other meat balls. The variety meats, white meats, game, and many fishes and crustaceans (particularly*

168

crab), and even starch vegetables like split peas, go very well with sauces that use mustard as an ingredient. Lettuce salad with mustard dressing is a pleasant change.

Myrtle

(*Myrtus communis;* French, *Myrte;* German, *Myrte*) A Mediterranean shrub formerly considered sacred to Venus, is remarkable for its evergreen leaves. A member of the noble *Myrtaceae* family, the clove tree, and the allspice, it is a modest, hardly-known culinary aromatic. Its floral buds, kidney-shaped seeds, as well as its small firm leaves, are rather fragrant. Their aroma is like that of rosemary and juniper but their taste is a little resinous.

Cretan, Corsican, and Sardinian cooks, island people who stood apart from the spice trade for a long time, add myrtle to a number of dishes; to Corsican bouillabaisse instead of saffron, roasted thrush, boar stew, and roast lamb. Myrtle seeds are combined with pistachio in some delicatessen, sometimes even in the delicious *mortadella* sausage.

Pliny reports that his contempories doted on *myrtatum*, a pork or lamb stew flavored with a large quantity of myrtle berries. It was also used to prepare a spice wine, *myrtidanum.*

N.B. Myrtle and myrrh should not be confused. The latter is a resin gum taken from the Oriental turpentine tree, *Balsamodendron myrrha.* This violent aromatic is destined to be burned like incense in a perfuming pan.

Nard (Spikenard)

This word comes from the Latin *nardus,* a transcription of the Persian *nardy.* Nard was a favored aromatic in antiquity and in the Middle Ages. Today, even its name is forgotten. Cookbooks of the last century sometimes mentioned it, without further explanation.

The true kind is the Indian nard, *nard indien* in French, the rhizome of one of the tropical *Valerianaceae; Nardostachys gangitis.* It was more costly than ginger in the markets of ancient Rome. Its taste is somewhat like that of ginger and vervain. Fibrous and brownish, it has always been used in making Oriental perfumes and in Ceylonese and Malayan cooking.

CELTIC NARD, which perked up the foods served to the first Capetian kings, can be called a substitute. It is the root of a European plant that grows in marshy areas *(Valeriana dioica).* Both acrid and perfumed, this stump became a minor condiment as soon as the first Crusaders were taken by a taste of Oriental spices.

FALSE NARDS are rather numerous: asarabaca *(asaret sauvage),* Italian lavender as well as some mountain graminaceous plants. Indian nard is almost unobtainable in the West. As for the other *Valerianaceae,* lamb's lettuce is appreciated by gourmets for its delicate, bitter leaves. Zoologists have disclosed that the Himalyan mouse deer, or chevrotain, from which the musk so sought after by perfume-makers is obtained, eat a great quantity of Asiatic *Valerianaceae.*

Nasturtium

(*Tropaeolum majus;* French, *Capucine;* German, *Kapuzinerkresse*) A very pretty, decorative plant whose culinary and dietetic properties are too often forgotten. Professor Léon Binet,* Dean of the School of Medicine of Paris, has analyzed the nasturtium and found it contains a good deal of sulphur. The German and Finnish hygienists (Kraut, and Virtanen) even consider it a powerful natural antibiotic. But to get back to our cooking—we recognize that nasturtium has a unique taste rather close to that of cress. It used to be called Mexican cress *(cresson de Mexique)* or Indian cress *(cresson d'Inde).* Its leaves can be used in making soups. Its orange flowers have a spicy, lightly peppery taste and embellish a lettuce salad from all points of view. Its flower buds, like its still-green seeds, can be treated like capers. Alsatian wine-makers add nasturtium flowers to their casks of fermenting *Gewürztraminer*.

Nenuphar

An improper name given to lotus (which see) in some cookbooks.

Nettle

(*Urtica dioica;* French, *Ortie;* German, *Nessel*) The large "dead" nettle is today considered a vegetable of poverty. Nevertheless, the ancient Greeks liked to eat it in the spring, before the swallows arrived. The young leaves, a little bitter, are still esteemed in Russia where they are blanched and strained with veal broth (*zélionye stchi*). Some old country recipes of France make use of dead nettle and burning nettle *(ortie brûlante)* like sorrel or spinach, notably to garnish *anguille au vert* (green eel, a dish of eel and herbs).

Needles of the two varieties are full of formic acid, which hardly encourages their gathering. The stringy stems of nettles

* See APPENDIX.

172

are retted to make *filasse* when they are dried. These plants are appreciated by cows. They give an agreeable taste to the milk and are sometimes grown as fodder in the Nordic countries.

Another plant, white archangel *(lamier blanc—Lamium album)*, can be used as a spinach substitute. Highly aromatic, without prickly bristles, it is considered by herbalists an emollient and resolvent.

Niaouli

A volatile oil extracted from the leaves of a Melanesian tree *(Mélaleuque Leucadendra)*. It has a lemon odor, close to eucalyptus. In North Africa, refreshing beverages of the same name are prepared by macerating vervain and southernwood.

A Malay tree of the same family, *Mélaleuca cajuputi*, furnishes an aromatic essence, *cajuput,* which smells like rose and camphor. These rather odd smells are sometimes elements in exotic cooking. They are especially sought after by cosmetic manufacturers.

Nigella

(Nigella arvensis, N. sativa) A name, borne by several European and Asiatic ranunculi, coming from the coal-black look of their seeds. The field nigella, which used to be called *poivrette* or *herbe de capucin,* is distinguished from love-in-a-mist *(Nigella damascena)* or *sounegh* and the Bengal nigella or *kaladjira.* All are small, slim plants with blue blossoms, also used as garden flowers.

Until the sixteenth century, nigella played an important role in cooking. The spicy, perfumed taste of these tiny seeds is close to that of pepper and poppy seed.

USES: *The seed of the nigella (duly identified for reasons that will be explained), can support coriander and allspice in all their Western uses. Their normal look is hardly pleasant but they can be crushed in a mortar, then sieved. They are elements in many variations of curry,* garam masala, ras-el-hanout, *and other Oriental mixes. Whole seeds can be heated in hot oil before use in seasoning a dish of lentils, vegetables, or Indian rice. We have followed this advice in preparing red beans, using nigella, savory, smoked bacon, and a hint of chili with very agreeable results.*

N.B. The gastronomic botanist should not confuse wild nigella with corn cockle (Lychnis githago), which has red flowers and poisonous seeds.

Nitre, Niter

A word today more or less reserved for the jargon of fireworks-makers it appears, nevertheless, in numerous culinary works of the last century. It then meant saltpeter, or potassium nitrate (generally mixed with salt), that is used to redden meats in brines. (*See* SALTPETER.)

Alexander Dumas in his *Grand Dictionnaire de Cuisine* manifestly confused nitre with certain purified salts. Nitre has also been associated, mistakenly, with *natron,* a natural salt used by the ancients that contains sodium carbonate. (*See* BICARBONATE OF SODA.)

North Africa

The cooking of the people of North Africa is rich in spices, aromatics, and flavor harmonies. A very strong tradition, undoubtedly earlier than our own, governs their use. The expansion of Islam introduced the powders and spices of the Orient to the North Africans in the seventh century, before they influenced the food of Languedoc in the ninth century, brought by the Moors of Spain.

True cumin (*kemoun*), coriander (*kosbor*), red pepper, or Sudan pepper (harissa), cardamom, and even ginger are the strong consonances of the culinary harmony. A mixture of spices, *ras-el-hanout* (literally, summit of the shop) dominates the lot, as its name would lead one to believe. Garlic, mint, almonds, rose petals also play an important role. As for fats, the Moroccan cooks—undoubtedly the most skilled of North Africa—are familiar with several oils as well as *smeun* (strong butter).

The Jewish cuisine of North Africa is an interpretation of local recipes according to Talmudic precepts. The obligation not to "cook the lamb in the milk of its mother" makes the Jew use oil when it is necessary to "butter" a *couscous,* to the regret of gourmets. On the other hand, it is necessary to give credit to the Sephardic cuisine for its excellent distillation of such alcohols as *boukha,* Tunisian fig alcohol, and for the contribution of amusing variations on traditional *couscous;* for instance, *nikitouche* with wheat patties, and *bkaìla* with fried spinach. (*See* COUSCOUS, HARISSA, RAS-EL-HANOUT, ROSE *and* SMEUN.)

Nuöc-Mam

Also *nuokh-mam,* or *nuq-mum.* Malays and Thais say *ballichong, balla-chan,* etc. The most famous Vietnamese condiment, there is no equivalent in the West, although there was in antiquity: the famous *garum* of the Romans. Like garum, nuöc-mam is made of small fish coated with salt and exposed to the sun for a long time. Once they have been "self-digested" by the intestinal microbes, they are crushed in a press. The juice gathered is preserved in jars and bottles and can be recognized by an odor that makes one think of anchovy sauce and mushrooms.

There are several "growths" of nuöc-mam among which Asiatic gourmets differentiate, just as the wine-lovers do with Beaujolais. *pho-quoc,* named after an island of the Siam Gulf, is said to be the most delicate.

Without a doubt, nuöc-mam will displease palates unaccustomed to the very interesting Vietnamese cuisine. It is nevertheless irreplacable for seasoning Indo-Chinese dishes and a good source of nitric salts and vitamins. It can be cut with lemon juice, seasoned with a little red pepper or soy sauce. The principal failing of nuöc-mam is that it goes badly with Western wines. Aromatic tea with sugar or, if necessary, a cold rosé wine goes better with a dish of rice seasoned with nuöc-man than do other wines.

Nuöc-mam oxidizes rapidly on contact with air. It is necessary to keep it in well-closed jars, filled to the top, even if it means diluting the brine with a little boiled salt water. (*See also* ANCHOVIES *and* PISSALAT.)

Nutmeg

(French, *Muscade noix*; German, *Muskatnuss*) A brown tough nut, so marvelously scented that magic virtues were ascribed to it. It is found in the heart of an exotic apricot, borne by a beautiful tree, *Myristica fragrans,* cultivated in Indonesia and the British Antilles.

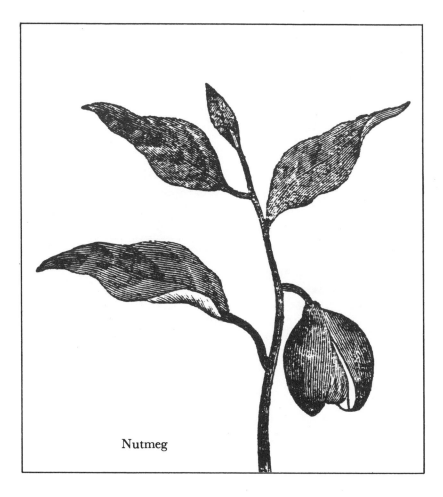

Nutmeg

On maturity, the fruit bursts open, and the nut appears, enveloped in a network of fibers. This fiber is called mace or the nutmeg aril. It is improperly called "nutmeg flower." Dried, then powdered, mace becomes a salmon color, its aroma somewhat like that of cinnamon. (*See* MACE.)

The nutmeg tree is a delicate plant that is vulnerable to tropical cyclones. In 1955, following a cataclysm that ravaged the plantations of Grenada, one of the Caribbean Islands, the price of nutmeg doubled. The nutmeg is dioecious, that is, secuate. It is cultivated in thickets. A male tree is sufficient to fertilize a "harem" of twenty female plants. It does not begin to bear fruit until its sixth year and furnishes 1,000 to 2,000 nuts a year.

This spice has only recently been used. The ancients knew only mace, and that not very well. "It is the red bark of an unknown tree," wrote Pliny the Elder. Nutmeg appeared in Europe at the end of the first millenium B.C., first in Byzantium, then in Capetian courts and in the German emperors'. The *Roman de la Rose* mentioned *noix mugades*. For once, the Chinese do not seem to have had the advantage, for nutmeg is not among the "five powder perfumes" of China and Vietnam.

The leaves of the nutmeg, which look like those of the peach, are green on one side and whitish on the other. When rubbed between the fingers, they give off a smell sweeter than bay leaves. In the Celebes and the Philippines, they flavor grills and soups. They cannot be found in the West, unfortunately.

USES: *First, it should be said that varieties of nutmeg, as such, don't exist. Choose fat, heavy, ashy-brown nuts unpierced by worms when buying in bulk or simply buy them in a good grocery. This last recommendation goes especially for powdered nutmeg and mace.*

Nutmeg should be kept in cans or well-closed jars, to keep away from moisture and to ensure that the odor does not influence neighboring foods.

BEVERAGES *A touch of grated nutmeg accents creole punch and sundry cocktails-with-milk, like the Alexander. Nutmeg is an element in most sweet vermouths and in many aperitifs and aromatized spirits (melissa water, four thieves vinegar,* raspail, quinquina, *etc.).*

PASTRIES AND SWEETS *Some splinters of nutmeg give a characteristic touch to the famous* leckerli *of Bali, to many small lemon or honey cakes, pear or cherry compotes, English cakes, milk shakes, and vanilla sweets, and possibly fruit tarts.*

EGGS *Nutmeg (or mace, preferred by some chefs), admirably seasons ome-lettes and especially soufflés, whether salted or sugared, as well as all stuffings where eggs* (godiveau) *are an element, including baked eggs.*

CHEESE DISHES *These represent the best area for experimentation by cooks intimidated by this heavy nut. Whether used in a cheese soufflé, a gratinated dish, Welsh rarebit, or even onion soup covered with cheese, there is scarcely a risk of making a mistake. Avoid it, however, in Swiss cooking* (fondue, raclette)*, or Italian (when Parmesan cheese is combined with tomato).*

SPECIALTIES *Grated nutmeg is an element in many preparations where it might be overlooked on the spinach that accompanies a roast, or even a dish of baked sardines,* sauce béchamel, *meat balls, rice croquettes (if they are covered with a smooth sauce), in meat and potatoes, on hash in mashed potatoes (seasoned with cream and egg yolk), on grilled blood sausage, on snails, and if necessary on a leg of lamb that smells of grease.*

In compound spices, (quatre épices)*, both nutmeg and mace find an almost universal use. Nutmeg should not be used in Mediterranean and exotic dishes, as it goes poorly with cumin, anise, and most other aromatic herbs. This subtle but somewhat showy spice, native to the Moluccas, tends to remain alone on the stage, at most in combination with pepper and cloves. (See also* COMPOUND SPICES.)

NUTMEG BUTTER *is a solid oil, prepared in the tropics from broken or inferior nuts. It is presented in longish loaves, often wrapped in palm leaves. Crumbly and fragrant, it can be used as a cooking fat. It is valued in pharmacy.*

Oak

(*Quercus;* French, *Chêne;* German, *Eiche*) The shoots of oak trees have a subtle, bitter taste recalling that of green walnuts. They are sometimes used as aromatic ingredients. The Slavs, for example, add them to the preparation of *kvass,* the light Russian beer, and to marinades. The Germans drank acorn coffee as the national drink during the rationing of the First World War.

Oils

Food oils of vegetable origin are extremely numerous and ancient. The need to make foods slide with the aid of a lubricant other than animal fat had already appeared to the cave man. Very quickly, our ancestors distinguished some vegetable fats by their pleasant flavor. For thousands of years, they also had the role of aromatics. Today their taste has singularly degenerated. The best-selling oils praise themselves for their insipidity. Curnonsky* was indignant about this, adding, "A good eating oil should smell of its fruit, as good wine smells of the grape on the vine arbour." Here is their tasty hierarchy:

* See APPENDIX.

OLIVE OIL is the queen of table oils, the soul and secret of the Mediterranean gastronomes. Maligned by the butter-lovers—and still badly known in our times—it was rehabilitated for the first time by Racine. "I ate it in sauces, and without lying, (I can say) there is nothing better." (*Letter from Uzes, 1661*.)

Virgin or natural olive is preferable, if it is guaranteed cold pressed and first pressing. The oil called "extra de Nice" discreetly fruity, is without a doubt the finest of all. Greece, Italy, and Tunisia export excellent kinds. (There is also a Greek dietetic olive margarine.) Spanish oils, from fermented fruits, are a little acrid and become rancid quickly. Olive oil is indispensable in fish soups, unequaled in salads, and lends itself very well to deep frying because it tolerates, without changing, a temperature of 550°F. It should always be stored in a dark place, free from temperature changes.

SESAME OIL is spicy and sharp. It takes the place of a condiment in Chinese cooking and its taste is found in the *halva* of Oriental candy-makers. It should not be heated. It coats composed salads and hors d'oeuvres very well.

WALNUT OIL, greenish when it is fresh, has a pronounced taste like green walnuts. While not everybody likes it, there are fervent admirers. It is especially suited to Paris salad (lamb's lettuce, celery root, and beet), and to chicory and dandelion. A trout, that is to be broiled on coals, can be dabbed with walnut oil.

BEECHNUT OIL, extracted from the small triangular nut of the beech is, unfortunately, almost unobtainable. Its fine taste resembles that of chestnut and hazelnut. It is amber-colored when well prepared. Beechnut oil can be compared with olive oil and cures in aging.

CORN OIL, SUNFLOWER SEED OIL, AND GRAPE SEED OIL, have appeared on the shelves of food stores and specialty food shops. Highly recommended by dietitians, they are light and digestible, but their taste is reduced by the manufacturers. Sunflower oil is found in a number of commercial French mayonnaises.

RAPE OIL comes from the seed of the rape colewort cultivated in the West and North of France. Yellow and sweetish, it is only used

180

as food when very fresh, as its country flavor quickly becomes too pronounced.

SWEET ALMOND OIL is fine and delicious, but very costly. Like hazelnut oil, it is not used much except in candy-making and perfumery.

CORNEL TREE OIL is extracted from the drupes of this small rustic tree whose wood is noted for its hardness. The Italians like its fruity smell and its viscosity. In Piedmont, it is used for deep frying or to brown the onion and celery in the *minestra*.

PEANUT OIL, extracted from the peanut, has a light taste of almond when very fresh and when it has not been deodorized in a vacuum-pack.

POPPY OIL, taken from the seed of the black poppy, was the best known of neutral-tasting oils before the commercial exploitation of peanut oil.

COTTON OIL, pale-yellow, and without appreciable aroma, comes from cotton seeds stripped of the fine fluff that is the principal value of the plant. It is used to make various vegetable fats and also to imitate olive oil or goose fat.

PALM OR COPRA OIL, taken from the pulp of coconut, is a solid oil that solidifies at 68⁰ F. Some of it has a rather fruity, spicy flavor. It is used mostly to make margarine.

COLZA OIL, the extract of rustic cabbage seeds, is yellow, viscous, with an intense aroma of the *Crucifeae.* It is only agreeable when diluted with many other oils.

OTHER OILS: Most of the inexpensive table oils sold in French groceries are mixtures of peanut, poppy, colza, and sunflower oils neutralized with soda and filtered over activated charcoal, etc. Their principal merit is found in reducing the cost of frying potatoes.

Food oils of animal origin are extracted from marine animals. Viscous, stinking whale oil is almost entirely used in the soap industry. Cod liver oil is valuable for its vitamin richness—its taste is something else. Herring oil, obtained by the Scandinavian fish processors, finds many fans among canneries in Northern Europe. One exception to marine sources for animal oils is neat's-foot oil, obtained by boiling shinbones and feet of cattle, which used to be prepared in the country. Bland and very fluid, it was used to lubricate watches, and to soften leather.

MINERAL OILS are, for the most part, dangerous poisons. Many soldiers have died, without help from the enemy, by eating fried potatoes cooked in machine-gun oil. Vaseline and paraffin, nevertheless, have been used in times of scarcity as food, without too many accidents.

AROMATIC OILS: Sundry preparations and macerations of table oil with ingredients of animal or vegetable origin exist in cooking. Crustacean oil is made with the trimmings and shells of crabs and lobsters, pounded in a mortar with olive oil and then sieved. Oil steeped several weeks with basil branches and whole garlic cloves becomes basil oil. Lemon oil is extracted from little Oriental lemons, first preserved in coarse salt.

Okra

Or *Gombo, Gombaut, Gumbo,* etc. It is the hornlike fruit of *Hibiscus esculentus,* of the *Malvaceae* family, grown in the Levant, Africa, and Antilles. There are two kinds of okra, the *bamiah* or *corne grecque,* small and rounded, and the American variety, which is longer. This condiment vegetable has a peppery, amusing flavor. In cooking, it gives off a mucilaginous substance that makes gumbo soups syrupy and "ropy."

Another variety of gumbo, the *ketmia-sorrel* of Guinea, is sought out for its leaves, which have an acid taste. Almost all gumbos have musk-tasting seeds, which, dried and roasted, can be used as a substitute for coffee.

Gumbo should not be underestimated. It finds its best use in Oriental mutton stew, in the *calalou* from the Antilles, in chicken with okra and sweet peppers, which is prepared by the descendants of French colonists in Louisiana, and elsewhere in the southern United States.

Olives

Fruits of *Olea europaea,* a tree that is the very symbol of Mediterranean civilization. Bearing gracious, persistent greenery on a

Olives

picturesque framework, the olive tree often attains a thousand, sometimes even two thousand years of age. Whether we speak of the olive branch that the dove brought to the ark, or the Mount of Olives, it plays a role in the Scriptures. The Greeks revered olives to such an extent that for a long time only virgin females and pure men were used for its cultivation. Its lanceolate leaves, shorter when the tree is wild, remain the emblem of peace. Two olive branches appear on the United Nations banner. The very hard olive wood, veined with brown, is almost rotproof. Ancient sculptors preferred it to all other woods for their work. The olive wood is used to make very beautiful table utensils. Its dried branches are used for spits in Haute-Provence to cook meats.

The oil extracted from its fruits by cold pressing is one of the finest of vegetable fats. (*See* OIL.) On the other hand, the oil of fermented olives is a little acrid and becomes rancid quickly. The oil obtained from boiling the residue of the first pressing (*huile tournante* or *huile d'enfer*) is used only for making soap. Olive margarine is a valuable Greek dietetic product.

The olive itself was appreciated as a food and a condiment from earliest times. Gathered green, before ripening, or black, when completely ripe, it has an acrid, disagreeable taste in the raw. Green olives are marinated in a lye wash of wood ash while black olives are dried before being preserved in brine or oil. Sundry aromatics are elements in this maceration: bay, fennel, orange or bitter orange peel, coriander, and marjoram. The people of Provence much prefer the black olive, which they call *facho-ouiro* (oil-maker). Often the only treatment it receives is being steeped for a long time in fine salt and herbs.

Among the most valued kinds of olives are those of Nice— very small but deliciously perfumed—and the Ascoli olives of Italy, as well as the Calmata of Greece. As for green olives, there are the *pitchoulines* of Provence, firm, greenish or brownish and rather large to contradict their name, Nimes, and Lucques (Tuscany) olives. The *verdales* olives of Seville are the most prized.

USES: *Green olives are often eaten stuffed. The stuffing is made of anchovy butter, tuna fish, and sometimes grilled pimiento or eggplant. In Italy, olives are stuffed with ham before being fried. Blanched, they can garnish the famous duck with olives* (canard aux olives). *Black olives are used in* tapenado sauce *and in the tasty* salade niçoise. *They are also prepared on many Mediterranean shores, in stews with duck or other fowl, rabbit, or even veal. An olive with an anchovy filet wrapped around it like a wreath decorates certain* tournedos à la toulonnaise. *The black olive combines perfectly with meat glacés, seasoned with garlic or tomatoes, diluted with dry white wine, with all olive-oil fricassees, and many other foods. Pitted, the black olives can also be an element in the stuffing for a fowl or large fish. In the time of Brillat-Savarin, a beef filet was studded with truffle slices and black olives before being marinated in white wine.*

N.B. There is, of course, another variety of olive tree in China, called lan-hoa. *This is Linnaeus'* Olea fragrans. Its greenery and wood are very aromatic. The dried, pulverized leaves are used in some varieties of tea.

One-Hundred-Flavors

A pretty name to some very expensive concoctions of Chinese cooks. Hence it permits intrepid gourmets to demonstrate the richness of their spice cabinets and sometimes their skill as well. (Carrots with one-hundred-flavors combine the flavor of our familiar comestible roots with those of a series of ingredients: parsley, bay, thyme, tarragon, nutmeg, Chinese five spices, star anise, fennel, cloves, cassia, Chinese pepper, etc.)

Onion

(*Allium cepa;* French, *Oignon;* German, *Zwiebel;* Italian, *Cipolla;* Scandinavian, *Loek*) When we peel this noble bulb, we cry, but it would be sadder for us if it were missing from our cooking. No country can lay claim to it, not even Egypt, which formerly gave it divine honors. It is supposed to be native to the shores of the Aral Sea because it is found wild there. However, it followed very ancient human migrations, even before being known it embarked on Phoenician boats.

These are the principal kinds:

WHITE ONION is harvested early in April in France. The varieties most sought after proclaim their Italian origin: Florence, Barletta, Noccra. It is sweet, discreet, and lends itself to being eaten raw with salt. The white onion, *gros plat italien*, is very fleshy and autumnal, large and flat.

SPANISH ONION is generally slow to put on flesh. Sometimes it is pear-shaped. Its husk varies from straw-yellow to purplish-red, passing through coppery-red; it is mild-flavored. Its principal merit is that it keeps well, permitting it to be stored for the winter.

BULB ONION is an odd variety, bearing bulblets at the end of its stem instead of seeds. These bulbs are called rocamboles, red garlic (*ail rouge*), Spanish or Egyptian shallots (*échalotes d'Espagne ou d'Egypte*). It is somewhat similar to garlic (*Allium scorodoprasum*), but used in the same way as shallots. (*See* ROCAMBOLES.)

The bulb of *Allium cepa* has always been an element in therapy. The Turks, according to Cuvier, ate onions to prevent goiter. Doctors in Molière's time prescribed it for gravel and for dropsy. Today, dieteticians confirm that onions contain allyl sulphide that permit the body to eliminate urea and sodium chloride. Some scientists, like Professor Virtanen of Helsinki, are convinced that the alliaceous bulbs, like onions and other vegetable aromatics, act as bacteria-killing bombs. They give off aerosols in food gardens and could be antibiotics of great value. In sum, the Pharaohs were very well advised to have enormous quantities of garlic and onion given to the pyramid builders when this huge labor force was threatened by many epidemics.

USES: *The modern gourmet is fortunate. He can not only obtain many kinds of onion, but onion flakes, powdered onion and onion salt. Their uses are as obvious as they are numerous. Some first truths about onions are onions cause the eye to tear because, when cut, they give off a caustic vapor. By peeling the bulb under running cold water or by chilling it in the refrigerator, one is protected from this mist.*

Raw onion, finely chopped, is appreciated in the Balkans as a condiment. Traditionally it accompanies kebab cici *(Serbian meatballs), and appears in sundry Hungarian and Bulgarian onion salads. A white onion finely cut, washed several times under the faucet, and finally twisted in a cloth, loses its volatile juice but not its aroma.*

The new onion, held by its stalk, is a delicious condiment which garnishes Oriental skewered mutton.

Burnt onion (onion charred in a frying pan), is an aromatic coloring that is tied in a cloth to pep up and season a consommé or pot-au-feu.

In some cases, onion should not be chopped on a board, but grated finely (as in Russian or Rumanian meat balls.)

The rather strong taste of this bulb should, in principle, accent a dish and not make itself felt too strongly. There are several exceptions to this rule:

oignonade à l'ancienne, *Chinese-style beef with onions, Turkish stuffed eggplant and peppers*, pissaladière *from Nice, as well as the garnish made of onions stuffed with garlic, in honor of the Côte d'Azur, or fish with onions, to name a few.*

New onions can be marinated à la grecque *(like artichokes) or preserved in vinegar. In addition to French condiments of this kind, English-style pickled onions, Italian* sottaceti, *German* Perlzwiebeln, *and Indian* atjars *are available.*

Orach

The name given to several very common plants of the *Chenopodium* family (*belle dame,* follette, or atriplex). Rather like market spinach, they used to be an element in the preparation of cooked herbs and refreshing soups.

The old French cookbooks proposed the use of orach leaves, but they do not possess gastronomic virtues. Neither the English nor the Germans, who call it *Melde,* have found any really original uses for it.

Orange

(*Citrus sinensis* and others; Arab, *Narandj;* English and French, *Orange;* German, *Apfelsine, Orange;* Italian, *Arancia*) Fruit of the orange tree, which should be distinguished from many others of the *Hesperidium* family, such as lime tree, lemon tree, citron tree, bitter orange tree, grapefruit tree, etc. "Of all the fruit trees," an old botanical treatise tells us, "none is more beautiful or more useful." Its greenery gives a perpetual shade, its flowers perfume the air with a sweetish odor, and finally, its fruits, the *Hesperidiae,* quench the thirst of the traveler and refresh the palate of the ill. It is believed that these plants are native to tropical Asia and that they were carried very early to Persia, thence to Egypt, and from there to Europe during the Crusades.

In cooking, the sweet orange is nothing less than a substitute. It is substituted for the bitter orange in the preparations famous as duck *à l'orange.* Its zest is less robust. Quarters of orange can be mixed with a lettuce salad, but are less pleasant than those of tangerines; its juice loses much of its aroma after a few seconds of boiling.

In Provence, dried orange peel is also a discreet aromatic that complements thyme and bay in the cooking of beef stew, breast of veal, sauce for *supions,* stuffing for partridge, guinea hen, etc. It is combined with saffron in the extrapolations of Spanish *paella* in Languedoc. In Sweden and Germany, rolls with grated orange-peel decorations are found. In California, housewives prepare beef and fowls with whole oranges, simply cut in quarters. This way of cooking would make Cromwell rejoice if he were alive, for the historian Guizot reports that Cromwell, the famous "protector," enjoyed roasted veal with oranges above all other dishes.

In French cooking, the expression *à l'orange* or *en robe orange* qualifies sundry cooking processes, sauces, etc., which always profit by livening up with the zest and juice of the bitter orange —the Seville orange much used for marmalades. Young fowl, or tender winged game (duckling, woodcock, etc.) prepared with orange, pike stuffings, fish marinades, as well as certain mousseline sauces may be seasoned with grated peel of the bitter orange. Doubtless the bitter orange may be difficult to find. If so, it is possible to substitute sweet orange zest combined with a drop of curaçao (which see).

ORANGE BUTTER is butter mashed with orange or bitter orange zest and a whisper of nutmeg. It is used in slices on white meats.

THE BERGAMOT ORANGE is a sourish orange borne by the *Citrus limetta.* It can also be considered a sweet lemon. Its epicarp and pulp permitted the Italian chemist Farina to perfect his famous eau de cologne. This pale-yellow fruit, scarcely acid, is an element in Mediterranean recipes: *harira tangeroise,* veal *à la calabraise,* etc. Its aroma is like grapefruit.

Bergamot orange and bitter orange in Latin America often season peppery sauces, tempering the violence of chili and tabasco. In Brazil, an orange salad is served with the national stew (*feijoada*).

Oxygarum

A very spicy condiment formerly prepared in Norbonne Gaul with benzoin, mint, caraway, and native and imported seeds. (*See* BENZOIN *and* RESIN.)

Paprika

A flamboyant pulverized spice made from the Hungarian pepper. In the Hungarian language this word means both the cooking powder and the vermillion pods of *Capsicum annuum szegendense*. (See the botanical details under RED PEPPER.) These peppers are dried in the sun and milled with or without their seeds. Paprika is the only good reminder the Hungarians have of the Turkish occupation of their country which ended in 1699. In the eighteenth century, it was still called Janissary pepper. The soldiers of the sultan, in fact, doted on the pods of the American *Solancea* brought back to Europe by Columbus and adopted by the Moroccans and other Islamic people.

The Hungarian professor Albert Szentgyörgi, a Nobel Prize winner, has demonstrated that red pepper is richer than any other vegetable in vitamin C. On the other hand, he has forgotten to state whether or not temperate or vocanic peppers should be chosen in the name of nutrition. In the groceries of the city of Pest, six tones of paprika are found: *without bite* (without capsicin and dietetic), *sweet, half-sweet, pink, strong,* and *special.*

USES: *In Magyar countries, paprika is a part of all celebrations and almost all meals. Gathered when its green covering yellows, it is eaten raw with salt alone, like all the little red peppers of Spain and Africa. Reduced to a powder, it colors and flavors a thousand recipes: meat soups,* pörkölt *of beef, veal, chicken, fish; sauerkraut with fat and paprika, noodles with paprika. (The Hungarians use the word* pörkölt *instead of* gulyas *for all those stews we specifically call Hungarian goulash.) The fragrance of this red pepper is supported by some caraway seeds and a sprig of marjoram. The fat used is lard because it is traditional in this country of pig-raising and cold winters. But paprika, like its Iberian homologue* pimentón, *goes well with oil.*

Let us not forget that paprika is equally at home in other parts of Central Europe: Rumanian Transylvania, Bulgaria, Serbia, Slovakia, and other places. The Balkan or even German recipes that call for paprika have only transcribed the secrets of Hungarian cuisine. A single oddity is worth noting —the Czechs and the Austrians moisten many goulashes with light beer.

*In French cooking the red vegetable gives a hot note to a recipe that must also be used in other countries; Gypsy sauce (*sauce Zingara*); molded eggs, and langouste bathed in a creamy sauce with paprika are often called* à l'archiduc *in France, in honor of other more fortunate wanderers.*

The many uses of paprika can be summarized: it accents crustacean dishes very well, lobster and langouste à l'américaine, *sautéed oysters, and many fresh-water fish like carp sautéed in white wine with aromatics. It can be used in a risotto, in a vegetable cream, especially cauliflower, fish in mayonnaise, mushroom omelette, brown sauce, or béchamel, if it is absolutely necessary to give them a high flavor. It goes very well with cheese, notably the famous* Slovak Liptauer, *and white cheese. Among the meats, in addition to many goulashes, it is suited to* veal escalope *and chicken fricassee. In German countries, paprika is used in the cooking of some roots like black radish, Jerusalem artichoke, and oyster plant. Sometimes delicatessen-makers use it in making blood sausages and dried blood sausages.*

Parmesan

An Italian hard-paste cheese with a light saffron color, made from skimmed cow's milk, cured two or three years in humid cellars. The Italians sometimes say *cacio parmigiano*, but more often *formaggio di grana, grana* being the name in the peninsula for cochineal, which often colors this kind of cheese. *Stravecchio* is the first choice.

Dietitians reveal that of all cheeses currently consumed, Parmesan contains the most mineral salts and nitrate substances. It is also one of the least rich in fat and the poorest in water—30 per cent against 32 per cent in Gruyère and 54 per cent in Brie. During its ripening in the cellars, the Italian cheese-makers cauterize suspect fermentations with a hot iron. The crust is dabbed periodically with a mixture of grape-seed oil and burnt earth.

Parmesan cheese plays a most important role as a culinary ingredient and as a condiment (see uses under CHEESE), but it can also be eaten alone with butter or walnuts. Natives of Ravenna like to eat chunks of Parmesan with luscious pear quarters.

Parsley

(*Petroselinum hortense;* French, *Persil;* German, *Petersilie;* Italian, *Prezzemolo*) The most widespread of all *fines herbes.* A food writer of the last century said, "To take parsley away from a cook is almost to make it impossible for him to exercise his art." Dumas proclaimed parsley "a condiment obligatory for all sauces." We have restrained ourselves from participating in this concert of praise. Parsley is spicy, aniselike, more robust than chervil, but a much less noble herb than tarragon or basil. Easy to grow, often offered as a bonus by the most miserly French butchers, it has become commonplace. It lends itself to the worst hustling of pseudogastronomic restaurants and permits housewives to imagine that they really know aromatic botany.

COMMON GARDEN PARSLEY (or broad-leaf parsley) Native to Greece, naturalized in continental Europe for a long time, it has ceded its place more and more to another variety, because of the gardeners' efforts.

CURLY PARSLEY is today the most widespread in France, and widely available in other countries Its leaves are dark-green, dwarf, and very curly. It is also called double parsley. Its leaves are hem-stitched, finely denticulated, and very decorative.

HAMBURG PARSLEY (*Persil bulbeux, Persil-navet, Persil de Hambourg*) is a variety highly valued in Slavic and German countries. Its tap root is agreeably flavored, as it plays a role in cooking Russian soups (bortsch, *stchi*) and stews.

NAPLES PARSLEY (*Persil-céleri, Persil de Naples*) is very close to Hamburg parsley. It is esteemed in the Italian peninsula for its large roots that are eaten blanched like celery hearts.

FALSE PARSLEY *Umbelliferae* that are closely related are also called white parsley, black parsley (*persil noir*), and *horse parsley.*

CRAB PARSLEY (*persil arabe* or coriander), white parsley (*persil blanc* or Cretan carrot). (*See* CRETAN CARROT, CORIANDER, *and* HORSE PARSLEY.)

The present use of parsley makes doctors rejoice, for the leaves contain a great quantity of calcium, iron, vitamin C, and trace elements, notably manganese. Professor Léon Binet* cites the case of a famous doctor who attributed his spryness to "acres of parsley" eaten during his long life. In ancient times, parsley was considered a magic herb. The winners in the historic Isthmian games, dedicated to Neptune, were crowned with garlands of parsley. In the Middle Ages, it was thought that a parsley seed had to encounter the devil seven times before germination. (Its germination is very slow, it is true.) Even today, in some places, there are superstitions surrounding parsley-growing; it is bad luck to transplant it, it should be sown by a simple-minded person, and so on.

USES: Juvert, *as parsley is called in Provence, is an aromatic vegetable for all occasions. It can tolerate the longest boiling and even frying without losing its aroma. In Périgord, fried potatoes are garnished with frizzled parsley.*

Combined with garlic, shallots, and chives, it is useful in all sautéed or fried dishes. Tied with thyme and bay, it becomes the everpresent bouquet garni *that bathes in a* pot-au-feu *and in numerous stews. Dried and reduced to flakes by foreign grocers, called* Petersilienflocken *in German, it is used in recipes in countries where they lack fresh parsley. A piece of beef or mutton can be studded with parsley and bacon as our ancestors did, as is the case with the rack of mutton* gourmandé de persil, *which is found in Molière's* Bourgeois Gentilhomme.

Finely chopped parsley or "tufts" of parsley can be mixed with many sauces and salads. We will not belabor these uses; everybody knows them. Besides, they tend to make parsley an omnipresent and omniscient herb. We refuse to let ourselves believe in the existence of an aromatic panacea.

* See APPENDIX.

Pastis

Pastis is a variety of anisette with the sugar absent and a small quantity of licorice tempers the ardor of the essence of star anise and dill.

In cooking in the south of France, pastis is a relatively new ingredient. It can replace seeds or greens of anise, dill, fennel. A few drops of this apéritif can be sprinkled on fish or snails before they are cooked in the oven, or used in flaming a lamb chop. It can also be used in bouillabaisse.

Pastrami

Also *pastourma, bastorma, pastrama.* A very tough dried meat coming from the Levant. It can be mutton or goat, as well as beef or even Egyptian buffalo (*gamousse*). Before being dried, pastrami is macerated several days with garlic, powdered fenugreek, and paprika. Its very spicy taste makes it suited for *mézés.* Finely chopped, it can be used to make some stuffings or meat balls full-bodied, and in a number of Armenian dishes. (Editor's note: In America, pastrami is a sandwich meat. Highly seasoned beef, usually a shoulder cut, is boned and has fat removed, is rubbed with spices, smoked and cooked. It is served hot or cold.)

Peanut

(*Arachis hypogaea;* French, *Arachide;* German, *Erdnuss*) A plant native to America, its fruit, peanuts (*cacahouètes* in French), have a name of Aztec origin. They are also called ground nuts (*pistache de terre*) because the pods that follow the flowers drag on the ground at the moment of ripeness. Today their neutral-flavored oil is widespread. The fresh or roasted nut is an element in a great number of African culinary preparations: Congo *sanga d'arachides,* Cameroon shrimp and peanut pastry, Senegalese peanut sauce. Crushed or pounded peanuts are almost always used, cooked for a long time with a little hot water, pepper, and then mixed with fried onions, crab meat, vegetables, and fruits. The pastries are rolled in blanched banana leaves, reheated in the steam table or on hot coals. Peanuts can also be used in pastry-making as substitutes for almonds or pistachios.

PEANUT BUTTER A commercially made product with an amusing taste and great nutritional qualities, highly enjoyed by children. It can be used on canapés decorated with slices of radish, or watercress.

Pebre D'Ai

(French, *Pebre d'ai, Pebre d'ase*) The provincial name for winter savory. (*See* SAVORY.)

Pepper, Black, White, Etc.

(*Piper nigrum;* French, *Poivre;* German, *Pfeffer;* Italian, *Pepe;* Arab, *Felfel*) All these names come from the Sanskrit *pilpali* that appears in the ancient Vedas. The pepper belongs to the *Piperaceae* family that also numbers many tropical vines. Its fruit displays many colors: they are red when ripe, black when dried, gray or white in the jargon of grocers.

Only the seeds of *Piper nigrum* can be truly called pepper. There are, nevertheless, other peppers borne by other vines: cubebs, grains of paradise, allspice, etc. They are generally more acrid and have less scent than the Asian black pepper of the botanist, which is cultivated in India, Indonesia, Ceylan, Madagascar, and Brazil. The world commerce in pepper exceeds 50 million dollars each year, which is why it is protected by numerous regulations in many countries.

Known for twenty-three centuries, at least, by the Mediterranean peoples round pepper of Asia was very early placed first among spices. Through the ages, it has supplanted a great number of rustic condiments like myrtle, nigella, and juniper seeds. It was, until quite recently, very costly. In common language, the name "pepper" has been lent to other fruits or berries from very different plants, such as Cayenne pepper, a powder made from a Caribbean red pepper. We discuss this condiment in a separate article.

GRAY PEPPER (grocers call it "black" pepper) is the whole fruit of the *Piper nigrum.* Gathered before it is completely mature, dried in the sun or artificially, it has a lined epicarp and a burning taste, and it slightly colors sauces and foods.

WHITE PEPPER comes from the same fruit; that is, the "black pepper." The berry is gathered very ripe and soaked in salt water where it rids itself of its dark-red bark, with only the light nut remaining. White pepper is less strong than whole pepper. Its net cost and sale price is a little higher. It is preferred for white sauces, and generally, in French cooking.

The best growth of pepper very often bears the name of the port from which it was shipped to the West: white from Tellichéry (India), black from Lampong (Sunda Islands), Mangalore from near Madras, very large black from Saigon and Singapore. There are also sizeable qualities of pepper from Cambodia, Madagascar, Nigeria, and even from Brazil where it is called *aguaxima.*

Generally, it is thought that pepper should be very dense, so that heavy pepper, the most valued, is distinguished from medium-heavy and light pepper. The pepper lover prefers pepper heavy, compact, not crumbly (unless it is a question of a pepper mixture of *Piper nigrum* from several sources filled out with allspice, sold in some groceries). Not only the strength (the bite) of the pepper should be considered, but also its aroma, and its taste after trying it out on potatoes, salads, etc. Finally, the amateur should examine it under an eyeglass to reveal mixtures—light seeds, dust, etc.

GROUND PEPPER, even of excellent quality, is less worthy than whole pepper freshly ground as needed. It rapidly loses its aroma but keeps its acridity. Besides, it is often adulterated with sundry ground plant substances (date pits, peanut shells, etc.).

Among the less common offerings of pepper, there is *mignonnette,* crushed, but not ground, and mixed pepper, a veritable aromatic cocktail whose composition should always be indicated.

BETEL PEPPER (*Poivre Betel*), of earlier times, comes either from the betel (which see) or the chaba pepper, below.

CHABA PEPPER (*Poivre long, Poivre de Java*) (Trans. note: this is not *our* Java pepper) coming from the *Piper lonum* or *chaba,* is not a seed, but a little cob that is used whole. The ancients were already familiar with it in the time of Taillevent,* the medieval cook, who used it in *sauce cameline,* a reddish cullis for salt-water fish, and for *chaudemer,* a fish stew. The chaba is very spicy, looking a little like some red peppers and, though replaced by them generally, still used in some English sauces and pickles.

KISSI PEPPER (*Poivre de Kissi, Poivre de Achantis, Poivre de Guineé*) (Trans. note: this is not our Guinea pepper) is borne by a vine authentically African, the *Piper guineensis.* It is not as fine as the common pepper.

CHINESE PEPPER (French, *Poivre de Chine* or *Anis poivré*) Not a true pepper but the fruit of a tree of the Far East, *Zanthoxylum piperitum.* Its taste is lemony. (*See* ANISE.)

GRAINS OF PARADISE (French, *Malaquette* or *Poivre des Nègres*) often confused with Kissi pepper. Highly valued in the sixteenth and seventeenth centuries, grains of paradise are the seeds of an African amonum also known as *habzéli, zélim, xylopie,* etc. (*See* GRAINS OF PARADISE.)

CAYENNE Made from certain red peppers (which see).

PEPPER TREE PEPPER (French, *Poivre du Pérou* or *mollé*) Fruits of the *Schinus mollé,* a little South American tree of the *Terebinthaceae,* of which there are several decorative varieties. It has a spicy-flavored nut. The leaves are also aromatic and can be used in sundry spicy sauces called *mollé.* Another Guinean tree, *Fagara peperita,* lends itself to the same uses.

SUBSTITUTES FOR PEPPER Many berries, seeds and plant leaves are chosen by cooks for their spicy taste: myrtle, juniper, etc. The *poivrette* is the seed of nigella. The *petit poivre* is the fruit of the agnus-castus *(gattilier, Vitex agnus castus). Poivre d'eau* is that of the persicaria or crowfoot (*Polygonum hydropiper*). The *poivre de muraille* comes from the leaves of the white archangel *(tripe-madame* or *orpin blanc).* Finally, the *poivre d'âne,* or the *pebre d'ase,* is nothing more than winter savory.

PEPPER AND NUTRITION Highly prized by ancient doctors, who prescribed a decoction of *Diatron piperion,* as a plaster or salve,

* See APPENDIX.

pepper is rather criticized today. A little bit facilitates gastric secretion, but more is very irritating and binding. It has fewer vitamins than red pepper. The alkaloid it contains, *piperine*, has some antifebrile virtues, but it is mostly used to make *peperiline*, a scented essence like heliotrope, valued by perfume-makers. Doctors and gourmets join in their efforts for a reasonable and moderate use of pepper in all its forms.

USES: *They are innumerable. Some meats and preparations take their name from this spice.* Poivrade *is a very spicy sauce that accompanies meat.* Steak au poivre *is rolled in coarsely ground pepper before being placed under the broiler.* Piperade *is a Basque recipe for scrambled eggs with red pepper, flavored with black pepper or cayenne. In foreign countries,* pepper pot, *a mutton stew with onions, is strongly flavored with pepper. White pepper potato soup is another British specialty, and* Pfefferkuchen, *German gingerbread, are familiar. But almost all cooks know that pepper is always called upon to play supporting roles. Used too generously, it masks the food's own flavor. The only recipes where it is advisable to use pepper furiously are in some salad seasonings.*

Pepper as such is never used in beverages. It is known, however, that Frederick the Great peppered his black coffee and cut it with champagne! In Oceania, the roots of the intoxicating pepper plant (Piper methysticum) *are used to prepare the heady wine* kawa, *whose effects are a little like those of hashish.*

Peppers, Red

(Trans. note: What we currently call peppers, e.g., red peppers, chili peppers, etc., are called *piment* in French, while our pepper, e.g., white pepper, ground pepper, black pepper, is *poivre.*) (*See* PEPPER.)

SWEET RED PEPPERS (French, *Piment doux, Poivron doux*) A variety of *Capsicum annuum,* an edible annual pepper, planted, cultivated, and relished mostly in southern Europe and the Middle East. Its pods are large, fleshy, round, or squarish, green, orange or red. It is the vegetable fruit with a sweet taste that we discussed under Bell pepper, which is the variety enjoyed in America.

HOT RED PEPPERS These have a more or less hot taste, depending on the size of the slender pods—the smaller the fruit, the more volcanic it is. It is another variety of *Capsicum annuum,* corresponding exactly to the *agi* of the Caribbean natives that Columbus brought back to Isabella of Spain.

The hot pepper has seduced the African and Asian more rapidly than the Westerner. Transported from America to Asia by Magellan's companions in the seventeenth century, it passed for some time as a native plant of the East Indies. The botanist Alphonse de Candolle (1806–1893) destroyed this legend. Today, hot peppers are most appreciated in the southern countries, North Africa, Mexico and Latin America. Fearless gourmets eat them with salt alone or with *méchoui.* In Italy, they are sometimes called "little devil," notably in the preparation of the *capretto al diavolino* of the Abruzzi—a roasted kid surrounded by little peppers. In Hungary, Bulgaria, Rumania, and Spain, paprika and Spanish paprika are made from the hot pepper, dried, milled, and ground with a little oil. The English use small hot peppers in marinating pickles. (*See* PAPRIKA.)

CHILI PEPPER A bush of the same family, reaching at maturity to about four feet high. It lives several years. The botanists call it *Capsicum frutescens,* or perennial pepper. Its very small, curved fruits are called chili peppers, chilis, *piments caraïbes, piments enragés, piments-oiseaux.* The perennial pepper is best known because one of its varieties, with particularly caustic tiny fruits, is made into cayenne pepper. (*See* CHILI *and* CAYENNE PEPPER.)

The red peppers, burning, explosive, herbaceous or perennial, are a highly favored condiment in hot countries. They appear on the tables of the Chinese, Indonesians, black Africans, Antilles natives, just as mustard and ground pepper appear on ours. Their taste, very strong, often murderous, is part of a gastronomic tradition that is difficult for us to accept in our temperate countries. Only Hungarian paprika and Tunisian *harissa* have acquired citizenship. *Harissa* is made of the *soudania* African peppers borne by a perennial variety of capsicum, relatively more temperate than the Mexican or the Antilles perennial pepper. In Black Africa, *pili-pili* (a corrupt form of the Arab word *felfel* which means pepper) is a fiery spice that is rather like cayenne pepper. Pili-pili, like Mexican chili, cannot be used except in exotic recipes. Cayenne pepper, used with moderation, can easily substitute in French or Western cooking for all other pepper seasonings. Pepper figures,

198

in small quantities, in mixed Oriental spiecs like curry, etc. (*See* HARISSA, PAPRIKA, PILI-PILI, *and* CAYENNE PEPPER.)

USES: *The small fresh pepper or the chili pepper, preserved in vinegar, can occasionally season a mayonnaise or a spicy sauce (a half pepper is finely chopped, then crushed in a mortar before being added to a sauce, which will then be sieved). The fresh pepper, rather than being eaten by a fearless guest, takes the place of the "spice bag" in cooking dried beans, lentils, or Havana-style paella. It can be used very prettily in the final presentation if the guests are warned of the presence of the little devil. It can also communicate its aroma by simply being rubbed like garlic on a salad bowl.*

Perce-Pierres

Also called *casse-pierres* or sea fennel, it is Samphire (which see).

Persillade

A chopped mixture of garlic and parsley that flavors a reheated dish, or a meat at the end of cooking, is called *persillade*. This condiment, perhaps a wee bit vulgar, is also sold as a green powder in little jars. *Persillade* is an aromatic, capable of helping a hurried cook, but it should be used with discretion in a sauce or cooking liquid.

N.B.   The adjective *persillé* also qualifies foods that look as if they had been sprinkled with sprigs of parsley; *boeuf persillé* indicates meat streaked with fatty veins; cheese *persillés* are those with greenish molds, like Roquefort or Fourme d'Ambert, etc.

Pe-Tsai

(*Brassica sinensis*) A plant close to chicory and cabbage. It was introduced into France in the nineteenth century by missionaries returning from the Far East. Its taste is less strong than cabbage, being rather like that of cooked chicory. The leaves of *Pe-tsai*, or Chinese cabbage, can be mixed in with those of spinach, chicory, or mixed salad.

Piccalilli

An English condiment combining pickles with a rather diluted mustard. (*See* PICKLES.)

Pickled Turnip

The charming turnip of our food gardens can also be a condiment. Its fleshy roots, white or red according to the variety, are bitter but scented. For a long time, French cooks have observed that it sponges up the grease of fatty meats (mutton or duck, etc.). In China and in the Arab countries, cooks use its absorbent power in aromatic marinades. Turnip sauerkraut, marinated with lemon and fennel, is a classic garnish in Canton and Saigon. In Tunisia and Egypt, sliced turnips are bathed for several hours in the juice of lemons and bitter oranges, or even grapefruit juice, seasoned with red pepper. This preparation is called *tarchi* and it is like pickles, but finer. Vinegar is too spicy for this use.

Pickles

The most common of English condiments. They are made from vegetables (cucumbers, gherkins, onions), preserved in a very highly spiced vinegar sauce. Pickles probably came from the *atjars* or *achards* of Madras and Bombay.

Pili-Pili

An African variety of chili peppers. This word is a corruption of the Arab *felfel* meaning pepper. It is offered pulverized, looking like cayenne pepper, and also in purée, like the North African *harissa*, although stronger. (*For the uses of* PILI-PILI, *see* RED PEPPERS.)

Pimiento (Spanish)

A Spanish spice very close to Hungarian paprika, often called Spanish paprika in English. It is made from a rather sweet variety of *Capsicum annuum.* (*See* RED PEPPERS.) In the Murcia region at the end of the summer, the fields of red peppers are picturesque spectacles. The red pods are carefully gathered, then dried on wattles in full sunlight. They are then ground under granite millstones, sieved, and mixed with sea salt, or cochineal, and a little olive oil. In spite of its southern origin, Spanish paprika is less appreciated by cooks than the many and very fine varieties of *Gyula* and *Kolocza* (Hungary). Their red powder has a large role in Spain in making *chorizo* and sundry delicatessen as well as the cooking sauce of *bacalao* (salt cod) and *pollo en pepitoria* (chicken fricasse with sweet pepper). (*See also* PAPRIKA.)

NOTE: Pimientos (or pimentos) in the United States are used for garnishes, in relishes and sauces, not dried but preserved in juices in bottles or cans. Also, green olives are pitted and stuffed with them.

Pine-Almonds, Pine Nuts

(*Pinus pinea;* French, *Pignons;* German, *Pinienkerne*) Sweet pine nuts, or *pignoles,* are the nuts borne by the cones of the sea pine tree, a very widespread variety of conifer on Mediterranean shores. The sea pine nuts are larger than the seeds of other pine varieties. Oblong and a little angular, they enclose an oily white nut, with a stronger flavor than almond, in a tough envelope.

NOTE: A similar pine nut is found in Western America.

USES: *In Mediterranean countries, the pine nut is eaten with walnuts and hazelnuts and it is used in a number of pastries, (macaroons, tête de mort crackers), but also as a valued condiment as such. In Smyrna or Salonica, it has a considerable role in stuffings for fowl or winged game. It is present in* Itch pilau—*rice soup with pine nuts and raisins. In Spain, it is found in peasant soups very closely resembling the Ligurian soup with grated hazelnuts. (See* HAZELNUTS.) *In Italy, where it is called* pignoli, *it is most appreciated by cooks, almost indispensable in sweet and sour sauce for hare or ham hock, or in romagnole sauces, with rabbit, and in omelettes. In a general way, grated or crushed pine nuts can be recommended for use in wine sauce, minestrone with beans, or whole in Turkish* pilaf, *and meat balls.* (*See also* ALMOND.)

Pineapple

(*Bromelia ananas,* French, *Ananas;* German, *Ananas*) This delicious fruit, borne by a plant resembling the aloe, is an ingredient in making many desserts and sweets, but it can also be used as an aromatic condiment in sundry exotic preparations: chicken stuffed with pineapple (Creole cooking), sautéed pork with pineapple (Vietnamese cooking), and fish with pineapple (Pacific cooking).

In the Netherlands, little bits of pineapple are added with cheese to mayonnaise, and in Germany, some gourmets extol sauerkraut with pineapple.

Pineapple cider, Jamaican fashion, can also be prepared by steeping quartered pineapples in sugar water for five days. Press the fruits after this maceration, then filter the liquid and keep it in well-corked champagne-style bottles.

Pink (Dianthus)

(*Dianthus caryophyllus;* French, *Oeillet;* German, *Nelke*) A very pretty flower having varieties called *oeillet granadin* and *oeillet à ratafia,* which interest pharmacists, liqueur-makers, and cooks. Its scent is comparable to that of cloves. Its Latin name was borrowed by Linnaeus from clove tree. In German, the word *Nelke* is used for both. Distilled pink water and a pink vinegar were formerly made, and employed to aromatize potions, *ratafia,* sherbets, and even sometimes sauces. Pink petals can still be sprinkled on a fowl or a roast pork flavored with cloves, but it is an amusing curiosity, nothing more.

Pissalat

A condiment from Provence that resembles the famous *garam* of the Romans and Vietnamese nuöc-mam. It is a brine of the little fish that is called *poutine* or *melet* in the South of France. It is similar to anchovy butter, and should be mixed with olive oil, the resulting mixture emulsified. It can also be made with whitebait.

Pistachio

(*Pistacia vera;* French, *Pistache;* Italian, *Pistachio;* German, *Pistazie*)
Seed of the ungrafted pistachio, a large bush of Asia Minor, acclimated to Mediterranean countries, the pistachio nut is generally a beautiful pale-green, more rarely yellow. It is contained in a white woody shell that is removed by drying, leaving an inner reddish husk. Grocers recognize several qualities: the Sicilian pistachio is the most esteemed, the Syrian pistachio the strongest tasting and largest. (Unfortunately, it is yellow.) The Narbonne pistachio is very fine but difficult to hull.

Their exquisite taste and very pretty color makes them brilliant vegetables, highly appreciated by confectioners, bakers, and delicatessen-makers. Made into a praline with sugar, they make a delicious candy and can season a Montélimar nougat. Preserved in salt, they are part of the *mézés,* a Greek or Turkish cocktail snack. A pistachio pastry covered with chocolate, and a very expensive pistachio oil used for beauty products are also made. A pork galantine or a *mortadella* seasoned with pistachios are, in principle, first-choice products.

USES: *In the most sophisticated Western and Eastern cooking this rather costly seed has the role of a deluxe almond. The people of Provence, the Italians, and the Arabs add it to stuffings and sauces for tender fowl, or to chopped veal or chicken dishes that will be eaten cold. Florentine* soppressata, *a* ballottine *of fowl or pig's head, Moroccan* djerdad imer, *chicken with ginger and honey, etc. In faraway countries, notably Madagascar and India, the pistachio is used considerably as a condiment, purée, or as a vegetable in* pilaf (*Hindu* pulao). *It should be remembered that the pistachio, unlike the sweet almond, cannot be ground or shredded. Remove the reddish husk only by soaking in hot, but not boiling milk. This also tenderizes the nut. (See* ALMOND *and* LENTISK.)

Pistou

This is not an aromatic herb, nor a soup, contary to what many culinary tracts say. Without a doubt, basil can be called *herbe à pistou,* and one could familiarly say "tonight we'll eat pistou" when the *soupe au pistou* will be served. But *pistou,* for gastronomy and for semanticists, is a cooking *pommade,* used to season a soup, a dish of macaroni and, rarely, as a substitute for *sauce béarnaise* for a grilled meat or *steak tartare*. It comes from the Italian *pesta*, which means "trituration," or pounded. It is a thick, oily substance, very spicy, that can be bought in deluxe food shops as little jars of imported Italian *pesto*.

In Genoa, the name always indicates an emulsion of olive oil, basil, and grated cheese (Parmesan, ewe's cheese, Gruyère, Edam, etc.) Should several cloves of garlic also be crushed in the mortar and added? The people of Provence say yes. The Genoese cooks are more skeptical because garlic, in their opinion, should dominate another *pommade* (*agliata*), made with crustless white bread and a little vinegar. But in Liguria, in San Remo for example, everybody is in favor of garlic. So are we.

Another problem divides the people of Provence: should tomato pulp, fresh or browned in oil, be added to this mixture? The people of Marseilles say yes; the people of Nice and Cannes protest. In Toulon, they hesitate. We tend to favor the side of Cannes. The dispute grows bitter when the composition of the grated cheese is brought up. We refer our readers to our article on grated cheese. (An excellent gourmet from Marseilles, says: 3 ounces of Gruyère, 3 ounces of Edam, and 2 ounces of Parmesan.) Old cooks from Hyères are convinced that a lump of blue-mold Gorgonzola should be added. Their demonstrations, if not orthodox, are tasty, indeed.

Plankton

All the microscopic animals and plants that float in shallow oceans, taken together, are called plankton. Edible and even nourishing, as was demonstrated by Doctor Alain Bombard* during a heroic crossing of the Atlantic. Only an island people reduced to bare subsistence—the Japanese—have thought to make it figure among taste treats! Plankton soup, we have been told, has a delicious taste similar to chicken or veal. It is composed mostly of phytoplankton, of purely plant origin, rich in chlorophyll and proteins. The whale, eating it as a daily diet, is not well known as a gourmet. (*See* AGAR-AGAR.)

* See APPENDIX.

Plantain

(*Plantago coronopus;* French, *Corne-de-cerf;* German, *Wegerich*) (Trans. note: Both the bananalike tropical fruit and this small tropical plant have the same name in English. The tropical sort is a perennial herb, *Musa paradisiaca*, growing to thirty feet, and producing the above-mentioned fruit.)

A small annual plant of the genus *Plantain* with yellow flowers and widely split leaves grows in rubbish in northern climes. The young shoots of this variety are used as salad plants. Dumas made a big deal of them, and his example is still followed in certain parts of Southern and central France. The taste of plantain is close to that of garden cress. (*See* CRESS.)

Pomegranate

(*Punica granatum;* French, *Grenade;* German, *Granatapfel*) The large, tough reddish berry of the pomegranate, a middle-sized tree, native to Afghanistan, that has been cultivated in Mediterranean countries for a long time. It flourishes in soils and climates too sterile for the orange tree. Only the very numerous seeds, covered with a kind of transparent gel, are edible. They have a pleasant, sugary taste, a little on the acid side. Grenadine syrup is made from juice extracted from them. Rich in pectin, the juice of the pomegranate is used in the preparation of many food gels. Pomegranate concentrate is as common in Iran as tomato concentrate is elsewhere. Mixed with grated walnut, it lends itself to making dark sauces with an acid taste.

In the tropics, the seeds of the pomegranate are often elements in salads, decorating them like beautiful vegetable rubies. They also can flavor a sugar *couscous* (semolina cooked in milk steam, sprinkled with honey water, and served with curdled milk, pitted dates, fig quarters, etc.).

Poppy Seed

(*Papaver somniferum;* French, *Graines de pavot;* German, *Mohnsamen*) This large plant with violet flowers yields many kinds of products. The laciniate tender green leaves are often eaten like spinach.

Poppy

Blanched in salt water, then cooked in meat juice or cream, they are rich and delicate. The milky sap that flows from the fruit pod, cut when green, dries in brownish tears. This is raw opium, smoked as such by the Asiatics, but from which the pharmaceutical industry extracts morphine and laudanum.

Its bluish, kidney-shaped, very small seeds, freed by the ripe pod, furnish poppy seed oil. They are also used as a condiment in many Oriental and Germanic countries. The sweetish, oily taste goes especially well with sugar, as in Turkish poppy nougat. Egyptian pastries made with sesame and poppy seeds, and Balkan rolls and crescents are covered with poppy seeds. Pounded or coarsely crushed, they can be used in sesame mayonnaise. (*See* OIL *and* SESAME.)

WILD POPPY (*Papaver rhoeas;* French, *Coquelicot;* German, *Klatschmohn*) A wild member of the *Papaveraceae,* commonly seen in wheat fields after the harvest. Its petioles and leaves give off a noxious, slightly nauseous odor. This common wild poppy and the thorny Mexican poppy (*coquelicot-argemone*), are sometimes used to take the place of other poppy seeds in rustic preparations. The use of poppy seeds as a condiment goes back to the ancient Egyptians.

Port

A Portuguese wine that does not necessarily come from the Porto region, where the only famous cellars are located, but from the sunburnt slopes of Haut-Douro. There are several types of port: *sec, demi-sec* or *doux,* golden-white, or coppery-red.

USES: *In cooking, this wine is less esteemed than its compatriot, Madeira. It is used in cooking domestic duck with port, teal with port,* sauce portugaise, *etc., but apparently it cannot withstand cooking as well as Madeira. It is a delicate seasoning for cold dishes: melon, consommé, blue mold cheeses.* (*See* MADEIRA *and* MARSALA.)

Pouliot

(Or Pouillot) The name of a variety of wild mint that is mentioned in old cooking treatises. (*See* MINT.)

Poutargue

Also written *boutargue;* the Italians say *bottarga,* the people of Levant, *battarikha.* It is a caviar of mullet eggs, compressed into flat, irregular sausages, dried, smoked, and even coated with wax. This preparation usually comes from Greece or the Middle East, but poutargue is also made in France, in Martigues and, in Italy, in Portoferraio.

PREPARATION: *Poutargue should first be removed from its waxy envelope, and then cut in fine slices or well grated. It is an amusing condiment for finishing an hors d'oeuvre plate, accompanying a* ratatouille *or* caponata *of eggplant. Grated poutargue can also be found in a Greek mussel stew and in some cold fish sauces with capers and gherkins. It is a good idea to mix and emulsify this second-class caviar with lemon, oil, and cream.* (See ROE.)

Prickly Pear

Prickly pear (*Figue de Barbarie*) is an egg-shaped orange fruit of the great racket-shaped cactus so common in North Africa. Of an unremarkable sweet taste, the *kharmouss,* as it is called in Morocco, is an Islamic delicacy. In Portugal, the pears of cactus opuntia are eaten in compotes and prepared as a vegetable with tomatoes and sweet peppers.

NOTE: A similar cactus fruit is found in tropical America and in the southwestern United States.

Primrose

(*Primula officinalis, P. veris,* and *P. grandiflora;* French, *Primavère;* German, *Schlusselblume*) A springtime plant widespread in central and northern Europe. It is also called in French *coucou, primule, oreille d'ours.* Its leaves are eaten in salad or cooked like cress. Its flowers are yellow, rarely violet. They may decorate a lettuce or beet salad. The root of the primrose has a taste, *sui generis,* like anise and clove. It was formerly used to flavor hydromel and some Nordic beers. (*See* FLOWERS.)

Prune

(*Prunus domestica;* French, *Pruneau;* German, *Gedoerrte Pflaume*)
Dried fruit of the plum tree. The prune is a healthy laxative food
that can be cooked a long while with red wine or, receiving less
obvious treatment, can accompany white meat or a fatty fish. Eel
with prunes is a rather odd Vendean specialty, and rabbit with
prunes is a succulent classic preparation.

N.B.   Prunes marinated in sugar and vinegar is a Danish delicacy
that accompanies cold meat canapés.

Pulque

The American agave, a large cactus, is improperly called aloe. It
is highly valued by the Mexicans, who, following the example of
the Aztecs, extract the milky juice and ferment it. This drink,
pulque, resembles bubbly cider at this point but is strongly alcoholic. By distillation, it is made into burning spirits called, according to the place, *tequila, mezcal, cocuy.* Tequila is drunk
according to ancestral tradition. A *camión* (a small glass filled with
alcohol) is held in one hand; in the other a small piece of lemon
with a pinch of salt in the palm. After dipping one's lips in the
tequila, one bites the lemon and licks the salt. Finally, the whole
glassful of tequila is swallowed once!

USES: *Pulque is often mixed with pieces of fruit,* chorizo, *or ham before
being consumed. Reciprocally, many Mexican sauces are rounded out by agave
must, that may be fermented or not. These preparations are close to those we
describe under the word chicha.* Tequila *is rarely used in Spanish-American
cooking. It is highly alcoholic, and is reserved for flaming. It is sometimes used
to flavor the Mexican version of* sangría.

Purslane

(*Portulaca oleracea;* French, *Pourpier;* German, *Portulak, Buerzelkraut*)
A plant generally wild in the South of France, rarely cultivated
under the name of *pourpier doré* or *pied de poulet.* (In America it is
known as a succulent garden weed.) Its leaves, which are rather

wide, have a spicy and refreshing taste. They are eaten like cardoon leaves, cooked in meat juice or under a leg of mutton. The
young shoots are an excellent condiment that can be perserved in
vinegar and salt or used in a salad, soup, or omelette. Purslane
used to be mixed with other aromatic herbs, particularly cress and
burnet. It can also be used in sauces—*béarnaise* or *paloise*—or a
mixture of adventitious salad greens under its Provençal name of
bourtoulaigou. (*See* MESCLUN.)

Quetsche

A large, oblong reddish-violet plum grown in Lorraine, Alsace, and Rhineland. Its name comes from the German *Zwetschke*. It used to be written *couëtche*. Quetsches are delicious in pies and sweets. A white, highly alcoholic liqueur of the same name is extracted from them and used in many Alsatian and Baden specialities, notably pheasant with sauerkraut, and flamed *tarte*.

Quetsche should be flamed in a small pot before use in flavoring these culinary preparations at the last moment before serving.

Quince

(*Cydonia oblonga;* French, *Coing;* German, *Quitte*) The fruit of the quince tree that the ancients called *poire de Cydonie,* has strongly acid, tough pulp that lends itself to the preparation of desserts only after long cooking with sugar, as in making quince jelly, for instance. This yellow fruit can give a very sweet flavor to condiments, such as apple and quince chutney, or to the apple sauce that garnishes a grilled blood sausage—one quince for every 5 apples, says an old recipe. In Morocco, the Fassi, the old middle class of Fez, cook lamb in a closed earthenware jar, with peeled quince, cinnamon, and a spoonful of honey.

Quince seeds, very rich in natural gelatin, were sometimes used to make food gelatins. They are known for their use in preparing *bandoline,* a lotion for the hair now out of style.

Raisins

(French, *Raisins secs;* German, *Rosinen*) There are many kinds: Smyrna or Sultana, Provence, Malaga (still on the bunch), and Corinth raisins, as well as American domestic types. The most esteemed in cooking are Corinth, used to fill out and flavor stuffings, fowl loafs, etc. The Corinth raisin is a tasty jewel in exotic cooking, indispensable in the preparation of Moroccan *couscous,* *tangine* stews, and Afghanistan pilaf. The cooks from Provence do not hestitate to combine raisins with sea foods.

GRAPES are equally choice condiments. Peeled muscat grapes admirably accompany slices of *foie gras* sautéed in butter and swished with Frontignan wine. They can also be stuffed in an *ortolan* (a tiny bird), a partridge, guinea fowl, or any other fowl wrapped in vine leaves and cooked in a casserole. (*See* VINE.)

Rampion

(*Campanula rapunculus;* French, *Raiponce;* German, *Rapunzel*) A perennial plant with blue flowers along a stalk, a member of the *Campanula* family. Its name comes from *rapum,* turnip in Latin. Doctor Henri Leclerc* has praised rampion in these terms: "Gath-

* See APPENDIX.

ered in the beginning of summer, this plant is an exquisite taste symphony in which one finds the aroma of hazelnuts and the fragrance of newly-mowed lawns." Alexander Dumas mentioned that the root and the leaves of this plant were eaten in salad and that they go well with celery root and red beets. Unfortunately, it is necessary to live in the country to enjoy this delicate vegetable, for it is not grown for market.

Ras-el-Hanout

A North African spice mixture unknown under this name east of Tripoli. It is most in favor with Moroccan cooks. These three words signify, "The summit of the shop," and are synonymous with aromatic nectar. In the *souks* of the Kingdom of Jordan, a related mixture is found called *hawadj-om-schekelé* (a little of everything).

What does *ras-el-hanout* contain? Undoubtedly, it would be easier to enumerate what it doesn't. From Gabès to Agadir, its composition varies from *souk* to *souk*. It may be defined thus:

INDISPENSABLE COMPONENTS:

True cumin	20 per cent
Turmeric	15 per cent
Guinean Ginger	15 per cent
Cardamom	10 per cent
Nutmeg	10 per cent
Coriander	10 per cent
	Total: 80 per cent

OTHER INGREDIENTS: Cinnamon, grains of paradise, Sudanese red pepper, allspice, rose petals, mastic, nigella, galingale (*souchet*), marjoram, ash berries, etc.

GALANT VARIETY contains the aromatics cited above with, in addition, a little ginger, galingale (*galanga*), *yohimbehé* bark, even Spanish fly and hashish!

Moroccan *ras-el-hanout* has a musky, sumptuous, choking odor. Its Tunisian equivalent is much more mild, impregnated with musky rose petals. This spice is necessary in the stews and the broth that acccompany *couscous* and other typical North African dishes. It is terrible in Western dishes, as it corrupts the original taste. The only exceptions are mutton stews and curries. Lacking *ras-el-hanout,* its first three elements can be used as a substitute: Oriental cumin, turmeric, and ginger. Red pepper (*harissa*) is used alone.

Raventsara

(*Evodia raventsara*, according to Gaertner) A large Madagascan tree of the *Lauraceae* family whose leaves and nuts are called cinnamon clove (*cannelle-giroflée*). After the leaves have been boiled, they are threaded on a string and dried in the sun. The angular, oily nuts are dried for a long time on wattles. This exotic spice is very worthy. Its aroma is like a mixture of cinnamon and cloves, with the cloves dominating. Unfortunately, its taste is a little acrid, which is why it is rarely exported. The Malagasy use it extensively, notably in *zebu,* or squirrel stews.

Red Peppers

(*See* PEPPERS, RED.)

Resin

The gums and resin obtained by the exudation of vegetable tissues have no nitrogen and are nearly worthless as food. They were, on the other hand, highly appreciated by the ancients and Eastern people as condiments. *Laserpitium* and the *Silphium* of the Romans, benzoin and styrax balm and finally opoponax were extracted from many *Umbelliferae* or *Styracaceae*. Highly scented, indeed fetid, these gums were used in stews as well as in electuary and cosmetic preparations. Today, in the Sahara, nomads still use the resins of the *Thapsia silphium,* an African *Umbelliferae,* to season fibrous camel or donkey meat. (*See* ASSAFOETIDA, BALM, BENZOIN, *and* SILPHIUM.)

Senegal gum, taken from tropical acacias, and tragacanth, coming from one of the Armenian *Papillionaceae,* are valued in pharmacy for making cough drops. Tragacanth is sometimes used by pastry cooks to stabilize whipped cream. In Greece, pine resin formerly was used to disinfect white wine musts. It has become, little by little, an aroma appreciated in the famous *retsina* wine that seasons the fried dish of little fish, or *marida,* served in all the Athens taverns. In the same region of the globe, lentisk resin, or *mastika,* perks up anisette and many condiments.

Nor can we forget, having mentioned a word close to masticate, the chicle gum of Central America, which is the base of chewing gum.

Resinous woods, juniper and fir, are often used to smoke sausages, even cheese. Finally. maple syrup, which is sweet and very sugary, is the product of an important industry in Canada and the United States.

Rhubarb

(*Rheum rhaponticum;* French, *Rhubarbe;* German, *Rhabarber*) A comestible plant native to Turkey, introduced to Europe by the Magyars, its leaves can be prepared like sorrel. The young shoots are sometimes eaten like asparagus. But it is the ribs and the flower stalks, used in making compotes and English rhubarb pies, that make rhubarb valuable.

The juice of the rhubarb contains oxalic acid, which means that the plant requires a quantity of sugar in cooking and serving. It cannot be used in salads, figuring at most in some versions of chutney and sour-sweet Anglo-Saxon condiments. The Poles and the Slavs sometimes use it in their acid soups. The Chinese use rhubarb to color and flavor some spirits.

Robinia

(*Robinia pseudoacacia;* French, *Acacia;* German, *Falsche Akazie*) The white acacia, or robinia, is a European tree that bears abundant bunches of white perfumed flowers in June. It should not be confused with the *Cytisus,* which flowers a little earlier; its yellow flowers are toxic.

Today the robinia flowers are used in fritters. Preserved in vinegar solution, they are combined with melon and banana in making some sweet pickle sauces in the United States. Some lovers of artistically decorated salads embellish a finely cut lettuce salad with finely chopped acacia flowers. It is also permissible to add these corollas to the cooking liquid for young fowls, especially

216

duckling; refrain from adding other aromatics, with the exception of a lemon peel. And they may be added to English cream for a vanilla flan or a nut torte.

Rocambole

(*Allium scordoprasum*) Also called Spanish or Egyptian shallot (French, *échalote d'Espagne* or *d'Égypte*). The name rocambole comes from the German *Rockenbollen,* in other words, a distafflike bulb. Rocambole is very different from pink garlic, improperly called "red" by some merchants. (*See* PINK GARLIC.)

Its tiny red bulbs are generally sweeter than those of white or pink garlic. In Andalusia, they are eaten raw. If they have not arrived fully ripe or if they have been grown in infertile soil, their taste can be very acrid. They are then used like shallots.

Rocket

(*Brassica eruca;* French, *Roquette;* German, *Wilde Rauke;* Italian, *Rochetta*) A small plant of the *Cruciferae* family related to cress, with white or yellow flowers smelling a little of orange. It is also called *riquette* and *rouquette.* It is highly appreciated in Italy and Provence for the spicy taste of the smooth leaves that look like small daggers. They are mixed with lettuce or other adventitious salads, sometimes with cold sauces.

Roquefort

A prestigious French cheese made with mountain sheeps' milk in the Saint-Affrique region of Rouergue. Its curd is inseminated with moldy bread, pierced by sharp needles, and finally aged in natural caves or very deep cellars. Roquefort is known in the entire world and badly imitated in many countries. It is used in many ways in America.

The use of Roquefort as a condiment is far from new in France. Notably, it is used in onion and Roquefort soup, celery hearts with Roquefort, pies and *gnocchi* with Roquefort, etc. In general, Roquefort is mixed with a white cheese or *provençale*

Rosemary

brousse, before being used as stuffing or being spread on bread or celery; slightly dry Roquefort can be crumbled between the fingers.

Rosemary

(*Rosmarinus officinalis;* French, *Romarin;* German, *Rosmarin*) A shrubby Mediterranean tree with blue flowers and very fine needlelike leaves. It grows wild in Sicily and Spain, but is generally cultivated in gardens as a border plant. Rosemary is one of the aromatic foliages in the large botanical family of *Labiatae,* which is very rich in scented herbs. Its name comes from the Latin *Rosmaris,* which means "sea dew." The Greeks and Romans numbered rosemary among the sacred herbs, which did not prevent it from being used in cooking. Even before humans, bees always doted on rosemary nectar, which flavors the excellent honey from Narbonne. The entire plant contains a strong concentration of essential oils containing camphor, pinene, etc. Many hygienic preparations were made from it.

USES: *Fresh or dried, even powdered, the leaves of rosemary are an aromatic highly prized by Mediterranean cooks. It is an element in many formulas, such as compound spices and turtle herbs (which see). Italian gastronomy reserves a top spot for rosemary in roast meats, baked fish, and some tomato sauces. It can be said without exaggeration that the rosemary needles might have been created to be used in cooking all forms of veal, but it is well suited to lamb or game as well. Some vegetables like eggplant, corn on the cob, and sweet potato accept this aromatic well, with its subtle, slightly caustic flavor. Spanish-American cooking has given its name to* romeritos, *corn breads stuffed with shrimp and sea food, dusted with rosemary. In Central Europe, suckling pig is stuffed with rosemary twigs before being cooked on a spit.*

Rosemary is often found, along with thyme, in a blanquette de veau *or on pork chops. It is important to use rosemary skillfully as its aroma is pervasive, and to avoid having the needles offend the guests' palates. As for powdered rosemary, it gives a rather bitter taste to sauces and foods. Freshly gathered rosemary, cut with scissors, is preferred.*

Botany also recognizes many false rosemarys, such as marsh tea (Ledum palustre; French, lédon des marais *) whose branches and leaves are downy. It is used to perfume the famous Russian leather. Its use in cooking is not advised; marsh tea is lightly narcotic and vomitive. All the same, it is used to season some Nordic beers.*

Rose Petals

The queen of flowers is not a stranger to gastronomy. She also knows how to flatter the taste buds, and not only through the use of the rose petal jelly, so prized in the Balkan and Middle East. The petals of *Rosa damascena,* are macerated with powdered sugar, then cooked to a syrupy consistency. This rose is one of the most perfumed and has an important role in Bulgaria and elsewhere in the making of rose essence. Many Oriental sweets borrow a mellowness from both the essence and the jam.

Tunisians like roses to the point of adding rose petals to their stews and *couscous* broth. Tunisian-Jewish cuisine admires it most of all. *Chachiouard* as it is called in M. Borguiba's country, is a veritable spice that is used, pulverized, even in variations of *ras-el-hanout.* However, it is not the *Rosa damascena,* but the *Rosa moschata,* a rose with a light musky smell. In Iran, dried rose petals combined with mint leaves and sliced cucumbers season *abdough,* a summer soup served cold with milk curds.

Apicius, the Roman gourmet, about whom Seneca speaks so much, would have enjoyed these many uses. He had a stew of nightingale and other songbirds' tongues served to his guests while sprinkling them, and the food, with rose petals. (*See* COUS-COUS, SWEETBRIAR, MUSK, *and* RAS-EL-HANOUT.)

N.B. The hollyhock (*rose trémière*), whose flowers are purple, has been used to color wine for a long time. It is not of the *Rosaceae* but is one of the *Malvaceae, Althaea rosea.*

Rougail

A creole, specifically Réunion, condiment. There are eggplant rougails as well as fruit rougails, which are very close to some chutneys. The difference is that rougails are served hot. Shrimp rougail is a highly spiced paste used to give a high flavor to scrambled eggs or stuffed mussels. (*See* CRUSTACEANS.)

The rougails of Réunion are so worthy that they reveal a certain French influence on the savage gastronomy of the shores of the Indian Ocean. They can skillfully be used alongside many exotic dishes: chicken creole, fish curry, pork with bananas, etc.

Rouille

A succulent *sauce-pommade* from Provence almost as famous as *aïoli*, its first cousin, or *pistou,* a relative from Genoa. Rouille admirably accompanies a boiled fish or a fisherman's soup like *aïgo-sau* or *bourride.* It is presented in a bowl on the table; it should have the consistency of loose mayonnaise and the color of rusted metal.

Rue

(*Ruta graveolens;* French, *Rue;* German, *Raute;* Italian, *Ruta*) A wild plant, rarely domesticated, with light-green leaves and bright-yellow flowers. The acrid, subtle odor of its leaves makes them a condiment of little value. Nevertheless, an English book recommends rue for use in sandwiches. The principal merit of rue is to reinforce the aroma of some wines like *Gewüztraminer,* or white alcohols, like Italian *grappa.* The Gauls added sprigs of rue, as well as lovage and lavender, to *oleogarum,* a condiment that was thoroughly milled in stone mortars.

Rum

A spirit made from cane sugar. True rum comes from the distillation of *vésou* (fermented cane juice), while *tafia* is extracted from molasses and sugar-refinery leftovers. On leaving the still, rum is colorless, acrid-tasting, and hardly pleasant. It must be aged for a long time in oak casks before becoming white rum that is, in fact, rather yellow. Colored rum is artificially dosed with caramelized brown sugar and curious aromatic and coloring mixtures: powdered oak tan, cloves, Norwegian tar, mahogany or rotra bark, indeed even a large quantity of scrapings from new leather. This last detail comes from the *Manuel de l'Epicier.* In the Antilles, the connoisseur distinguishes *rhum d'habitant,* the product of a plantation or habitation, from *tafia d'usine,* rum distilled by large firms where molasses is exploited without mercy.

USES: *Currently rum producers and merchants make meritorious efforts to call our attention to the fact that this spirit is very useful in cooking. There is a whole range of sweets that go well with rum, such as sugar, vanilla, and chocolate in confection and pastry-making. Dessert omelettes, seasoned with rum, coated with powdered sugar and branded with a hot iron are particularly delectable. Rum is also used in the cooking of spicy foods. It is also used in many creole recipes, Antilles chicken, rack of pork with sweet potatoes, turkey with pineapple, island-style rabbit. The aroma of rum combines with fruit and vegetables of the Caribbean—red pepper, ginger, grapes, and dried almonds, even with bacon, onion, and herbs like thyme, rosemary, marjoram. It is suitable to add a wine glass of rum to these dishes at the end of cooking and to season them with some other aromatic, even if it is only lemon zest. Rum is a supporting aroma. It is not suited to flaming meats, with the exception of tender fowl. (See* CANE SUGAR, BROWN SUGAR, *and* SUGAR.*)*

Russia

Russian cuisine and, more generally, Soviet cuisine, is as unified as the empire of Nicolas II, the last czar. There is some gastronomic regionalism in the U.S.S.R., such as the barely evident Oriental tendencies in Georgia, Armenia, Turkmenistan, etc., but the foreign traveler eats the same Caucasian *chachlik* in Tiflis, Vladivostok, or Murmansk. The turbaned kolkozens of Uzbekistan, and without a doubt the last muezzins of Samarkand, eat *stchi* and bortsch, the cabbage and beet soups invented in the Nordic *isbas*, or log huts.

Moscow gastromony is no doubt much less refined than that of Leningrad. No flavor accord shocks the palate, but the preparations are often a little fat and indigestible. One princely food, *ikra* (caviar), is uniquely Russian. A prestigious collection of hors d'oeuvres, *zakouski*, is closer to the Scandinavian cold table than to the Greek-Balkan *mézés*.

Of all the white race, the Soviet citizens are the most discreet users of spices. A little pepper, a bit of North Vietnamese cinnamon, even less of cloves and nutmeg, and that is the end. The strict rationing of the five-year plans are not to blame; the Russians are attracted to the flavors of their homeland. No doubt, there is some use of rhizomes like ginger (ginseng, varieties of spikenard, etc.) in Asiatic Russia, but the secret of the Russian-Soviet cuisine lies in the judicious employment of the many national plants: dill, caraway, Hamburg parsley, lovage, bay, oak shoots, red beet, horseradish, and a condiment of animal origin, *smetana* (sour cream). (*See all the food words mentioned, as well as* BEER, GHERKINS, POPPY, KVASS, *and* VODKA.)

Safflower

(*Carthamus tinctorius;* French, *Carthame*) A plant of the *Compositae* grown in Egypt and in America. Its flowers are saffron-colored but do not smell like saffron. In the Levant, the shoots are eaten in salads or used to curdle milk. The weakly-spiced flavor is negligible, but safflower blossoms are a valued food coloring. The Arabs call them *hosfor* and use them for coloring rice pilaf, stewed tripe, etc. (*See* FOOD COLORS *and* SAFFRON.)

Saffron

(*Crocus sativus;* French, *Safran;* German, *Safran;* Italian, *Zafferano;* Arab, *Zahfaran*) A plant similar to the garden crocus, native to Asia Minor, that was introduced to Spain by the Moors. The spice taken from this plant is not a seed, a leaf, nor even a root, but a very small part of the flower, the stigma (that is, part of the pistil), extending out to receive the pollen. A costly product, as might be expected, saffron is cultivated in France, in Gatinais, Angoumois, Comtat, and in Spain, in the Teruel and Valencia regions, and finally in Italy, Greece, Iran, and Latin America.

The yellow-orange powdered saffron is easily obtainable in groceries. Sometimes it is adulterated and often may be stale. The

Saffron

brownish saffron filaments (*safran en barbes*) are preferred, gathered from the hearts of the violet-colored flowers, and simply dried on a fine sieve over a brazier. They are once again dried before being used, placed in a paper near a heat source; then they are pulverized with the fingers.

In the Levant, cultivation of saffron is very ancient. It is the *karkhom* mentioned in the Song of Solomon in the Bible (unless, as some say, it is turmeric). It formerly was used in cooking, magic and medicine. Trimalcio, a character in the *Satyricon* of Petronius, dusted the bench, where guests to his feast were reclining, with saffron to keep them drunk. Dioscorides considered it a powerful emmenagogue. The Sybarites drank an infusion of saffron as a holiday preparation. In the Middle Ages, the bristles of *Crocus sativus* were an element in elixirs, love potions, beauty products, and leather dyes. Another plant, the American *Carthamus tinctorius*, was found cheaper as a coloring material before being supplanted itself by the industrial coloring, yellow naphthol. Today, safflower, yellow naphthol and even arnica, an Alpine plant, are used to imitate powdered saffron.

The taste of saffron is bitter and curious, but it is combined with a hot, inimitable smell. A gourmet without an olfactory nerve cannot appreciate a saffroned dish.

USES: *Saffron has known both ups and downs in gastronomy. Highly appreciated until the Renaissance, it slowly declined until the nineteenth century. Dumas had a pitiful opinion of its penetrating odor. He said, "It can cause violent headaches and even death." There are several countries where this flower is used as a seasoning or to give color to vermicelli cakes or butter. With the migration of people because of World War II, summer tourism, and so on, saffron has come back in full force. Two dishes have introduced it: bouillabaisse and paella. They would not exist without it. They also indicate that the two essential uses of saffron are coloring and seasoning rice, and giving a unique touch to fish soups. Mediterranean cooks, of course, are the most skillful in manipulating this aromatic. For them, saffron is an ingredient of great mobility whose influence must be measured carefully. Too much gives a pharmaceutical taste to preparations. Often, its flavor must be supported by anise, fennel, sage, tomato, pimiento, even by pastis, crustacean sauces, etc.*

There are many other ways to use saffron. In Lebanon, it is an element in cold entrées like red mullet à l'orientale, *or squid. Mussels, white meats, tripe, noodles,* couscous, *and white beans accept a discreet presence of saffron. It is more rarely used with beef or pork; for example, in an old recipe from Périgord,* mourtayrol, *a* pot-au-feu *of short ribs, pullet, and ham, which is saffroned and reduced like a bouillabaisse.*

In all these recipes, saffron is stewed. It hardly tolerates being cooked in boiling oil or burning butter, for its molecules burst easily in the heat. Saffron is an indispensable ingredient in many liqueurs, like yellow Chartreuse, and also in some cheeses, like Parmesan.

SAFFRON BOURBON (*Safran des Indes*) Other names for turmeric, whose rhizome yields a yellow and lightly aromatic starch. (*See* TURMERIC.)

Sage

(*Salvia officinalis;* French, *Sauge;* German, *Salbei;* Italian, *Salvia*) Another cooking herb in the rich *Labiatae* family. An herbaceaous plant that looks a little like some varieties of mint. Native to Europe, sage is grown in all European countries, particularly in Italy, Yugoslavia, and Albania.

Sage is recognized by its erect blue flower spikes and its grayish, downy leaves. There are several different-sized sages, even in the variety *S. officinalis,* or garden sage. The smaller the foliage, the more sweet and aromatic it is. The botanists record wild species that have little value in cooking: *S. pratensis* (marsh sage), *S. verticillata* (lilac sage), *S. sclarea* (common clary).

The garden sage gives off a subtle, lightly-camphored odor. Its leaves should be dried in the shade because salvianin, the plant's essential oil, is volatile. They should be wiped before drying, if not washed, as the papilla of their rough surface can contain dust or tiny insects. The leaves are kept in closed jars, out of the light. Since the aroma of the sage leaf is rather pervasive, it is not an element in compound spices or in turtle herbs (which see). The wise cook mixes sage with foods at the last minute and spares it contact with a hot grill or boiling oil because the aroma of sage disperses easily. (The most delicate perfumes evaporate, the bitter smell and the camphor remain.) Sage has an unusual and delicate aroma.

The doctors of the Salerno medical school regarded sage as a miracle plant. They said: *Cur moriatur homo, cui salvia crescit in horto?* (A man cannot die if there is sage in his garden), which was answered by *Contra vim mortis non est medicamen in hortis* (It is not in the garden that it is a medication against death).

The emperor Charlemagne had earlier ordered his farmers to cultivate sage and other royal herbs. In the nineteenth century, the famous doctors Trousseau and Cazin thought sage was very useful in the treatment of liver, kidney, and nerve problems. After a short eclipse, this scented vegetable has seemed to regain the favor of the neurologist and endocrinologists. Its Latin name is a synonym for cure. In perfumery, salvianin is highly valued, notably in making mouthwashes and toothpastes. For many reasons that have nothing to do with culinary art, the *officinalis* sage used to be called *herbe sacrée, thé de Grèce, thé de France.* It was purified with quince syrup.

USES: *In the great cooking opera, sage may be compared to a touchy and capricious diva. She demands to be alone, or almost alone, on the stage. Sage is detestable in beef broth,* pot-au-feu, *consommés, etc. It combines much better with white meats and vegetable soups.*

The Italian cuisine uses sage very knowledgeably with veal (piccata, saltimbocca, *and* ossobuco) *and more rarely with pork. No other aromatic is used for these fried or roasted meats, except the white wine that is used to swish the cooking dish. In the north of Italy, sage sometimes replaces basil in the mixed* pommades *used for minestrone; in that case, it is a vegetable soup with rice, not macaroni.* (*See* PISTOU.)

The Nordics use sage with onion in stuffings for winged game, turkey, and other poultry, suckling pig, etc. They may be sweetened with a piece of sugar, elderberries, gingerbread, etc. As for beef, sage does not seem acceptable except with Provençale nougat de boeuf (*cold stew) and many beef-in-aspic preparations. The Germans favor spit-roasted ham with sage, as well as tripe with sage and some eel matelotes.*

Sage is known and appreciated in Hungary and the Balkans. A whisper of sage can be mixed with marjoram in many paprika-based preparations— veal liver, mutton kidneys, etc. The Basques use it with grilled tuna or in sauces.

Sage leaves can also be used to cover a fowl before it is roasted. They are taken from the sauce before the final thickening; the same treatment can be used for spit-roasted ham. The people of Province are past masters in the art of combining sage with a great quantity of garlic.

Sago

The pith of many kinds of tropical palms, it can be white, gray or pink. The best of the plants for flour is *Cycas revoluta*, found in Indonesia and Oceania. In South Africa, an inferior starch is made from the *Encephalartos*, the Afrikaans "broodboom" (bread tree). Tapioca, the white sago of America, comes from the manioc root (which see).

All these products, rather close to arrowroot and potato starch, are especially nourishing. Their rather indefinite taste makes them suited only for thickening sauces and exotic soups, or for sweets.

Saké, Saki

The true name is *o'saké* in Japanese, a drink with its alcohol about thirty proof. In Tokoyo, it is drunk hot as an aperitif. Its aroma is a little like very light prune spirits, such as the Yugoslavian *slivovitz*.

Saké can be used to swish a frying pan in which an Oriental food has been sautéed. It is generally proper to sugar and season it with a little soy sauce. Light, perfumed saké vinegar is used by the Japanese to preserve bamboo shoots and other vegetable condiments. (*See* SOY *and* YELLOW WINE.)

Salep

The turbercles of Asiatic orchis or the starch made from them. Iran and Turkey export salep as a yellowish powder. Since the days of antiquity, salep has been considered invigorating. The Orientals season it with ginger, amber, and musk in aphrodisiac dishes. Mixed with cocoa, sugar, and vanilla, it becomes *racahout*, a porridge for children and convalescents. In Turkey and in other Moslem countries, salep is used in sugared beverages.

The odor of salep is sometimes like sweet clover or elder flower, while its flavor is almost nonexistent. This root seduces the lovers of sweets most of all. (*See* ARROWROOT *and* SAGO.)

Salt

(French, *Sel*; German, *Salz*; Italian, *Sale*) The common name of sodium chloride is salt. Food salt may be sea salt, obtained by the evaporation of salt water in salty marshes. It also contains small quantities of mineral substances, notably sulphates, as well as traces of iodine and arsenic. Modern nutrition insists on the usefulness of these trace elements, particularly the iodine. Salt is also a mineral, and may be sold as coarse rock salt or pulverized for table and other uses.

In the matters of salt, as in aromatics, the Mediterranean peoples are long-time past masters. *Sel du Midi* (salt from the South of France) is more white, more pure, and more beautifully crystalized than the ocean salt. One of the most ancient salt routes was followed by the Phoenician merchants en route to selling their precious commodity on the shores of the Baltic. This odorless, universal condiment used to figure in many magic rites. The ancient Semites shared bread and salt with their guests. The Bedouins still have an "alliance of salt" consisting of eating a flat bread coated with salt. Salt is also sought after by herbivores: goats, cows, deer, etc. Their organisms are, in effect, saturated with potassium and deprived of sodium, which results in the salt hunger observed by cattle-raisers. The human organism requires a ration of one-eighth ounce of salt a day, but doctors impose salt-free or limited-salt diets in cases of hypertension, obesity, or cardiac trouble.

A rather widespread prejudice has it that white salt, that is, highly purified salt, is less tangy than gray or raw salt. But, although many preparations of table salt, carefully refined, have a little lime phosphate added to preserve them against humidity, this belief is an error. Gray salt that contains some traces of magnesium is not really more flavorful.

Although present in all preparations, salt is the star in brines and in meats served with coarse salt (boiled meats, etc.). Representing the sea water from which all life came, found in blood plasma, salt is an irreplaceable element in human economy. A gourmet should consider salt without preconceived ideas. Did not Grimod de la Reynière* say, "Overturned salt shakers are only dangerous if they fall in a good dish"?

* See APPENDIX.

CELERY SALT Fine salt mixed with a third quantity of dried and pulverized celery root. Indispensable in tomato juice and other vegetable juices, consommés and apéritifs; it is also very useful in flavoring many vegetables.

LOVAGE SALT Stronger than celery salt, it seasons vegetable soups and some sauces. In Germany, fine salt is prepared with dried lovage root (*Liebstöckel*).

HICKORY SALT Highly appreciated by Americans for use in barbecuing.

CHINESE SALT (*See* MONOSODIUM GLUTAMATE.)

FISH SALT (*See* NUÖC-MAM.)

PINK SALT A salty preparation reinforced with saltpeter, used by French butchers and delicatessen-makers. It is also called *saumurade*. (*See* SALTPETER *and* BRINES.)

DIET SALT substitutes for salt, partially or totally without sodium chloride, for the ill, obese, or simply diet enthusiasts. There are three categories:

Slightly salty "salt," often called vegetable salts. They contain monosodium glutamate, tricalcium phosphate, a little sodium chloride, and many aromatics. They have an agreeable taste. Unfortunately, in using them there is a tendency to push the dose and to introduce a certain quantity of sodium chloride into the foods as well.

Medical salts are radically reduced in sodium chloride. They are reserved for the sick or as a reducing cure. Their taste is spicy and very bitter as they are very much an ersatz salt. The composition is seasoned with various chlorides—calcium, potassium, ammonium—as well as monosodium glutamate.

Monosodium glutamate (which see) is certainly the best of all salt substitutes.

Saltpeter

(French, *Salpetre;* German, *Salpeter;* Italian, *Salnitro*) The common name for potassium nitrate, also called *azotate de potasse*, etc. Today, it is industrially made, resulting in small, white, odorless crystals with a fresh spicy flavor. It used to be obtained by scraping and washing the walls of cellars, storerooms, and stables. Gunpowder is made of six parts saltpeter, one part sulphur, and one part activated charcoal.

USES: *In the food industry saltpeter is a preservative. One pound of butter is preserved by mixing into it 1 ounce of powdered sugar, one-half ounce of fine salt, and one-quarter ounce of saltpeter (a formula in favor with sailors over the last century). But it is most often used by delicatessen-makers to give a pleasant pink tint to salted meats, very often, employing colored saltpeter —called pink salt—tinted with dyer's moss. It should be used with discretion, as it hardens animal flesh.*

Saltwort

(*Salicornia herbacea*) A fleshy plant whose leaves remain in bud state, that grows in seaside dunes. Because of its salty, spicy taste, it formerly was prepared like gherkins. In Provence a related plant, samphire, is preferred (which see).

Sambal

This most popular Indonesian condiment is a red sauce, often pasty, containing very strong red pepper and grated onion, and possibly sliced green lemon, with a little oil and vinegar added. Sambal is useful in the gastronomy of a hot, humid country such as Borneo as it helps the gourmet to combat the debilitating monsoon. It is served with marinated octopus, buffalo rumen, or aged boar, with rainbow-colored fish, etc. The capsaicin contained in the red pepper disinfects meats spoiled by microbes and molds, but sambal also annihilates the taste of the foods. In Vietnam, there is an equivalent, *tuon-hot.* By extension, many dishes seasoned with this incendiary condiment are called sambal.

Samphire

(*Crithmum maritimum;* French, *Christe-Marine*; German, *Meerfenchel*) It is also called in French *casse-pierres, perce-pierres, fenouil marin, bacile.* A fleshy plant, almost without leaves, that grows on embankments by the sea, the rocks of coves in Provence, and in all salty soils.

The shoots of this member of the *Umbelliferae* have a very delicate taste of both iodine and anise. They are used as a country condiment. In Provence, it is preserved with pickles and capers in vinegar. It can also be used in stuffings and cold sauces. Saltwort and sea kale are similar, and lend themselves to the same uses.

Sandalwood

(French, *Santal*) Sandalwood, heavy, rotproof, and strongly scented, has been used mostly in perfumery and therapeutics. Yet, it sometimes has a modest role in Asiatic cooking. (*See* WOOD FIRES.)

Savory

(*Satureia;* French, *Sarriette;* German, *Bohnenkraut, Pfefferkraut;* Italian, *Santoreggia*) This name designates several rather close varieties of the aromatic *Labiatae.* It comes from the Latin *satyrus,* undoubtedly because of the aphrodisiac virtues formerly attributed to this kind of plant. It is also called *sauriette, sadrée, savourée, savorée,* and *herbe de Saint-Julien.* The savories are plants somewhat like thyme and of southern origin.

SAVORY *(Satureia hortensis;* French, *Sarriette commune)* is a small annual plant with dull, ashy-green leaves, a little more elongated than those of thyme. Its flowers are pink or lilac.

WINTER SAVORY (*Satureia montana*; French, *Sarriette de montagne*) is woody and perennial. Its leaves are somewhat more elongated, lanceolate, and stiff. Its flowers are white or pinkish and are grouped in terminal bunches. Its seeds and plants are obtainable at the nurseryman's. This plant is especially appreciated in Provence where it is called *pèbre d'ai, pèbre d'asa,* that is, "ass's pepper." There are many varieties of this savory: *S. thymbra* that grows around Thymbra, a city on the outskirts of Troy where was a celebrated temple to Apollo, and *S. capitata*, or Spanish savory, Both are very aromatic and were appreciated by ancient doctors. Two Antilles plants, *S. americana* and *S. viminea*, are equally redolent and esteemed by the natives.

In medicine, the sundry savories are considered eupeptic or, in other words, facilitate digestion. The fresh leaves, rubbed on a wasp sting, calm the pain and diminish inflammation, but their vermifuge and depurative properties are strongly disputed today. It seems very clear that with savory, like other aromatic vegetables, phytotherapy hesitates to commit itself. Nutrition was, nevertheless, invented well before the appearance of dietitians.

In groceries, garden savory has become a very common aromatic. It is sold dried or pulverized. Some mixtures known as *herbes de Provence* contain thyme, wild thyme, rosemary, and the sharp leaves of *pèbre d'ai.*

USES: *Despite what the spice merchants say, savory is infinitely better fresh than dried. (This also is the case with lemon thyme but not at all with common thyme.) The aroma of garden savory is more subtle and more delicate than that of thyme. It seasons slightly the bland seeds (salsify, lentils,* mogettes de Poitou, fèves de Séville, *chick peas, etc.) and the cellulose of vegetable fruits (tomatoes and Bell peppers).*

In addition, fresh savory is very subtle in many preparations of meat: Asturian raw ham, braised in sweet wine with savory, mint, and accompanied by new limas; veal grilled on vine-brand embers in the fashion of Var (a large pinch of fresh savory added in mid-cooking), roast rabbit, or rack of pork. Fresh savory is better than rosemary and thyme together, and mixes with basil and chervil more skillfully than they do, notably in that vegetable cocktail known as turtle herbs (which see). It is incomparable in omelettes and ramekins with broccio, or any other goat cheese.

Winter savory, or pèbre d'ai, has a more caustic, resinous flavor. It figures in a marinade, in barbecue aromatics, if necessary, in cooking a civet *or young boar, a* cassoulet *or* provençale panisses *(flat cakes of flour and chick peas). Dried and powdered savory can certainly give some personality to canned French peas, cucumber salad or snow peas.*

It also can be used in a number of other preparations, with acceptable results: fish soup, mutton stew, fresh sauerkraut, fried chicken livers, etc. Once dried this aromatic herb progressively loses its virtues. Some English cooks add dried savory leaves to the breadcrumbs used for meat and fish. (See also COMPOUND SPICES.*)*

Seasoning

A word that means both the adding of some substances to a culinary preparation and also the mixture of these ingredients. Dictionaries stipulate that "seasonings aid digestion by stimulating the appetite." The seasonings are variously salty, acid, bitter, or aromatic. Some purists among food writers have pronounced that there is only one true seasoning—salt.

We prefer to say that there are a thousand ways of seasoning and almost the same number of substances suited to this use, from the corolla of flowers to fermented fish. Seasoning is a difficult and typically French art. Dumas, in his *Grand Dictionnaire de Cuisine*, reports an encouraging example, that of the Knight of Albignac, a French noble who lived in London on the meager resources accorded by His Majesty to exiled royalists. Having to earn some money, he became the salad seasoner of the gentry. He went about in his private carriage with a servant carrying a chest with all the various oils, vinegars, and aromatics that made him a success. When conditions improved, d'Albignac returned to France with a small fortune. He finished his days in gentlemanly existence in Limousin.(*See* DRESSING.)

Sedum

(*Sedum album;* French, *Tripe-madame;* German, *Fetthenne*) The ancient and culinary name of white archangel or small white sedum (*orpin blanc* or *petite joubarbe*). This is one of the *Crassulaceae* with large yellow flowers that grows on old walls and roofs. The Germans also called it "wall pepper." Its small fleshy leaves were called mouse breasts! Sedum can be enjoyed in salads and the people of Northern Europe use it in cooking fatty fish.

Sesame

(*Sesamum indicum;* French, *Sesame;* German, *Sesam*) An oily member of the *Pedaliaceae* highly valued in the Levant and the Far East. It is called *chi-ma-tsé* in China, *béné* in Western Africa, and *ajindjolan* in Arab countries. The word *zinzolin,* synonym of purplish-red in French, comes from this Islamic word.

Sesame oil is delicate and tasty. The Chinese cooks use it raw in a number of dishes. (*See* OILS.) The seeds from which this oil is taken are yellowish or reddish, depending on where this fluted plant grows—Formosa, India, or the Middle East. They are sold in Europe under the Indian name of *ajonjoli.* Their principal use is in Oriental confections and pastry-making, notably the famous *halva.* But they are also used as a condiment, in sesame mayonnaise or Egyptian *tahina,* or to make the Syrian *hoummous,* a condiment made of ·chick peas pounded with sesame oil. (*See* TAHINA.)

Several elements extracted from sesame can be used to color margarine yellow, and to make the Japanese spiced salt *goma-510* that contains grilled sesame seeds mixed with monosodium glutamate and salt, a very agreeable condiment favored by dietitians.

Shallot

(*Allium ascalonicum;* French, *Echalote;* German, *Schalotte;* Italian, *Cipollina* and *Scalogno*) A bulb that takes its name from Ascalon, a city of ancient Palestine and is related to garlic and onion. Like them, shallot is native to the steppes of Turkestan and was introduced by Levantine cooks.

Its taste and smell are more cheery than that of other onions. The shallot is without acridity, and seems to be well tolerated by fragile stomachs. French cooks particularly appreciate it; they give it noble credentials with three famous preparations: *sauce Bercy, sauce béarnaise*, and the incomparable butter sauce. The raw shallot is superior to the onion in *steak tartare* and in salads.

A wise gastronome prefers the gray shallot with its small bulb and sad covering. Its aroma is incomparably finer than that of the full and ruddy shallot-onion called Jersey shallot. The gray shallot is rather rare in the French markets, because it does not pay as well for the market gardener and is harder to keep. It is a vigorous condiment, incomparable in wine sauces.

In Poitou, *bouilliture d'anguilles,* a sort of eel stew, is prepared with red Foye-Montjault wine, thirty or so cloves of garlic and as many shallots (added during the last hour of cooking). The Chinese and Vietnamese dote on shallots in vinegar. They are sometimes used with foods that are not at all exotic. Look for them in Oriental food shops.

N.B. *Echalote d'Espagne* is rocambole (which see).

Sherry

(French, *Xeres;* Spanish, *Jerez*) The king of wines of Andalusia. A dessert or aperitif wine, according to the type. It is subject, like champagne, to much adulteration and dilution. Sherry for the English market (they drink five million bottles a year) is golden color, dry, and fruity.

USES: *In cooking, sherry and its cousin manzanilla, are used like Madeira and port. But very dry sherry goes better than the sweet Portuguese wines with fish and crustaceans. Often it is cut with whiskey, Cognac, or kirsch. Some of the surplus of sherry and manzanilla is made into vinegar of the first order. It is an element in a number of American recipes, notably in one of the best, chicken à la king. The expatriated Chinese in the West enjoy sherry, as it recalls some of their rice alcohols. (See* YELLOW WINE.)

Silphion, Silphium

A resinous condiment highly prized by the ancients, sold at a very high price in the old Roman markets. All we know today is that silphium came from Cyrenaica and was extracted from one of the *Umbelliferae.* At the end of the last century a special envoy of the Paris Museum of Natural History, M. Jules Daveau, searched all over North Africa for this aromatic plant. He found nothing except certain other *Umbelliferae* used as condiments by the Bedouins and Touaregs—Linnaeus' *Thapsia garganica* or bastard turpeth, *Ferula narthex,* etc. It can be assumed it was an Oriental ferula, rather close to asafoetida, but with a less repulsive smell. (*See* ASAFOETIDA *and* RESIN.)

Smallage

(French, *Ache*) A name given to many comestible *Umbelliferae. Ache odorante* is nothing other than wild or domestic celery, while *ache de montagne* is lovage. (*See* CELERY *and* LOVAGE.)

Smetana

A Russian word synonymous with sour cream, in French cooking books it is sometimes written *smitane.* The Germans also like this lactic condiment, which they call *Sauerrahm.*

Sour cream should never be overheated. It is used with bortsch, *stchi* and other Moscow soups. It can also thicken a pepper or mustard sauce in a hot utensil removed from the fire. In Hungary, it simply caps the paprika preparations as they are presented on the table. In Rumania, it is very agreeable in the peasant *pot-au-feu* that contains veal, sweet pepper, and lovage stems. The composition of sour cream varies from one region to the other. Mildly acidulated double cream from the Polish Carpathian Mountains is nothing more than a mixture of buttermilk and top cream in the north of Russia and Scandinavia. It is prepared simply by diluting cream with a little lemon juice and seasoning it with ground pepper or even grated horseradish. It can also be thickened with a tiny bit of flour or starch (Scandinavian, *flötesaus*). Smetana is all the more pleasant as it leaves it up to the guests to entertain themselves by stirring up the contents of their plates. Besides, it is very digestible.

Smeun

Also written *Smênn,* this is a North African word meaning preserved butter. It corresponds to the Egyptian *sâmna* (fat), but is different from *tassemt,* the Algerian mutton fat.

Called "odious rancid butter" by European travelers who do not understand anything of North African cooking, which is older than the French, *smeun* is a fat of great originality. Like many other culinary specialties, it has economic necessity behind it: preserving the fatty part of milk in a region consumed by the sun. A close relative of the Indian cook's *ghi,* it is made of ewe's butter, more rarely cow's, melted, clarified, mixed with a little salt and semolina, and preserved in jars of earthenware or stoneware. In a Moroccan *diffa* it is considered chic to serve *couscous* buttered with seven-year-old *smeun.* Seventy-seven-year-old *smeun* is a gastronomic delicacy analogous to what a Cognac of the same age is for us. (The number seven plays a magic role for the Moroccans. The best *couscous* is the 777—seven meats, seven vegetables, seven spices.) On aging, this butter cures, taking on a flavor a little like almond butter.

NOTE: Clarified salt butter, seasoned with a whisper of saffron or a drop of orange water, can be used as a substitute for seventy-seven-year-old *smeun* with North African foods.

Smoke

Originally, smoking was the process of drying and conserving domestic game, fish, etc. It had a single aim—to allow meats and protein-rich foods to be stored. By chance, the very particular taste of some products aromatized by the combustion gases became a gastronomic delicacy.

In our time of large cold rooms and industrial canners, only a few foods of this type are still offered to the consumer. The situation can be summed up by saying that smoked salmon is a luxury food, while the pemmican dear to old explorers does not have a chance of finding a taker any more. In the article on Wood fires, we discuss which plant materials lend themselves to cooking on a grill as well as to smoking. Smoking is highly appreciated by Chinese cooks; they slowly "ripen" chickens, ducks, and vegetables over little braziers, burning little cinnamon branches, fennel, bay, brown sugar, poplar sawdust, etc. Spanish *chorizo* is smoked with juniper wood, but it is still necessary to find it or to prepare raw *chorizo*! In Sicily, and on other Mediterranean shores, ewe's milk cheeses like *cacio-cavallo* are smoked. In Scotland, salt haddock is smoked over a fire of marine algae.

Finally, for the information of smoked-fish lovers, amusing utensils for quickly smoking a trout or a quarter eel are found in the fishing supply stores. The appropriate sawdust is also sold by the same merchants sometimes.

Sorb (Service-tree)

(*Sorbus domestica;* French, *Sorbier;* German, *Eberesche*) Domestic sorb (*sorbier domestique* or *cormier*), is hardly cultivated any more, but grows wild on the slopes of southern Europe. Its flowers are small, white, and grouped in thick bouquets. In October, they become bunches of small, bright-red fruits. These sorbs have an acid flavor if they are not ripened on straw like medlars.

Sorb wine (*vin de cormiers*) was highly appreciated by our ancestors. It is still made in some eastern regions of France. Finer than cider or perry, but a little heady, it was also distilled.

In Alsace, Germany, and Slavic countries the must taken from the mountain ash (*S. aucuparia;* German, *Vogelbeerbaum;* French, *Sorbier des oiseleurs*) is directly distilled. Its red fruits are very acrid and astringent, but mountain ash spirit has a delicate flavor (*sui generis*). It is 100 per cent proof and, as we know, the lecherous and greedy Russian monk Rasputin doted on it.

Russian cuisine uses sorb spirits in fish stuffings and pastries. The Poles and Germans occasionally use it in cooking eel and crayfish. Its rather odd aroma goes very well with caraway, dill, fennel, and paprika.

Sorrel

(*Rumex acetosa;* French, *Oseille;* German, *Sauerampfer*) A common European plant, cultivated only since the Middle Ages, its more or less wide, blond leaves are appreciated as a garnish. There are several species; notably common sorrel, and patience dock (*oseille-épinard*).

Braised, that is, melted in butter, passed through a sieve, and thickened with heavy cream or egg yolks, sorrel seasons soups, and vegetables like the strawberry-spinach, or spinach. Vegetable fritters seasoned with sorrel (*farcidures*) are prepared in Limousin. The acid flavor of sorrel is due to the presence of oxalic acid.

Sorrel is rarely found among *fines herbes.* Lightly blanched, dried, then chopped fine, it can season a mustard and vinegar sauce. The water in which it was cooked can be enriched with lemon juice and take the place of sourish water for Balkan soups. (*See* BORTSCH.) Sorrel, to sum up, is an aromatic herb that should be used more often than it is.

Sour Cherry

(*Prunus cerasus;* French, *Griotte;* German, *Weichselkirsche*) Botanists distinguish the wild cherries (heart cherries and bigaroons) from the true cherries (among them the sour cherry or the English cherry). Borne by a very short stem, the sour cherry is characterized by a more or less acid taste. The red sour cherry from the Vosges and the Italian *marasque*, which is made into the famous maraschino liqueur, are the most valued kinds.

The sourish pulp of the sour cherry can be treated like the bilberry and used as a condiment. The leaves of the sour cherry tree, which are smaller and darker than those of the wild cherry, are lightly aromatic. In the Ukraine and the Balkans, they are used to season some sourish preparations, notably bortsch water and pickle marinades. (*See* BORTSCH *and* CHERRY.)

Sour Grape (Juice)

(French, *Verjus;* German, *Sauertraube, Agrest;* Italian, *Uva Agra, Agresto*) The acid juice extracted from green grapes or badly ripened grapes, makes an unfermented wine, kept from fermenting with coarse salt or vinegar, that used to be known under the name of *verjus en topette* (literally, sour grape juice in phial). Sour grape juice, almost unobtainable today, was used to moisten sauces. It has a spicy taste, a much more agreeable flavor than vinegar, and seasons green walnuts with salt, (*See* NUTS), *cèpes à la bordelaise,* etc. In salads, it combines very happily with chervil and chive. The makers of Dijon-style mustard still use it. This condiment, little used today, was already known to the Romans as *defrutum.* The botanists say *Uvae acerbae succus.* Very appropriately, *verjus* can be replaced by dry white wine with a little lemon juice.

The *verjus* sauce or *aigret* sold in the eighteenth century by Paris grocers was an acid liquid seasoned with *fines herbes,* cress, currants, lemon, and bitter orange juice, etc., as well as *verjus.*

Soy, Soya

(*Glycine hispida soja;* French, *Soja* or *Soya;* German, *Soja;* Vietnamese, *Dau;* Japanese, *Shoyu*) A common member of the *Papilionaceae* with lilac flowers and hairy pods, containing small, brownish-green or blackish seeds. Native to Manchuria the *pois chinois,* or *haricot oléagineux* as it is called, is apparently not a very attractive food. In America and Germany, soy is used mainly as green fodder or for making cattle cake, or semisiccative oil, but the inventive Oriental made a strong point of its gastronomic insufficiency. In the Far East, twenty-nine different foods and condiments made from the soy can be counted, ranging from coffee to cheese, from ersatz ham to vermicelli. This affection for soy is due to its richness in nitrogen and the ease of its cultivation. For at least 5,000 years, it was the principal native leguminous plant. The Chinese and Japanese having no milk products, make vegetable cheeses of soy flour to take their place.

N.B.   Many other beans, notably the *Adzuki* or *Phaseolus angularis* and the *Phaseolus aureaus* are grown and used like Chinese peas.

SOY FLOUR, rather difficult to find in the West, is of minor interest. It can be used to make pastries seasoned with star anise or jujube or, with sugar or vinegar added, to thicken sauces. Its flavor is undistinguished; soy only acquires some personality after germination or fermentation, or being submitted to various treatments.

SOY CHEESE is a spongy yellow cube. It can also be bought as canned bean curd from Hong Kong. Soy cheese and patties, often reddish, have a distinct taste and can only be used with Chinese or Japanese dishes: crab sautéed in lard, and vermicelli "pilaf." The red patties, fermented for a long time with salt and barley flour are sold under the names of *Tofu, Miso*, etc.

Soy cheese can also be prepared by boiling soy beans with very little water (no salt) for a long time. When they are at the point of bursting, pour off the water, and allow the beans to ferment for a day or two. Then, sieve them and mix them with the cooking water and some top cream. The resultant gel can be cured in a cool place like a true cheese, but we doubt that this procedure will be of great interest to our readers! Soy ham, soy coffee, soy wine, soy vermicelli, bean sprout sauerkraut, are gastronomic curiosities that one rarely has the chance to enjoy in the West.

BEAN SPROUTS, on the other hand (French, *Germes de soja;* German, *Sojatriebe*), are commonly sold in Europe and America. They can be harvested in the home kitchen in the following way: buy green varieties of dried soy beans; rinse them in cold water, and spread them out regularly on a moist towel placed in the bottom of a box or basket. Cover them with another wet towel, lightly wrung out, and repeat the operation until the seeds run out. This germination apparatus should be kept in a cool place, at a moderate temperature of 60-65⁰F., for eighteen days. The top towel should be sprinkled in the morning, noon, and evening. One pound of beans gives more than 4 pounds of *giâ* (the Indochina name for bean sprouts).

The *giâ* are eaten as a salad or used as a condiment in many Chinese, Vietnamese, and Japanese foods, notably, sundry *chop suey*, sliced pork or beef with bean sprouts. These little shoots, endive-colored, should be sautéed in oil or lard for three minutes at most. Bean sprouts, blanched for a minute in boiling water, can be mixed with a Western salad, particularly lamb's lettuce, celery, raw sliced mushrooms, etc. Long boiling makes them lose their fine taste and their vitamins.

SOY SAUCE This aromatic is found on all the tables from Bangkok to Seoul, passing through Canton, Peking, and Tokyo. Its name should be *tsang-yeou* because the Chinese invented and propagandized it ten centuries ago, through the Buddhist missionaries who were adept at Nirvana and also preparing good foods.

There are infinite varieties of *shoyu, shyou, souy,* soy sauces of Hong Kong and *si-dâu* of Saigon. The Oriental gourmet knows them as do gastronomes who choose this or that mustard. With the exception of Vietnamese *tuong-bâc,* which is pure vegetable, all soy sauces are seasoned with a little distilled nuöc-mam or pounded anchovies, toasted barley, caramelized brown sugar, salt, soy, or sesame oil etc. Our preference is for the Indochinese *si-dâu* or some "growths" of Japanese *shoyu*. All the formulas for making soy sauce are theoretically secret. Nevertheless, it can be said for sure that the seeds are boiled, fermented, and macerated with the grilled, smoked, and triturated pods of the same vegetable. Also, we note the presence of monosodium glutamate, ginger, mace, clove extract, etc. in many *shoyu* recipes.

The uses of soy sauce are extremely numerous. All the blackish liquids sold in the West as meat flavors, as well as Anglo-Saxon sauces, and solidified meat extracts contain some soy sauce, which is all to the good, as this sauce has a taste that combines well with meat juice, soups, etc. All the Southeast Asian dishes, in our opinion, imply a choice between sweetness and violence. The second alternative, represented by the fiery red pepper, can only be avoided by adding soy sauce and *nuöc-mam*. The mixture of soy sauce and red pepper is not very pleasant; in fact, it is foul. Lacquered duck, according to the famous "red cooking" of the Chinese cooks, dabbed with soy, pleads in favor of temperate aromatics. Western gourmets elect soy and *nuöc-mam*. Chinese pepper, with a light taste of anise, goes very well in this hypothesis. (*See* FIVE CHINESE SPICES *and* NUOC-MAM.)

In Western cooking, a few drops of soy added parsimoniously, can, all the same, give a high flavor to a beef broth, tomato sauce, a fricassee, a *daube,* and all the stews containing turnips, celery, carrots, Jerusalem artichokes, etc. Lentils, split peas, and even the beans generally reserved for *cassoulet* are delectable when sprinkled with meat juice seasoned with a little soy sauce.

Nutritionists have been interested in the many products extracted from the *soja hispida.* The stewed soy bean is a dish particularly suited to combating anemia and malnutrition (an equal weight of soy is twice as nutritive as the bean or lentil). Fermented patties of soy and barley seeds contain proteins, vitamins, and enzymes and are very useful to the human organism. The fresh bean sprout is a recommended food for diabetics. British poultry-raisers have learned that turkeys that eat some soy are free of lesion of the aorta, which is very common among fowl. Will the Scandinavian cardiologists who have already recommended the use of linseed oil against infarctus of the myocardium soon propose the soy by-products? Heart disease is, in fact, less frequent in the Far East.

Spain

Almost as large as France, and reaching from the Atlantic to the Mediterranean, the country of Cervantes shelters a great diversity of cooking traditions. There are all sorts of fish sold marvelously fresh. (Between Cadiz and Seville, the freight cars with the catch have priority over the passenger trains!) There are fruits and vegetables of an incomparable sapidity. Mutton is excellent, even if the beef is often execrable, while game, crustaceans, perfumed herbs, and olive oil abound.

Certainly Spain is not a country of restaurateurs. Dumas, the elder, blasted its innkeepers. The *paella* of Iberian purveyors in Paris is better than that of their native colleagues in Madrid or Barcelona. The best cooks of the peninsula are hidden in kitchens of the rich middle class and nobility. It is to them that one must go to get old recipes and unequaled secrets. This is not an easy chore in Spain which, like Germany, does not have a national cuisine, but is a jigsaw puzzle of regional specialties.

If it is necessary to attempt a synthesis, let us say that from a distance pimiento and saffron (red and gold like the national flag) typify this gourmet cooking. Enormous red *gambas* (shrimp), crimson *chorizo,* dark black olives, violet eggplant, white or red garlic, and an enormous green bouquet of mint, chervil, tarragon, and bay leaves complete this symphony of aromas and colors. (*See* ROCAMBOLE, CHAYOTE, CHORIZO, INK, ESCABECHE, PIMIENTO, *and* SAFFRON.)

Spices

(French, *Épices;* German, *Spezerei;* Italian, *Spezie;* Spanish, *Ultramarinos;* and, in Swedish, *Krydda*) In the section on aromatics we have already mentioned how difficult it is to classify the many substances of vegetable origin that are used to flavor and season foods. Rather than to stir up indefinitely the semantic ink bottle, it is better to recall that the use of most of our spices goes back to the most ancient oriental civilizations. The existence of cinnamon is noted, for example, under its ancient name of *kwei* in the oldest botanical tract in the world, edited on behalf of the Chinese Emperor Shen-Nung around 2700 B.C. With the exception of red pepper, vanilla, and cacao, which are of American origin, all our common aromatics were known to Pliny the Elder, author of a voluminious Roman natural history. Nevertheless, their rarity and their price caused the Romans to remain faithful to their traditional condiment *garum,* a very spicy brine made of fish, or to let themselves be seduced by mustard, a seed harvested by the Gauls.

It was not until the eleventh century and the return of the first Crusaders that the Europeans became acquainted with spices, even the rare and mysterious ones. (Cloves often were used as charms.) Our ancestors were also immediately infatuated with the hot tastes coming from the Orient. For four centuries Gothic cuisine had a debauch of all aromatic substances. Happily the Italian Renaissance came and, through the Florentine and Sicilian cooks, tempered the culinary ardors. For about a century, French food has manifestly fallen into an opposite extreme. At the risk of displeasing the believers in conservative puritan gastronomy, we rejoice on seeing the return of spiced meats in force. Tired of proper white sauces and vegetable broths inspired by hospital cooking, our contemporaries enthusiastically welcome Mediterranean and exotic specialties, like *paella, couscous,* pizza, and the spicy barbecue sauce. Saffron, *ras-el-hanout,* marjoram, and chili, to mention only a few, are beginning to appear on the shelves of the good groceries of the towns as well as in cities in this country.

Star Anise

(French, *Badiane;* German, *Sternanis*) Star anise is a small exotic tree related to magnolia, called *Illicium anisatum* by Linnaeus. Its fruit, also known as *anise étoilé, anis de Chine, semence de Zinghi,* is made of eight or twelve capsules joined in a star. It is easy to recognize. Each capsule encloses a brownish seed with a taste like green anise seeds, but a little stronger and more spicy.

The biggest consumers of star anise in the world are the Swedes, who dote on anise bread, and the Germans, who use it in their marmalades and all sorts of biscuits and pastries. Star anise is most used for making pastis and anisette liqueurs in France. In China, star anise discreetly flavors certain tea mixes, and is an element in mixtures of pulverized spices. (*See* ANISE.)

Strawberry Tree

(French, *Arbousier*) Name given to twenty or so species of shrubs and bushes, the most common being the *Arbutus unedo.* Another variety is the bearberry or bear-grape (*busserolle* or *raisin d'ours*) that grows in the mountains and is used by the herbalist. Its reddish fruits look like strawberries, but are sourish. They are made into many liqueurs and excellent vinegars. Arabs and Chinese value strawberry tree fruit jams.

Sugar

The most discreet culinary aromatic, this is condiment-food which enters only by the back door in some spiced meats. In fact, the

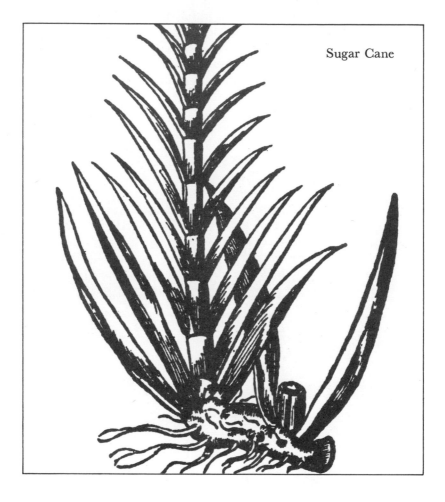

Sugar Cane

French palate demonstrates an extreme sensitivity, sometimes exaggerated, to sweet sauces or seasonings. Without a doubt, it is a reaction against the abuses of sweet or sweet-sour flavors that discredit some foreign foods. Is there a globetrotting gourmet who has not felt his heart jump before a Danish, or Scandinavian, or simply Germanic lettuce surrounded by a sugared vinegar sauce? Similar excesses are almost always present in cold countries where the organism requires a great number of calories. The use of sugar in Chinese or North African foods is much more skillful and worthy.

To proscribe sugar totally from spiced food would be a contrary and unpardonable excess. It is found, nevertheless, that many food authors willingly forget the little spoonful of powdered sugar that *must* season an onion purée, soubise sauce, polonaise sauce, mutton stew, and many fine sauces. The use of a piece of sugar in cooking some vegetables is better known. It combats the bitterness of endives, the acidity of tomatoes, or accents the natural flavor of French peas, carrots, red beans, squash, vegetable marrows, etc. In addition, the combination of salt and sugar is found in a number of sweet dishes, sugar dough, and other pastries, but then the salt has the minor role.

A hint of powdered sugar, caramelized or not, also seasons sauces containing paprika, cinnamon, nutmeg, curry, *ras-el-hanout*, etc., very well. This bit of sugar is indispensable in preparations where hot vinegar is used, if only to replace at a moment's notice white wine or Madeira, which are naturally sugared. But, we are approaching the concept of substitution. In our opinion, the piece of sugar is itself a substitute. Nothing equals a sweet wine, the pulp of a fruit, brown sugar or honey.

Sugar Cane

(French, *Canne à sucre;* German, *Zuckerrohr*) This "sugar reed," as Voltaire called it, is a large beautiful species of the *Gramineae* widespread in all tropical countries. (*Saccharum officinarum*). It had been cultivated for a thousand years before Christ, but the ancient Egyptians and the Romans were not aware of it.

The liquid extracted from it by cold pressing is heated and precipitated with lime. It crystalizes in coolers and becomes cane sugar. In Europe, it had replaced honey, the only sweet product known till then, before being dangerously challenged by beet sugar. The food uses of cane sugar are innumerable. The fresh stem in the Antilles and all of Latin America is used in making some more or less well-known spirits; rum, *chachaca,* etc. (*See* RUM *and* SUGAR.)

Sumac

(*Rhus coriaria;* French, *Sumac;* German, *Sumach;* Arab, *Sommaqh*) A bush of the *Anacardiaceae* group growing on the stony plateaus of Asia Minor. Its leaves and berries contain active principles that have been appreciated by dyers and curriers (from which the Latin descriptive name of this plant comes) for a long time.

In the spice *souks* of the Near East, sumac is sold as a powder, or rather a coarse, brick-red sawdust, prized by Arab cooks. It is made from berries gathered a little before maturity, dried in the sun, then ground in a mortar. Their taste is very acid.

USES: *Levantine cooking uses sumac to flavor or even replace lemon juice and vinegar in many vinegar sauces. A large handful of this aromatic is soaked in water, then pressed or milled.*

Sumac is also used to color Syrian fried onions, or season a chicken stuffing. Some historians believe that the dish of lentils that Jacob gave Esau was seasoned with berries of Rhus coriaria. *This culinary combination continues in Iraq and Kurdistan.*

Sweetbrier, Dog-Brier

(*Rosa canina;* French, *Églantier;* German, *Wilder Rosenstrauch*) A wild prickly, shrubby tree. There are several species. It is also called dog rose (*rosier des chiens*). Its fruits are knowledgeably called hips *(cynorrhodons)* commonly *gratte-cul* (literally, scratch-ass).

The Beltirel Tartars prepare a tealike drink with the shoots and roots of sweetbriar. The Germans make astringent, but nevertheless tasty jams with the berries, sometimes used as a condiment with grated horseradish. These red fruits must be carefully cleaned of the seeds and stiff hairs that cover the interior. (*See* ROSE.)

Tabasco

The name of a Mexican river given to an especially hot sauce, which is prepared with the red-hot tropical American chili peppers. Tabasco should be on the table when Mexican dishes are served; also for *fondue bourguignonne* or, perhaps, when a not very tasty boiled meat is served.

Tahina, Tehine

A condiment highly valued by the Syrians and Egyptians, it is an emulsion of finely milled sesame seeds and lemon juice, seasoned with pepper, coriander, nigella, etc. Tahina is a kind of sweet, very oily, mustard that traditionally accompanies the pickled salads and grilled meats of Levantine cooking. The same seeds pounded with sugar and almonds make *halva* a delicacy enjoyed by the heroines of Pierre Loti.

Mixed with chick-pea flour and fermented soy, tahina becomes a very nourishing but less delicate condiment paste. Excellent Egyptian tahina, as well as Turkish or Greek *halva* and cans of *hoummous* from Israel (guaranteed kosher), are to be found in Oriental specialty shops.

Tahina is particularly agreeable with Egyptian bean stew (*foul*), *falafel* (vegetable balls), and with fowl cooked in a fatty

broth, seasoned with Jew's mallow (*molokheia*). (*See* EGYPT, MO-
LOKHEIA, *and* SESAME.)

Tamarind

(*Tamarindus indica;* French, *Tamarin;* German, *Tamarinde*) The
tamarind is a large Asian tree also cultivated in Arabia and America. It belongs to the *Leguminosae-Caesalpiniaceae* family. Its fruit is
a 5-inch pod containing a reddish pulp and small shiny seeds.
Tamarind is also the name of the pulp or gel extracted from the
pods, which is consumed in great quantities by the Indians and
Malayans. This vegetable material is acid, slightly sugared, and
looks like a perdrigon plum, but is more heavily scented. It should
not be overused as doctors consider it a powerful laxative and
vermifuge.

USES: *Tamarinds are used in numerous Oriental condiments, British
Worcestershire sauce, many* chatnis *(chutneys), Hindu achards, Réunion*
rougails, *Indonesian macerated mango, with coconut. Turbaned cooks use
tamarind in fish brines,* chakhi, *vegetable stews, and even in fowl curries.
There are also tamarind soft drinks,* rassame *(tamarind broth), and tamarind flat cakes, an Indo-Malay specialty unobtainable in the West. In Africa,
the tamarind is less appreciated in spiced food, but it does season manioc flour
and sauces of karite butter, gombos, etc.*

*The very fruity, strongly acid aroma of the tamarind combines particu-
larly well with little green limes (Oriental lemons), ginger, grape seeds, red
pepper, and coconut meat. Dried tamarind is found in pharmacies and, more
rarely, in specialized food shops. It can always be combined with cherries,
bitter oranges, and vinegar in cooking young fowls.*

N.B. The tamarind should not be confused with the *tamarisk*, a
decorative shrub common on Meditteranean shores whose leaves
and bark are sometimes used to flavor beer. It has the Latin name
Tamarix gallica.

Tangerine

(*Citrus nobilis;* French, *Mandarine;* German, *Mandarine, Zwergapfel-
sine*) Fruit of the mandarin orange tree, a small tree native to

China. The tangerine is more flavorful than the ordinary orange and can advantageously replace it in many culinary preparations. The name *sauce maltaise* is generally given to the duckling sauce seasoned with mandarin. These fruits may also be used as an element in compound salads.

Tansy

(*Tanacetum vulgare*, French, *Tanaisie*, German, *Rainfarn*) A large composite related to mugwort, whose erect stems, finely denticulated leaves, and yellow flowers are seen on the steep banks of ponds and rivers. The entire plant gives off a subtle, aromatic, lightly camphored odor.

Also called in French *barbotine, sent-bon, larmise, remise, herbe de Saint-Marc,* tansy is a "hot purifying herb" much appreciated by medieval monks. Doctors acknowledge its vermifuge and tonic properties but in cooking, its uses are limited. The English, Flemish and Nordics have always added a little to puddings, stuffings, and pies, and roast goose can be flavored by interlarding it with tansy. It can be combined with chervil or rosemary in a fish sauce, but parsimoniously. Only a few finely chopped leaves should be used. Tansy is useful in marinades and in court-bouillons.

COSTMARY (French, *Chrysanthemum tanacetum; Tanaisie baumière*) or *costus* (Trans. note: this is not our costus) is a plant of the same family. Its oval, denticulated leaves have a sweeter smell, something like vervain, mint, and chrysanthemum. The English who import it from India use it to flavor certain beers, or fish pies. It is also called *alecost.* It would be very agreeable to use it in cooking duckling or guinea hen. Dumas knew it and prescribed it for use in some vegetable soups.

Tapenado

A Provençal sauce made of olives, anchovies, filets, and capers.

Tarragon

Tarama

(*See* POUTARGUE.)

Tarragon

(*Artemisia dracunculus;* French, *Estragon;* German, *Estragon*) An herb related to mugwort, native to Central Asia, introduced to Spain by the Moors as *tharkoum.* This word became *dragon* in French, *estragon,* and commonly *serpentine.* The Italians call it *serpentaria.* Tarragon's small lanceolate leaves are supported in tufts by branches. The variety called Russian tarragon has a lighter foliage and is more spicy.

Unknown to the ancients, in the sixteenth and seventeenth centuries, tarragon definitely conquered French cooking and became inseparable from many condiments. Nutritionists and gastronomes are agreed in recommending its use "for dyspeptics, suitable to a salt free diet." (Doctor Leon Binet.*) The essential oil it contains, *estragole,* is powerfully aromatic, appetite-stimulating, and without irritant effects.

USES: *An aristocratic component of the famous* fines herbs, *the flavoring of good vinegars, tarragon is the star in a number of excellent dishes. It particularly embellishes the cooking of young roosters. It is present in the most delicate cold sauces: gribiche, raviogote, tartre, vincent. A bravura use is in hot béarnaise sauce. This very interesting herb facilitates the most bold cooking experiments; grilled blood sausage with tarragon, young hare with mustard and tarragon, cold consommés with tarragon. Like all the plants of the genus* Artemisa, *tarragon tolerates drying and keeps its aroma even when powdered. It can also be blanched in boiling water, or browned over a flame, before being added to a stuffing or sauce.*

To have tarragon on hand during the winter, wash and clean a bunch in summer; remove all yellow leaves. Then blanch it for one minute, rinse under the faucet, and put it in a bottle of cold salt water (2 ounces of salt to 1 quart of water). Carefully close the bottle and place it in boiling water for three minutes. Cool it and store for future use.

* See APPENDIX.

Tea

(*Thea sinensis;* French, *Thé*; German, *Tee;* Chinese, *Tcha;* Russian, Turkish, and Arabic, *Tchai*) A tree quite closely related to the camelia, native to Assam, that is grown in Asia in rows, pruned to shrubs of four and a half feet. Its flowers are white and scented, but its oval, shiny leaves do not acquire their fine properties until dried. Tea has been known to the Chinese since 2757 B.C., and to the Japanese since 805 A.D., in Europe since 1636.

Chemical analysis reveals a strong concentration of *theine,* an alkaloid very similar to caffeine, tannin, and other aromatic and coloring substances. Green teas (Chinese, *tsing-tcha*), whose fresh leaves dry rapidly in the sun, is distinguished from black tea (Chinese, *hong-tcha,* which actually means red tea.) Black tea leaves are gathered when a little wilted, then boiled or macerated, and rolled by hand. There are many qualities of tea: Souchong, orange pekoe, mandarin, and Darjeeling—but their discussion is beyond this book's scope.

In the Far East, tea is the common beverage served during meals; and it is a digestive in North Africa. It is very often seasoned with jasmine petals, rose lotus, chrysanthemum, rose, orange (or orange water), even mint leaves, lemon peel, or star anise. It can also be smoked, combined with many vegetable aromatics, and even detheinated in Western factories. Tea flowers, the buds of the *Thea sinensis,* are made into a soothing beverage deprived of the exciting elements contained in tea.

In cooking, tea is rarely used as an aromatic. Tibetans make their flat flour cakes, *tsamba,* with butter, salt, and curdled milk, moistening them with tea. The Chinese use tea in the delicate smoking processes for fowl or crustaceans and crackers, and in France tea is used in ice cream and sherbet. The acrid taste of tea, coming from the tannin it contains, prevents its being used in formal cooking.

Tenderizer (For Meats)

(French, *Attendrisseur;* German, *Fleischmürbmacher)* A product, apparently inoffensive, that can replace salt in seasoning meats to be grilled while softening them at the same time. Through many soluble elements (calcium, sterates, papaine, etc.), it causes the

slackening of animal fibers. There are both neutral tasting tender-
izers and others more or less spicy.

Tequila

Mexican alcohol made from agave. (*See* PULQUE.)

Thyme

(*Thymus vulgaris;* French, *Thym;* German, *Thymian;* Italian, *Timo;*
North African and Arabic, *Alkil*) In the countryside of France, it
is called *pote,* because of its obligatory presence in *pot-au-feu.* The
people of Provence say *farigoule* (wild thyme is *farigoulette* there),
an herbaceous perennial plant with pink or sometimes whitish
flowers, which is generally cultivated. Garden thyme and wild
thyme (*serpolet*) are close cousins, like La Fontaine's city rat and
country rat. For a long time, it has been noticed that cultivated
thyme, developed by generations of gardeners, is much more
aromatic than its country or mountain relative that is, without
doubt, a Sicilian or Cretan variety that has had to propagate itself.
The ancient Egyptians and Greeks knew thyme and used it for
cooking and medicinal purposes.

Lemon thyme is another variety sold as plants by nurserymen.
Native to North America, it is called wild Canadian thyme (French,
Serpolet canadien), *Thymus serpyllum canadense* or *citriodora*. It is gener-
ally used fresh, finely chopped, in salads and fish cooking.

For ages, thyme was esteemed as a digestive tonic and a capillary salve because it contains a great deal of thymol, an ether close
to camphor. It is still a powerful antiseptic that preserves marinades from bacterial growth. Phytotherapy considers it the best
medicine for head colds (in infusions or inhalations).

USES: *In cooking, thyme is a fundamental aromatic. Some foreign authors
have named it the secret of French gastronomy. It is present, in fact, in most
meat broths and sauces of French cooking, whether alone or tied in a bouquet
garni with bay and parsley. It seasons* pot-au-feu, potée aux choux,
cassoulet, *many* civets, boeuf bourguignon, daube provençale, *fish
stews and innumerable other preparations. Thyme loses very little of its
properties in drying; it has more or less acridity depending on whether the*

flower tops are included or only the leaves are used. Winter thyme, more common in the markets, has more camphor than summer, or common, thyme. Thyme should be washed under the faucet after being gathered for, like wild thyme, it always has particles of dirt on its stem. Sprigs of thyme should be tied in a cloth bag and removed at the end of cooking.

Thyme also lends itself to many other dishes: scrambled eggs, omelettes, salads, tomato sauce, stewed lentils, etc., but at risk of being critized, we prefer other aromatic herbs in those cases: basil, marjoram, savory, etc. The great value of thyme is that it is always available, but why abuse it? The systematic use of a bouquet garni or a sprig of thyme day after day, in very different preparations, ends by boring the diner. Our spice shelves are too rich in aromatics for us to accept the concept of panaceas. The traditional domain of thyme should be shared by lemon thyme, marjoram, and savory. (See WILD THYME.)

N.B. *Thyme de Crète*, mentioned in old books, is garden savory.

Tomato

(*Solanum lycopersicon;* French, *Tomate;* German, *Tomate;* Italian, *Pomo d'oro*) An annual plant of the same family (*Solanaceae*) as the eggplant and the potato, it was originally imported from Mexico by Spanish sailors. It is queen of the cuisine in the Mediterranean countries. The primitive name of love apple or golden apple has stood in some foreign languages, but the Aztec word *tomatil* has prevailed.

One can hardly imagine what the Italian cuisine was without this precious condiment before the sixteenth century. Today, it is inseparable from macaroni- and spaghetti-cooking (another innovation in Italian gastronomy due to a Chinese influence). Whether it is cherry-red or yellowish, pear-shaped, or stiff-stemmed, the tomato is an element in non-Mediterranean preparations, too, among them Russian bortsch and Hungarian goulash. Its aromatic, slightly acid taste has always required the presence of meat juices and other vegetable aromatics. In Provence, where they are past masters in those things that concern love apples, it is always dipped in boiling water for a few seconds before being peeled and seeded, even if only for a simple salade niçoise. The Anglo-Saxons add sugar, soy sauce, and vinegar to make tomato ketchup. Although it is present in almost all brown sauces, tomato is especially associated with two southern sauces: *provençale* and *bolognaise.*

Tonka Bean

(*Coumarouna odorata;* French, *Fève Tonka;* German, *Tonkabohne*) The nut of a fruit of a large tropical Asian tree similar to the apricot, these "beans" contain coumarin, the scented element used by liqueur-makers, American cigarette makers, and Hindu cooks. The same sweetish, lightly vanilla odor is found in woodruff and fenugreek. (*See* COUMARIN.)

Truffle

(*Tuber cibarium;* French, *Truffe;* German, *Truffel;* Italian, *Tartufo;* Spanish, *Criadilla de terra*) Although they were the "diamond of cooking" of Brillat-Savarin, and "pearl of Périgord" on some menus, for the naturalist Pliny, truffles were the "scum of the earth." The most famous edible mushroom is certainly a plant of the *Ascomycetes* order, but it is a very curious one. It has neither stem nor roots and for a long time was thought to be a mineral concentration. Its musky perfume is like that of ambergris, an animal secretion.

Black truffles, the best of all, are most often found in France (Périgord, Quercy, Dauphine), but can also be found in Italy (Umbria, Tuscany), and Spain (Aragon). The white truffle (*Tuber griseum*), rare in France, is common in Piedmont, notably in the Mondovia region. Its flavor is something like garlic. The snow-white truffle (*terfez* for Moroccans) grows in the Atlas forest, particularly at Sidi-Yahia near Rabat. Unfortunately it is not very fragrant.

Despite many tries, the truffle has not yet been cultivated. In winter, long searches are necessary. Harnessed pigs on leashes, free-roaming dogs, and even goats find truffles at the foot of green oak, chestnut and hazelnut trees. In Périgord, the thickets of truffle oaks are called *raysses.* In Sarlat, the world capital of the truffle, the price of this mushroom is quoted like one of the most famous stock shares. It is presently worth more than sixty dollars a pound. The peelings and trimmings, canned and sold, cost half as much.

Known to the Etruscans and Romans, truffles used to be washed in white wine and cooked on hot coals. An antique text, attributed to Apicius, *De obsonus et condimentis,* has a recipe for truffles with honey, skirret (an Orental herb similar to caraway with edible roots), and meat juice.

Exciting and slightly indigestible, this *Ascomycete* has a gallant reputation: "Truffles stir up erotic and gluttonous memories for the fair sex and gluttonous and erotic memories for the other." (Alexander Dumas)

French cooking of the last century abused the use of truffles and *foie gras* as condiments. Today, French chefs are more judicious with these very rich foods. Some "slices" of truffle are sufficient to give great distinction to a sauce, if not to the soul of a *foie gras.* In the words of the Academy of Gastronomes, "Let's be truffle lovers, and truffle eaters, but let's beware of truffle-mania."

Forgetting about the use of the very expensive whole tubercle here are some uses for the modest truffle peels as condiments: *Poularde en deuil* or *en demi-deuil,* which is a hen with *sauce suprême,* stuffed and decorated with truffle slices. All the pâtés of white meats and winged game are proud of containing this fragrant confetti. Omelettes *à la quercinoise,* Périgueux sauce, and a number of white and brown sauces are ennobled by a few small pieces of this royal mushroom. In Italy, white truffles are inseparable from *bagna caudo alla piemontese,* a sort of melted truffle and anchovy dish, and from all the sauces named after Turin and Piedmont. Risotto with truffles is a princely meat, if the grains of rice are not stuck together in a gluey mass, as is too often the case in Italy. The white truffles go much, much better than do the black with Parmesan cheese and olive oil.

In stuffing a fowl, the truffles become more and more generous of flavor the longer they are left inside the bird. Economical cooks simply leave a chicken stuffed with truffles overnight in the refrigerator. The next day they roast it or braise the fowl, but without the truffles.

Turkey

Turks are not great gourmets. Merely going a little way into the interior of Asian Turkey confirms this. But, in the fourteenth and fifteenth centuries, these Ural-Altaic people successively occupied

Baghdad and Constantinople, the two most civilized cities of the time. The cooks of the seraglio learned both the Arabic science of aromatics and the secrets of Phanariot cooks. Turkish cooking became a mother cuisine and followed the sultan's soldiers into the Balkans and North Africa. Its influence is found from Morocco to Bessarabia, passing through Belgrade and Alexandria. Behind the Turkish names that exist more or less everywhere, a filigree of the ancient imperial Byzantine cuisine shows through. Even in Turkey, this culinary art is regional, according to the tastings of H. J. Duteil, a sociologist-gourmet, author of *Loin dans la Turquie.*

Garlic and onion, part of the heritage of Asia Minor, the tomato and the Bell pepper, which are recent acquisitions, and the eggplant, a *Solanaceae* plant native to India, are the vegetables most appreciated on the shores of the Bosphorus. Okra is an element in some soups and stews. Meat is rare, except for lamb, mutton, and fowl. Among the condiments, white cheese and yogurt have a large role. Spices are used with great discretion. Saffron heads the list, while cardamom more often seasons the famous Turkish coffee than cooked dishes. Damask rose, sesame, and calamus are used in sugared preparations such as *halva*, for the Turk, who loves the sweetness of life, also adores the sweets that aid the siesta. Turkish-Byzantine cooking has also taught us to stuff vine leaves, called *Yalantzi dolmas.* (*See* VINE LEAVES.)

Turmeric

(French, *Curcuma;* German, *Kurkuma*) A spice that has a large role in Indo-Malay cooking, it is hardly used in the West, although it has been known in Europe since the days of antiquity. It used to be called *safran bourbon* because it came from the island of that name, and *terra merita,* a curious Latin transcription of the Hindu word *turmeric.*

This very hot yellow powder, also used as the base color in pastry glazings, comes from a milled rhizome. The whole roots, or "fingers," can also be found in some Oriental food shops. This exotic saffron comes from *Curcuma tinctoria*, that is closely related to ginger. The spicy taste of ginger is found in turmeric, but it is only a slight fragrance, suffocated by a rather bland starch.

Turmeric, with its light taste of medicine, is above all a coloring spice. In any case, it can not replace true Spanish or Gâtinais

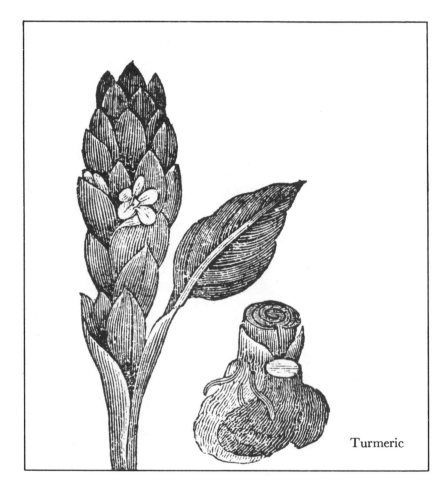

Turmeric

saffron in *paella*, bouillabaisse, etc. Its finest role is giving curry its yellowish color. It is also used in a number of English mustards and spicy sauces.

It should be considered a final-touch-spice; a little turmeric in an Oriental fish soup, in a crab pilaf, or in celery remoulade, or even in spiced compound butter. It is better not to add turmeric to a dish prepared with curry or *ras-el-hanout;* these mixtures are already carefully balanced. Turmeric should never be added to boiling oil as it blackens immediately.

Turtle Herbs

A cocktail of vegetable aromatics frequently used by restaurateurs to season turtle soup and other preparations. Below is one of the most classic of formulas:

Basil	3 parts
Marjoram	2 parts
Chervil	1 part
Savory or Thyme	2 parts
Fennel or Dill	½ part

In addition (but optional), a sprig of rosemary, one or two sage leaves, a few chopped chives, and a pinch of cayenne are often suggested.

Turtle herbs can be used not only for clear turtle soup, but oxtail as well. Infused in a half glass of aperitif wine, they are then strained out before being added. Myrtle seeds or leaves can also be added.

Urchin Roe

(French, *Corail d'oursins*) The red-orange seminal glands found in the inside of the carapace of sea urchins is a substance that, crushed with a fork and sieved, is used by Mediterranean cooks to flavor mayonnaise sauces and other fish sauces, as well as stuffings or soufflés. *Langouste* roe, although it is more delicate, lends itself to the same preparations. The Japanese export canned urchin roe to Europe; it can be used to garnish sole filets and as an element in seafood quenelles. (*See* CRUSTACEAN *and* ROUILLE.)

V

Vanilla

(*Vanilla planifolia;* french, *Vanille;* German, *Vanille*) A cosmopolitan word taken from the Spanish *vainilla* (little seed) that designates the pod of the vanilla plant. These rambling, climbing plants are a close relative of the florists' orchids that were discovered in Mexico by Cortez, who observed that the Emperor Montezuma was very fond of cocoa with vanilla. Today, vanilla is cultivated in Madagascar, Tahiti, Maurice Island, Mexico, etc. Generally, *leg* or *ley* (genuine Mexican) vanilla is distinguished from fine vanilla's long, highly scented pods, *vanille pompona bouffie* and finally *vanille simarona* or *vanillon*. This last kind, from the Antilles or India, has a less balsamous taste and is relatively more peppery. Mostly, it is used to flavor Havana cigars. Mexican vanilla is dry and reddish, but highly scented, while that of Réunion and Madagascar is black, very sweet, and has a more volatile aroma.

Vanilla sugar, sold commercially, is flavored with an aromatic aldehyde that, in principle, comes from the crystalized vanilla sap, but sometimes vanilline, an extract of allspice, is used as well. The sticks of vanilla offered by grocers are greased with cashew, coconut or castor oil, to preserve the pulp, which is more aromatic than the grains within. The fresh pod is odorless, but it is sometimes sold mixed with the flowers of *Pothos odoratissimia,* a tropical American plant. Oak seeds, which are rather fragrant, were formerly

267

used as a substitute for vanilla. Industrial vanilline has replaced the aromatic in this country.

USES: *They are innumerable for sweet dishes: ice creams, sherbets, frangipane (invented by the Marquis de Frangipani, an Italian perfume-maker who flavored ice creams, stuffings, as well as gloves and handkerchiefs with vanillaed essence of bitter almonds). Vanilla is indispensable in many aperitifs— creole punch, Spanish* sangría *etc. Vanilla seasons cocoa and chocolate in all their forms and is even found in the Mexican condiment* salsa el mole.

In spice cooking, the use of vanilla is very limited. Some Provençal recipes for fish soups or mussels call for a little vanilla. Its particularly sweet aroma can only combine well with saffron and the pulp of some fruits, like cherries. A little grated vanilla can always be added to the quatre épices *used in cooking young fowl. In Denmark, where sweet tastes are not feared, braised young rooster is garnished with a rhubarb purée seasoned with vanilla. A little grated vanilla with some orange zest can also be used, very carefully, in a stuffing for fresh-water fish, a pike quenelle, etc., but it takes great skill to manipulate this aromatic in that way.*

N.B.   *Vanille de Marseille* is the old, humorous name of garlic.

Vegetable Ashes

Our ancestors, and not only the cavemen, seasoned their foods by dusting them with vegetable ash; salt was unknown or too costly, and their organisms demanded mineral substances, as ours do. This practice has left some traces in modern gastronomy; ashes, like smoking, communicate a distinct, agreeable aroma to some foods. Who has not enjoyed the taste of potatoes simply buried and cooked in the hot coals of a hearth? Many French cheeses, like Vendôme, profit by the essence that an ashy covering transmits. In the Aegean Islands, ancient recipes for the clarification of wines with resinous ashes and sea water are still used. The Incas mixed wood ash with their corn meal.

The herbs growing on the crags of the Mediterranean shores (samphire, saltwort, etc.) have been dried and burnt for this purpose since the time of the Etruscans; this subtitute for salt was widely used in the Middle Ages. In Norway, the curious *lutefisk* eaten on Christmas Eve, is salt cod cooked in a brine made of birch ashes.

N.B. A small bag of wood ash can be used to sweeten the water in which lentils and chick peas are soaked prior to cooking them.

Verbena (Lemon Grass)

(*Lippia citriodora* or *Verbena triphylla*) A shrubby bush native to Chile with pink flowers, widespread in the gardens of the South of France, its lanceolate, slightly sticky leaves give a sweet, aromatic odor like that of vervain. It should not be confused with the bitter astringent vervain (*Verbena officinalis*) used in digestive teas. Lemon-grass verbena can be used like many other lemon-scented herbs.

Vervain

(French, *Citronelle*) The common name of several wild and cultivated plants that smell like lemon. Notably, southernwood (*Artemisia arbronatum;* French, *aurone* or *garde-robe*); several varieties of vervain, among them *Lippia citriodora*, and finally melissa or lemon balm (*Melissa officinalis;* French, *melissa officinalé*).

Some ancient elixirs such as Barbados water, *eau des carmes déchaussés,* were flavored with cinnamon and vervain. In addition, the oil and essence of niaouli (which see) contains vervain. It should be remembered especially that the fresh leaves of these sundry plants can occasionally aromatize a salad, a fish stuffing, a ginger sauce, or young cock, as well as many *ratafias*. (*See* MELISSA.)

Ve-Tsin, Vetsing

(*See* MONOSODIUM GLUTAMATE.)

Vinegar

(French, *Vinaigre;* German, *Essig;* Italian, *Aceto*) The product of the acetic oxidation of wine or many other alcoholic beverages, this fermentation is accomplished by an aerobic microbe *Mycoderma aceti.* It first forms a skin on the liquid, then a gelatinous mass, submerged in it, called mother of vinegar. A single mother is enough to inseminate hundreds of quarts of liquid to be soured.

Vinegar has been used as a condiment since earliest times. The Chinese have practiced the acid fermentation of rice or strawberry tree spirits for more than 4,000 years. In the Old Testament, Boaz invited his companions to dip their bread in vinegar. In Rome, the *acetabulum* (vinegar bottle) appeared on all the tables; in the heat of summer, the Romans also appreciated *oxycratum,* a beverage made of fresh water, vinegar, and mint leaves. Many different vinegars, often of foreign origin, are available in good food shops.

WINE VINEGAR is the finest of all. It is made of good quality red or white wine, as *besaigre.* Accidentally turned or soured wine never makes good vinegar. Choose a clear, light-colored liquid, at most pinkish, if red wine is being used. Like other spirits, it improves with age and acquires bouquet and bite after two years of maceration. Orléans, a city already renowned for its pâtés, undoubtedly produces the finest of wine vinegars. Containing the white wines from the shores of the Loire, it is slowly acetified in *poinçons,* oak casks that contain 236 liters. Unfortunately, the German method of acetification has generally supplanted the Orléans method. It involves turning vats, filled with beech shavings in which the wine oxidizes in only ten days.

The expression "wine vinegar" is not a sufficient guarantee for the gourmet. His only alternative is seek out and buy an old wine vinegar from a reliable food shop.

SHERRY VINEGAR is made with the excellent Andalusian wines of Cadiz (sherry, manzanilla, etc.). It is very fine, rather full-bodied, with a light taste of muscat grape or hazelnut.

AROMATIC VINEGARS are wine vinegars prepared for the table, using many plant spices. The use of tarragon to give vinegar a high flavor has become routine, but there are many other variations: elder (*surard*), rose petal (*rosat*), cumin, champagne, celery, rasberry, corn, etc.

ALCOHOL VINEGAR is generally colored with caramel. It has very little taste and often alters in aging. It is prepared with many alcoholic musts or mediocre spirits cut with water and wine, fermented by the German method. Vinegar extracted from wood alcohol is acrid and dangerous to the health.

BEER VINEGAR is naturally yellow, with a rather bitter taste. This taste, coming from the fermentation of hops, is masked with brown sugar and molasses. It is not very much esteemed by good cooks.

CIDER VINEGAR is sweeter than wine vinegar and has an appetizing golden tint. Highly appreciated by believers in natural medicine, it counteracts the overalkaline reaction of our organism, according to Doctor Jarvis.* It is found in health food stores and also in most markets. It is agreeably used in many macerations of condiments where the aroma of wine would be superfluous (pickles, chutneys, etc.). It tolerates the presence of garlic and onion in the salads that it dresses. There is also a perry vinegar, made from pears.

MILK VINEGAR, an amusing Swiss curiosity, is very light and recommended for people with stomach ailments. Its aroma combines well with Gruyère in a compound salad.

There are also many foreign and exotic vinegars, such as tamarind, commonly used in Bombay, Canadian maple vinegar, palm vinegar from Oceania and Africa, saké made in Japan, and malt vinegar, highly valued by the Anglo-Saxons. Going back in time, forgotten formulas are revealed: arbutus berry, date, fig, marc, and glucose vinegars. Some of these acid solutions can be very useful to the cook, but their taste varies considerably according to their formulation and the region they came from.

Modern medicine, which no longer uses the vinegar of four thieves, an ancient medication against plague, is very much interested in the utility of vinegar in foods. It is never prescribed for people in good health. A powerful digestive acidifier, it makes up for certain organic deficiencies and is supposed to combat migraines. The drops of vinegar that the Slavic and Balkan cooks add to invigorating dishes like bortsch and goulash make them much more digestible. Salads, well seasoned with oil and vinegar, play a large role in nutrition.

USES: *Evident every day, vinegar is not only an element in almost all salads, seasonings for salads, court-bouillons, marinades, etc., but is an element in*

* See APPENDIX.

many hot preparations. Many sauces are made of vinegar reduced with garlic, shallot or fines herbes; *among them* sauce Bercy *and* sauce béarnaise, *often diluted with white wine, seasoned with a little powdered sugar or chopped gherkins and capers, for example, in* sauce charcutière *and black butter. Vinegar is indispensable in German sweet-sour preparations. The Italians themselves, who willingly use lemon instead of vinegar in salads, give it a place of honor in* aceto dolce *and* sotto aceti. *In the Levant, all raw vegetables are macerated at least an hour in vinegar or* mokhalel. *In China, vinegar is mixed with soy, sugar, and pineapple juice in a number of recipes.*

N.B.   Among the counter indications are the use of vinegar in a salad that accompanies a *foie gras* and in most acidulated cream preparations.

Vine Leaves

Very useful to the sculptor, they also have a discreet role in cooking. First of all, they are used in Turkish or Greek stuffed vine leaves. They are also used to season some of our cooking, notably quail, grouse, and partridge covered with both a layer of vine leaves and bacon. Léon Frapié*, the food writer, who has had his hour of fame, recommends that snails should be cooked in a white wine court-bouillon perked up with a bunch of vine tendrils. Their bitterness disappears once they are blanched in a little water and lemon juice. They can also be prepared as fritters.

In Oriental groceries in Paris, vine leaves in brine canned in Istanbul are found under the name *Asma Yapragi.* (*See* LEAVES.)

Violet

(*Viola odorata;* French, *Violette;* German, *Veilchen*) A small perennial plant, without a stem, the fragrant violet is the symbol of grace and modesty. Pharmacists use it in making cough drops. In perfume-making, violet essence is worth its weight in gold. (A ton of violets gives about one ounce of essence.) The sweet, slightly transient aroma of violet is appreciated in candy-making. *Violettes de Toulouse* are well known. Pills, pralines, pastries, and sherbets are flavored

* See APPENDIX.

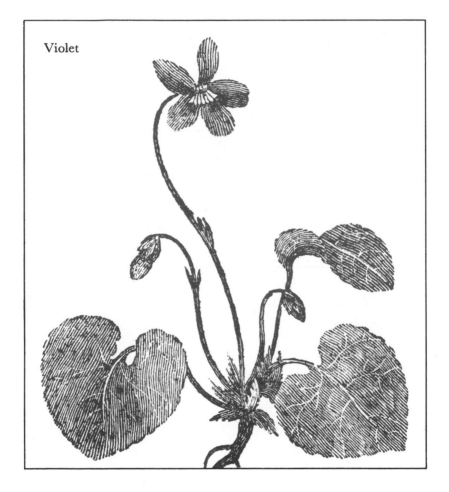

Violet

with violet extract, but in cooking this flower has a negligible role, and is used only to decorate salads. As an exception, violets can be mixed with the stuffing for squab or trout, etc. (*See* FLOWERS.)

Vodka

A Russian or Polish grain alcohol. Generally, it is a white alcohol, with a burning taste, that is best drunk iced. There is also a red pepper vodka, lemon vodka, and buffalo grass vodka. Seasoned vodka is not improved by heating or cooking. The Slav cooks prefer fruit alcohols or white local wines, or light beers like *kvass.* However, it is permissible to sprinkle a smoked fish, a herring, or a filet with beaten curdled milk with vodka and *fines herbes,* as is done in the Karelian region of the Soviet Union. (*See* ZUBROWKA.)

Walnuts and Green Walnuts

The walnut (*Juglans regia*) is a large tree native to Persia. From there it went to Greece, then Italy, and finally to the rest of Europe. The tough, large leaves have a subtle agreeable odor, quite perceptible when they are rubbed. They were used during the last war as a tobacco substitute. The wood itself is lightly aromatic. It is particularly suited, as coals, to grilling trout, and other fresh-water fish. (*See* HICKORY.)

The fruit, or walnut, is surrounded by a fleshy, tough envelope called the shell, which contains a widely used coloring substance that has a very acrid, fragrant taste. This shell is used in the preparation of some *ratafias,* in coloring marc, and even in some marinades used for imitating the taste and appearance of venison. The nut itself, when gathered a little before maturity, is called green walnut. Very ripe, and dried, it gives an oil whose taste is highly appreciated by connoisseurs. Pounded, it is used to cover a cow's-milk cheese. (*See* NUT OIL.)

Grated nuts are mixed with Parmesan for some Italian specialties (minestrone, etc.). They can also be used in the sauce for *cerchez taougu* (chicken *à la circassienne*), in the stuffing for Toulon-style snails, in a salad, croquettes, canapés, etc. They have innumerable uses in pastry-making. Green walnuts are also used as a condiment in cooking. The English pickled walnuts are based on an old French recipe. *(See* CASHEW, ALMOND, PEANUT, ARECA, CHESTNUT, NUTMEG, PINE NUT, *and* PISTACHIO.)

Whisky

Famous grain spirits made by Anglo-Saxons, *scotch* coming from malt barley, *rye* from rye, and *bourbon* from maize. Some kinds of rye are flavored with peat smoke. Scotches are generally aged in oak casks that first contained sherry or port, which explains the amber color.

These alcohols with their malty or smoky flavors are used in cooking, but their flavor is less glorious than that of Cognac or Armagnac. They are used to flame fowl or dilute very fruity spirits. Scotch whisky flavor goes well with sweet Mediterranean wines and Armagnac. Once burnt, it leaves a light taste of hazelnut. Rye is suited to smoked ham, sprats, and dried herring. As for bourbon, its job is to flame some barbecue meats, and lobster timbale with bourbon, New Orleans fashion, is not to be scorned.

Wild Raspberry

(*Rubus chamoemorus;* French, *Muron arctique*) An orange-colored fruit much like the raspberry that is borne by a small thornless bramble of Lapland, Siberia, and Canada. The Swedes call it *hjorto-ron,* the Norwegians *mylter* and the Canadians *chicouté.* Its extremely delicate taste and nasturtiumlike aroma make it a deluxe food. The wild raspberry, prepared in compote, is often used as a condiment for snow patridge. An excellent liqueur, *lakka,* is made from it in Finland.

Many other European or American false mulberries with an agreeable-tasting reddish fruit are occasionally used in cooking. In the Mascarene Islands (Indian Ocean), the fruit of a related bramble, *Rubus mascarinensis,* is used in making *rougails* (which see). The young shoots are generally edible, like those of some fodder plants or hop shoots.

Wild Thyme

(*Thymus serpyllum;* French, *Serpolet;* German, *Quendel;* Italian, *Sermollino;* Provençal, *Farigoulette*) A wild variety of thyme known by its creeping prostrate stems, pink flowers heads, and leaves that are smaller than those of cultivated thyme. Wild thyme is a feast for Garenne rabbits and other small mammals. Its aroma is sweeter than that of common thyme, and it can be used more freely in cooking. Some varieties have a smell that is somewhat like that of sage or eucalyptus, but these nuances are very subtle. Wild thyme leaves or powder may be preferred to cultivated thyme when preparing a fowl or white meat. (*See uses under* SAGE *and* THYME.)

Wine Cooking

Dumas thought that wine was the intellectual part of a meal, while food was only the material part. He devoted the longest article in his *Grand Dictionnaire de Cuisine* to wine, but forgot to treat wine-cooking. This mixture of solid foods with the most spiritual liquid is a very old invention. Archestratus of Syracuse and Timachidas of Rhodes, the first poets of the table, celebrated vinious preparations in pentameters. More recently, in 1936, R. Brunet and Pellaprat went into greater detail in their *Cuisine au Vin.* This fashion of cooking exists in all wine-growing countries, especially in Italy, Hungary, Rhineland, Spain, but it is willingly modeled on French examples.

The art of cooking with wine has its rules. The white, red, or rosé that impregnates a dish must be of excellent quality. The growths that do not cook well should be eliminated, and an honest, standard brand of not too young wine should be chosen.

Cooking never improves a bad wine. It is better to eat a chicken cooked in Morgon while drinking a coarse red wine than to drink the Morgon with a chicken cooked in a common red wine. Sour wine or corky wine cannot be used. Mature Bordeaux and Burgundies should be decanted to eliminate the lees.

A wine for swishing a sauté pan or a frying pan can be lightly acid and used as is. On the other hand, a wine used for long cooking, especially a white wine, should be deacidified, that is, first boiled for ten minutes, then flamed. If not, one runs the risk of a sourish sauce that will be impossible to change. The very good reds can be spared this treatment if they are boiled for five minutes, uncovered, when they are added as moistening. A dish moistened with wine should be tasted only after twenty minutes. If the taste is a little acrid, a piece of sugar or brown sugar can always be added to make the sauce more mellow.

WHITE WINE is mostly reserved for white meats, fish, and all the white stews. It is preferred to red wines and even Madeira for swishing fried meats, *tournedos, noisettes* (lamb), etc., which can then be flavored with lemon juice or Cognac. The most famous of all the preparations with white wine is *pauchouse,* a river fish bouillabaisse from Franche-Comté, containing carp, eel, tench, and eel pout.

SAUCES WITH WHITE WINE are innumerable, and one can only mention some of the rules of French cooking. White wine, with or without vinegar or lemon, goes well with everything spicy and exciting: shallot in Bercy sauce, tarragon in Béarnaise sauce, gherkins in *charcutière* sauce, crustaceans in many preparations *à la dieppoise;* finally, cayenne pepper, paprika, turtle herbs, white truffles, capers, fish essence, etc. Rarely, is it combined with cream, chopped ham, mushrooms, which it does not support as well as Madeira and fortified wines do.

RED WINE combines harmoniously with red meats. Braised kidneys with Chambertin, *civet de lièvre, boeuf bourguignon,* and *daube provençale* would be very sad if they were deprived of ruby red wine. But, in Dijon, Libourne, and Marigues, wine is loved to the point of adding it to chicken, rabbit, even fish dishes. *Meurette bourguignonne* is a red wine eel stew like its Cisalpine cousin, *caciucco* (an Italian bouillabaisse). Red wine is also an element in court-bouillon, but that does not allow it to be used to prepare a *truite au bleu!* (*See* COURT-BOUILLON.)

RED WINE SAUCES are a regionalistic aristocracy where two branches are especially remarkable: *bourguignonne* and *bordelaise.* They are the symbols of mellowness. Seasoned with mushrooms, truffles, garlic, or onion, perfumed with thyme, savory, or bay, they are thickened with brown flour, egg yolk, cream, *beurre manié,* or blood. Fried croutons are their most beautiful ornaments. Red wine is also used to cook red beans and even prunes! In Spain, tripe and a seafood stew, *zarzuela de mariscos,* are seasoned with red wine.

Wine is rarely used as a condiment if it is not heated and cooked. All the same, let us mention strawberries in red wine and sabayon sauce with white wine. In Limousin, red wine is often added to the last spoonfuls of country soups, called *chabrot* (or *goudale* in Béarn). This picturesque finish for a dish may be disputable from the gastronomic point of view.

Some sweet wines are sometimes used to soak the meats grilled on the barbecue (which see).

Many apéritifs or invigorating beverages are prepared with hot or cold wine and aromatics: Oxford wine, cinnamon wine, bischoff, etc. In our opinion, the best of all is the Iberian *sangría.* The use of many alcoholic beverages is discussed under: CHAMPAGNE, CIDER, CHICHA, HYDROMEL, HYPOCRAS, MADEIRA, MARSALA, PORT, PULQUE, SAKE, VERMOUTH, YELLOW WINE, *and* SHERRY.

Wood Fires

The cooking of meat or fish on a wood fire, or a barbecue as it is called today, necessitates some skill. The quality of the fire depends upon the fuel choosen. The best wood to be burned under a grill is certainly vine stems. In the southwest of France, refined gastronomes try to use the vines of *picquepoule* grapes, in which they find, it seems, the essence of Armagnac. A beef rib, *master of wine-shop style,* a spitted roasted hare, or grilled snails Toulon fashion, are incomparable if they are grilled with these crackling embers.

Oak logs give a good ember, with a light bitter smell, because of the tannin they contain. Beech and hornbeam are sweeter burning and not as good as chestnut. With all these woods, the smoke should be fortified with aromatic twigs and dried herbs (thyme, bay, myrtle, cistus).

According to an old Bavarian tradition, a live trout should be placed on the embers of a particularly aromatic walnut. American hickory, which has a large role in barbecue, is a variety of walnut. According to the Spanish *paella* purists, a large frying pan filled with saffron rice should always be heated over an orange-wood fire.

Resinous woods (pine, sea pine, thuya, cypress) are not advisable, as they give meats the smell of turpentine. Nevertheless, pine cones are used in Provence to grill small birds, and in Savoy sausages are smoked with pinewood.

The best *cassoulet* should be simmered, it is said, in an earthenware casserole place in a bakers' oven heated with genista and furze of the Montagne Noire (and some pine branches can be added). These shrubby trees give off a very strong heat, as well as a saffron odor of the best quality. The Laplanders smoke enormous salmon, barely skinned, with birch bark. The Berbers cannot make a true *méchou*, except with oak and Atlas heather embers. (*See* BARBECUE, AROMATIC WOODS, ASHES, CHARCOAL, SMOKE, *and* HICKORY.)

Woodruff

(*Asperula odorata;* French, *Asperule;* German, *Waldmeister*) This is a pretty sylvan plant to which herbalists attribute cardiotonic virtues. A *Rubiaceae* plant that in different places is also called *petit-muguet, reine des bois.* It is very different from the common lily-of-the-valley (*muguet, Convallaria majalis*).

The leaves of woodruff contain coumarin, which is given off more powerfully when they are dried. Germanic people especially appreciate woodruff and use it quite justifiably as an element in making some sausages and most often in the preparation of their famous *Maitrank* or *Bowle,* a delicate and exciting May wine, which is the Nordic counterpart of Spanish *sangría.* (*See* COUMARINE.)

Worcestershire Sauce

A very robust English sauce, that takes its name from a humid county in the west of England. The bottle of Worcestershire sauce is part of the panoply of the perfect Anglo-Saxon cook. Its contents are not at all mysterious: malt vinegar, soy sauce, strong red pepper, sugar, salt, and meat essence. This aromatic Niagara is destined for the seasoning of soups and boiled meats of good Old English cooking. Two or three drops of this elixir are always used in a marinade, brine, the trituration of *steak tartare* or in the mellow English stuffing (with a little powdered sage) in the crackling Wiltshire pork pies of the neighboring county.

Wormwood

(*Artemisia absinthium;* French, *Absinthe;* German, *Wermut*) A perennial of the family of *Compositae,* related to mugwort. There are numerous varieties. It used to be called *alvine* and *herbe aux vers.* Cattle dote on it, perhaps because of its vermifuge properties. Dumas thought that the incomparable flavor of *prés-salés* (salt marsh mutton) was due to the proliferation of wormwood on the shores of the Atlantic.

The denticulate and cottony leaves of wormwood, as well as its yellowish flowers, give off a strong aroma and have a strong bitter aftertaste. For thousands of years, its properties have been used in the preparation of alcoholic beverages together with hyssop, anise, fennel, etc. Ammianus Marcellinus, the Latin historian, reported that in the huts of the Saintonge Gauls, absinthe liqueur was drunk. Dumas affirms humorously that absinthe-based beverages caused more harm in the French African batallions than "yataghan or Arab guns." Later, Verlaine, and other famous writers devoted themselves to *fée verte,* made of *génépi,* a mountain variety of absinthe, aromatized with angelica and star anise.

The leaves and the flowers of absinthe are too bitter to be used directly in cooking. Mugwort, or even the sweet wines known as vermouth (taken from the German name of this plant) are preferred to it. Absinthe with celery is used in oysters Rockefeller, an American specialty.

Xylopie

(*See* GRAINS OF PARADISE.)

Yellow Wine

Also called Chinese wine. Its true name is *houang-tsieou,* but this is harder on our tongues than the beverage itself. Yellow wine is colored rice alcohol, flavored with flowers and fruits, about 34 per cent proof. The Chinese drink *houang-tsieou* with meals, even from the jar that holds it, using bamboo drinking straws. Distilled yellow wine makes *mei-kue-lou,* a light spirit, 50–60 per cent proof.

Innumerable Chinese recipes, some of which are mentioned in Western books, use yellow wine for flavoring sauces and other preparations. According to Chinese cooks, it can be replaced by sherry or white port, cut with a little marc or plum wine. It can accompany lacquered duck. *Vin de paille* from Jura or a *clairette* from Languedoc can be substituted.

Yogurt

Curdled milk that is prepared by the Turkish or Bulgarian method is a food recommended for the sick by their doctors and also a condiment. Before briefly summarizing the culinary roles of yogurt, let us enlarge this article to include all of the Oriental fermented milks: Caucasian *kéfir,* Arab *lebenn,* and Tartar *koumys.* In different countries, it may be made from ewe's milk, goat's milk, cow's, mare's or even camel's milk. The product is always rather spicy and has a weak consistency. Simply beaten with a fork, it becomes liquid and is used in a number of iced beverages, Turkish *ayran,* Iranian *dough,* Indian *lassi,* for instance.

As the Syrians, Turks and Afghans do not use alcohol, which is forbidden by the Prophet, curdled milk is used to cook meats, vegetables, or to dilute herb marinades. Most often used to season it are fresh mint, marjoram, chives, powdered cumin, and saffron. These uses are quite similar to the way Slavs or Balkans employ sour cream. Curdled milk is used to season soups, or on skewered grilled meat like shish-kebab, etc. Salted and cured, and thus changed into white cheese, it is an ingredient in *beureks,* a kind of cheese turnover, in raisin tarts, or may even be crumbled in soups. It is called *brinza* in Bulgaria and Rumania, *chorba* in North Africa, and *kouroute* in Afghanistan. Turkish cuisine has implanted itself all over the world.

In the cuisine of the ancient Romans and the Gauls, *mesgus,* their curdled milk, had an identical place. Even today, *brousse* and *broccio* are elements in some Provençal and Corsican recipes. (*See* BROCCIO.)

Zahtar

The Arab name of a variety of marjoram, *Origanum cyriacum*, which is like the ancient dittany of Crete. Fresh, or dried and powdered, *zahtar* adds a joyous green note to all the markets of the Near East. In Egypt, it is pounded in a mortar with chick peas and salt. (*See* MARJORAM.)

Zedoary

This is the name given to many tropical rhizome plants, notably Linnaeus' *Kaempferia longa* and Roxburgh's *Curcuma zedoaria*. The Arabs and Indians use them in condiments and medicines, but the principal culinary merit of zedoary is as an element in curry. Its aroma is a little like that of ginger.

Zubrowka

A Polish word meaning a plant and also a variety of vodka that it flavors; it is buffalo grass (*Hierochloe odorate;* German, *Darrgrass*), which is a gramineous plant like vernal grass (*flouve* or *Anthoxanthum odoratum*). Both are commonly called in French *avoine odorante*, or *houlque parfumée*. They contain coumarin (which see).

Augé, Claude: Famous French grammarian and lexicographer of the nineteenth century; author of grammars widely used in the French schools.

Binet, Leon: (1891-1967): A medical doctor and professor, also President of the French Academy of Sciences, he was a physiologist, enormously interested in nature, animals and gastronomy.

Bombard, Doctor Alain (1924-   ): A biologist as well as a doctor, he became famous by crossing the Atlantic in 1952 without assistance on a rubber raft, simulating a shipwreck.

Brillat-Savarin (1755-1826): Author of *La Physiologie du Goût,* which has become a classic of gastronomic literature (also available in English) and widely cited in cooking literature. Although it is seldom read, the aphorisms are widely quoted in both languages. For example, he wrote, "Tell me what you eat and I'll tell you what you are."

Carême, Antonin, (1784-1833): Cook of kings, king of cooks, and author of a number of major works early in the nineteenth century, his school of cooking became completely identified with the French cuisine while his recipes, in modified form, are still used to create *la grande cuisine.* He signed his works as Antonin Carême, although his first name actually was Marie-Antoine.

Curnonsky (1867-1957): Prince-elect of gastronomes and founder of France's most prestigious food magazine, *Cuisine et Vins de France.*

Dumas (1802-1870): Alexandre, "Dumas pere," was the author of scores of novels, *The Three Musketeers* being the most famous. His last work was *Le Grand Dictionnaire de Cuisine.* a monumental effort that is witty, exhaustive, and untroubled by historical accuracy or scholasticism. Available in a new French edition, it is also published in an abridged English paperback edition.

Escudier, Jean-Noël: An elderly gentleman from Toulon who is President of the Gastronomic Society of Provence and Nice and author of *La Veritable Cuisine Provençale,* the only recent valuable work on this marvelous subject. There is also an English edition.

Frapié, Leon (1863-1959): A typically French writer, author of the famous *La Maternell,* but related to gastronomy only in this work.

Jarvis, Doctor D. C.: Contemporary American who wrote *Folk Medicine,* published by Holt, Rinehart and Winston, relating how country folk used cider vinegar and honey to treat illnesses.

Leclerc, Dr. Henri: Author of *Les Épices* in 1929, also other books on medicinal and food plants. His books justifiably consider the scientific bases of his studies both in France and abroad.

Littré: One of the most authoritative of French dictionaries.

Lycurgus: A Spartan leader of the ninth century B.C. who was chiefly responsible for fashioning the body of law that made Spartan life more rigorous, more ascetic and martial.

Montagné, Prosper: One of the last of the great nineteenth century chefs, continuing the tradition of Carême. He wrote several books, the most notable among them being *Le Grand Livre de la Cuisine,* and co-authored *Larousse Gastronomique.*

de Pomiane, Doctor: Originally from Poland, he was about eighty when he died in 1950. He was well versed in cooking and invented the "gastro-technique." He wrote many books in French, the most famous being *Bien Manger pour Bien Vivre,* published by Albin Michel, Paris, and *Le Code de la Bonne Chere 'Same,* both published before the late war.

de la Reynière, Grimod (1758-1838): One of the most noted, eccentric and opinionated gastronomes of his time, and author of *Le Manuel des Amphitryons* and *Almanach des Gourmands.*

de Serres, Olivier (1539-1619): One of the best of Renaissance writers. He was the author of *Le Theatre d'Agriculture et Mesnage des Champs,* which had eight editions during his lifetime.

Taillevent (1310-1395): One of the earliest of major French food writers. As chef to Charles V, he wrote his famous *Viandier* while in service to the King. His real name was Guillaume Tirel. His grave may be seen in the Paris suburb of St. Germain-en-Laye.

Vuvier (1769-1832): A famous French naturalist, creator of the comparative anatomy of paleontology.